EVERYTHING
YOU NEED TO KNOW ABOUT...
Witchcraft

EVERYTHING

YOU NEED TO KNOW ABOUT...

Witchcraft

MARIAN SINGER

D&C
David and Charles

A DAVID & CHARLES BOOK

David & Charles is a subsidiary of F+W (UK) Ltd.,
an F+W Publications Inc. company

First UK edition published in 2005
First published in the USA by Adams Media, an F+W Publications Inc. company,
as The Everything® Wicca and Witchcraft Book in 2002

A catalogue record for this book is available from the British Library.

ISBN 0 7153 2316 4

Printed in Great Britain by CPI Bath
for David & Charles
Brunel House   Newton Abbot   Devon

Visit our website at www.davidandcharles.co.uk

David & Charles books are available from all good bookshops;
alternatively you can contact our Orderline on (0)1626 334555 or
write to us at FREEPOST EX2110, David & Charles Direct,
Newton Abbot, TQ12 4ZZ (no stamp required UK mainland).

Everything You Need to Know About Witchcraft is intended as a reference
book only. While author and publisher have made every attempt
to offer accurate and reliable information to the best of their
knowledge and belief, it is presented without any guarantee.
The author and publisher therefore disclaim any liability incurred
in connection with the information contained in this book.

Contents

Introduction

Of late, you may have noticed that the words Witch, Witchcraft and Wicca pop up all over the place – on television and radio programmes, in films, at bookshops, in magazines, on the Internet and even in casual conversations. The terms are not new, but they have finally lost their negative connotations: TV witches are no longer portrayed as ugly, evil crones – no more warts, wrinkles and black pointy hats – instead, the characters and people presented could live next door – and probably do!

Note the important difference between Wicca and Witchcraft: although the two are related and share similar practices, the beliefs behind them are often different. To keep it simple, remember that Wicca is a religion, like Christianity, while Witchcraft is a methodology. Wiccans generally practise Witchcraft, but Witches may not necessarily share Wiccan beliefs and therefore would not consider themselves Wiccan.

Confused? That's OK, as sometimes even those who have been practicing magick for decades still have to pause and consider how to define themselves in easily understood terms. The book you hold in your hands is one such pause for explanation and definition.

The goal here is to provide you with a plethora of useful information. It is, in fact, a guide that will cover everything you need to know in order to better understand both Wicca and Witchcraft, and even learn some magick to practise yourself. Here you'll discover where these two systems fit into the broad-based Neo-Pagan community, and you'll get an overview of their origins. You'll also find out how each system is practised, and who exactly is shaping this swelling spiritual wave.

As you read, bear in mind that Wicca and Witchcraft comprise many vision-based faiths and practices, shaped intimately by the individuals walking their chosen Paths. This means that no book can be the 'final authority' on Wicca and Witchcraft. The information provided here is generalized – a broad view, if you will, of what's common and popular in Wicca and Witchcraft. It's quite possible that you could meet a Witch or Wiccan who does things differently from the way they are portrayed in these pages – there's a lot of elbowroom for improvising, borrowing from other cultures and Paths, and personalizing these practices. In fact, the ability to transform and adapt with the earth, society and each person's individuality is among the cornerstones of eclectic Witchery and Wicca, as well as of many Neo-Pagan traditions.

Having the option of adapting custom and heritage does not mean that either should be thrown out with the proverbial bathwater. Some Witches and Wiccans only follow older or familial systems with specific rules and rites; they honour tradition, believing that it draws its power from use and refinement over generations. But nevertheless, even the most stringent of magickal traditions has room for spontaneity and ingenuity at suitable moments.

Finally, I should point out that both my perception of and my communication about Wicca and Witchcraft are certainly influenced by my own experiences. I consider myself a Witch, specifically a folk magician. Magick is an intimate part of my everyday life, and I am very pleased and excited to be sharing its wonders and blessings with you.

Important Safety Notes

Never leave a burning candle unattended, and always set a candle on a secure surface away from flammable items.

When using smudge sticks (herb bundles for space cleansing), carry the stick over a saucer or other heatproof dish after lighting, as embers may easily fall to the floor or onto clothing or other flammable items. Extinguish by dampening the end of the stick after use, then trim with scissors or a knife ready to use again.

Do not use essential oils directly onto the skin – always dilute them with a carrier, or base, oil such as almond oil. Do not ingest essential oils, because some can be toxic. Do not use essential oils if you are pregnant or are suffering from any serious medical complaint. If in doubt whether to use them, seek medical advice first.

CHAPTER 1

And Harm None: Philosophy and Ideology

It's impossible to cover the ideals, ethics and philosophy of Witches and Wiccans completely in one chapter, or even in one book. Nevertheless, these pages aim to provide a condensed version of how the magickal community envisions and interacts with the world, striving to improve both the self and humankind as a whole.

Dispelling Myth and Misunderstanding

Witches do not eat babies, and they're not Satanists. They're more likely to wear a business suit than a pointy black hat, and only a few regularly hug trees! Most drive cars rather than ride broomsticks and enjoy pizza over eye of newt any day.

A newt is a type of lizard, about 12.5cm (5in) long, that lives in lowland, watery regions. In Roman mythology, Ceres, goddess of the Earth, turns a youth into a newt for mocking her.

Here are some common stereotypes:

- ☾ **Witches are imaginary beings who sell their souls to the devil in return for special powers.** This folkloric image was picked up by mainstream religions.
- ☾ **Witches are humans who have psychic abilities.** This assumption may or may not be true. Some psychics may be Witches, but not all Witches are psychic.
- ☾ **Witches are sorcerers.** This term is accurate from an anthropological point of view.
- ☾ **Witches are modern worshippers of ancient gods and goddesses who also practise some form of magick.** This description is fairly accurate for Wiccans, but not always for Witches.

Only education and understanding can uproot misconceptions and prejudices about Witchcraft and Wicca, so you are on the right path. It's time to start thinking of Witches and Wiccans in a whole new sense – as people who are simply living their lives in a uniquely magickal way. We'll begin by examining the basic ground rules and core concepts that most Witches and Wiccans hold in common.

Who's Who and What's What?

By the way, it's good to remember that a male Witch or Wiccan is *not* called a Warlock. He is a Witch or Wiccan too. *Warlock* comes from an Old

English word for *oath breaker*, and during the mid-1400s came to mean *liar* (whether male or female). So to call a male Witch a Warlock is a rather nasty insult! For the purposes of simplicity, I will use the word *Witch* for both male and female Witches or Wiccans throughout the book.

The words *wizard* and *sorcerer* can be used for a man or a woman. *Wizard* derives from a term meaning 'wise', and *sorcerer* means 'witch' or 'diviner'.

As a point of interest, the word *magician* is also appropriate for both sexes and for both Witches and Wiccans. If we turn back the pages of time to Zoroaster in ancient Persia, the priests he taught were called Magi, and they relied heavily on astrology as an art. Depending on the cultural setting, *magician* then came to describe people adept in astrology, sorcery or other magickal arts. Note that the word *magick* in Wicca and Witchcraft is spelled with a *k*, to differentiate it from stage magic (or sleight of hand).

As with any religious or spiritual movement, Wicca and Witchcraft share some core concepts, but they incorporate various schools and traditions of magick that are distinctive and unique.

Which Is the Witch?

Despite the ugly face that competing religions have tried to put on Witches, the heritage of these fine people is that of helping and healing individuals and communities. Yes, some used their knowledge and abilities for bane, but history indicates that they were in the minority.

Wicce, an Anglo-Saxon term meaning 'one who practises sorcery', is the root of the words *Witch* and *Wicca*. At first the term was applied equally to wise men and women, especially those who practised herbcraft (sometimes also called 'cunning arts'). After the Crusades, however, the term pertained mostly to women and carried negative connotations.

Most witches learned their art as part of a family tradition in which they were carefully trained. (For more on the history of Witchcraft, see Chapter 2.) Villages and cities both had their honoured cunning folk to whom people would turn for all kinds of help – from helping crops to grow to mending a broken heart. In exchange for such services, the Witch might receive a chicken, a measure of grain or other necessities. (The barter system is *still* alive and well in Witchcraft!)

Witches learned their skills as just that: a Craft. There was rarely any ethical or religious construct involved unless it came from the family or cultural influences or was imposed by the individual's own sense of right and wrong. Witches do not need to believe in divine beings in order to use magick. They do not necessarily have a 'code' or tradition to which they adhere, unless it is dictated by familial custom.

Why are Witches not necessarily Wiccan?
The short answer is that Witchcraft implies a methodology (for example, the use of magick), whereas the word *Wiccan* refers to a person who has adopted a specific religious philosophy.

Again, however, the lack of an ethical or religious construct does not mean that all Witches are without ethics or religion. Magick is simply a means to an end and is morally neutral (except in how it's wielded).

As Far as Wicca

Writers such as Gerald Gardner and Sir James Frazier are commonly given credit for coining the term *Wiccan* and kick-starting the modern movement in the 1950s. Although the methods and tools of the Wiccan are often the same as those of the Witch, the constructs within which Wiccans work are a little different. The primary variance is that Wicca is considered a religion, with specific rituals and moral codes similar to those of other world faiths.

Wiccan Gods and Goddesses

An additional difference is that many Wiccans follow a specific god or goddess, and others worship several deities. These beings or personages may be chosen by the individual or dictated by a group, magickal tradition or a cultural standard. In this case, the Wiccan looks to the Divine as a copilot in the spiritual quest, and as a helpmate in effectively and safely guiding magickal energy.

Several divine figures show up as popular favourites in the Wiccan community. Among them we see:

APOLLO (Greece and Rome) HERNE (Celtic Europe)
BRIGID (Celtic Europe) ISHTAR (Middle East)
DAGDA (Ireland) ISIS (Egypt)
DIANA (Rome) PAN (Greece)
HECATE (Greece) RA (Egypt)

Karmic Law

A third difference is that Witches may or may not concern themselves with the potential results of a spell or ritual, while Wiccans are bound by the threefold law. This means that the way Wiccans and Witches view the cause and effect of their magick is different; it doesn't mean Witches don't respect magickal power, nor does it mean Witches are unethical.

What is the threefold law?
The threefold law has similar overtones to the concept of Karma. The law basically states that whatever actions you do, whatever energies you 'put out', return to you threefold (three times over) in this lifetime or the next.

Personalized Magick and Ritualistic Witches

One thing that Witches and Wiccans do have in common, however, is that both approach magick in very personal ways – ways that can be incredibly complex or very simple. Kitchen Wiccans and hedge Witches, for example, rely heavily on pragmatic, uncomplicated magick, much of which originates in folklore and superstition. Hedge Witches traditionally do not belong to a coven. Solitary practitioners, they depend on self-study, insight, creativity and intuition as their main guideposts. Hedge Witches may be self-dedicated, but they are rarely publicly initiated. Similar to village shamans and cunning folk in past generations, they provide spells and potions for daily needs.

In earlier times people didn't have the spare time to weave complex spells and rituals, so old wives' tales, sayings and superstitions were followed with tremendous respect and trust. The hedge Witch's magick depended on placing faith in such beliefs and enacting them purposefully (willfully, with intention).

Others practise magick with more ritualistic overtones, drawing inspiration from the Kabbalah (Jewish mysticism and magick) and other mystical and spiritual movements. The ritualistic Witches look to every aspect of a spell or working as being part of a huge puzzle, where each piece needs to be in the right place for everything to work as it should. For example, the astrological phase of the moon should be suited to the task, and every part of the working should be carefully contrived to build energy towards a desired goal. A large majority of such workings have been used for a long time and are honoured as part of the tradition from which the Witch originates. That is not to say that a ritualistic school has no room for variety or improvisation; it's just that the improvisation usually happens within a set framework.

Are You a Good Witch or a Bad Witch?

This classic question is among the favourite responses that might follow anyone saying, 'I'm a Witch'. So what is the answer? Are there 'bad' Witches who use their knowledge and power for personal gain and ill will? Yes, of course there are, just as there are 'bad' Christians, 'bad' Muslims, 'bad' Jews and so on. People are people. If you shake any figurative tree hard enough, a couple of rotten apples are liable to fall off. That's just human nature. The good news is that these rotten apples are the exception, not the rule.

Just like everyone else, Witches confront issues that require them to make an ethical choice. For instance, should magick be used as a weapon, even if it's only to fight back?

Some witches believe that you cannot effectively bless if you do not know how to curse. The reasoning behind this belief is quite simple: if you don't recognize the cause of a magickal problem and fully comprehend the processes used to enact it, how can you possibly hope to discharge it?

Wiccans and Witches alike see magick as ethically neutral, just as an electric socket is neutral. Magick is gathered from the life energy in all things; that energy is then turned and directed by the Witch towards a goal. So it's how each person uses magick that makes it white, black or grey. In addition, each person's perception of what constitutes white, black and grey isn't always the same. This is definitely one of the frustrations of vision-driven, personalized faiths: defining anything in concrete terms is nearly impossible.

The White Magick Codes

White Witches (those who abide by a simple code that instructs them to work for the good of all) have some general guidelines they follow. For example, as previously mentioned, many believe in the threefold law, which basically translates as *what goes around comes around, not just once but three times.* This seems to be a very good reason to make sure your motivations are positive!

White Witches believe it's highly unethical to attempt to manipulate another person's free will with magick. Such manipulation occurs most commonly in love magick, if one person tries to force or change another's attention. The problems inherent in this practice are pretty obvious – a Witch who casts a love spell will always wonder if the object of her affection truly loves her, or if it's just the magick! And in any case, this type of spell is selfish; it is certainly not cast for the good of all.

There is a universal motto that many Witches use in prayer, spellcraft and ritual: 'For the greatest good and it harm none'. Basically this phrase is added to any process so that the Universe can step in and guide energy where it might otherwise have been misdirected.

Magickal people recognize that while the human mind and spirit have unlimited potential, their ability to recognize all possible outcomes of their magick is *not* unlimited. Human beings are not omniscient, and sometimes good intentions lead to terrible results. The universal motto, therefore, acts as a request for higher (and wiser) powers to direct the magick towards the best possible outcome.

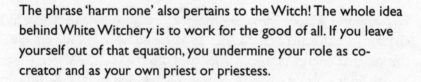

The phrase 'harm none' also pertains to the Witch! The whole idea behind White Witchery is to work for the good of all. If you leave yourself out of that equation, you undermine your role as co-creator and as your own priest or priestess.

Finally, both Witches and Wiccans believe in religious tolerance and respect every Path as having potential for human enlightenment. Since people are different, it only stands to reason that the Paths they choose to walk are different. In keeping with this outlook, you will never find a Witch or Wiccan standing on a street corner preaching about magick or faith. Both groups believe that people must choose their own Path. In fact, by virtue of coming from other religious backgrounds, many Witches and Wiccans have done exactly that.

It's important to stress that this brief overview is a broad generalization at best. Each Witch relies heavily on his or her inner voice (or conscience, if you will) in decision-making and in the way he or she wields magick. That is because Witches believe that each person creates his or her own destiny by action, inaction, karma and so on. There is no cut-and-dried answer to whether anyone is a good or a bad Witch. Most Witches hope to be the best Witches they can be!

'If you believe you can, you probably can. If you believe you won't, you most assuredly won't. Belief is the ignition switch that gets you off the launching pad.'

Denis Waitley, motivational speaker

The Afterlife

Christianity has heaven. Buddhism has nirvana. Where do Witches go when they die? Many of them believe that their souls go to Summerland, a resting place before reincarnation into a new body, in an ongoing cycle of birth, life, death and rebirth.

Gnostics, Hindus, Buddhists, Kabbalists and Druids alike subscribe to the idea that the soul of a human is not limited to a mortal shell. After the body dies, this soul is released into another dimension, where it waits to be reborn and begin the process of learning again.

For insights or ideas, Witches often look to other cultures where the belief in reincarnation has existed for a long time. For example, some African tribes claim the soul goes into the belly of the earth to await rebirth; in China, the spirits of the dead are said to be waiting in the underworld (which is not hell, but simply a place for spirits); Hindus believe that the spirit waits to be reborn from the stars.

Memories from Past Lives

Since each soul had previously inhabited other bodies, why can't you remember your previous lives? It seems as if some time between death and rebirth, memories of past lives are erased, only to be reawakened in dreams, meditations, through hypnosis and/or some type of traumatic life-changing experience. Exactly why past lives are irretrievable without external facilitation is uncertain. Perhaps wiping the slate clean gives human beings a better chance to start again.

Nonetheless, the fact that these memories can (in theory) be retrieved means that the imprint from all our past lives shapes our spirit in the mortal realm. It also means that those memories must be important – perhaps because they can prevent us from repeating past mistakes.

> In general, these memories are awakened by someone or something that ties into the past life experience. In addition, the information from that past life is usually pertinent to what is happening in the here-and-now.

How long a spirit waits between incarnations is also uncertain (mind you, all of this lies in the realm of faith anyway). Most people believe that at least several years (if not decades and centuries) pass between sojourns in this world. Facing the changes in social structure, technology and so on provides a greater opportunity for spiritual growth.

And what about animals? Do they come back? Can we come back as animals? No one knows for certain. If you ask the most devout magickal pet owners, they'll tell you animals have uncanny psychic abilities and seem to have a soul or spirit with which they interact.

Although the idea of reincarnation cannot be validated, many Witches seriously consider the karmic implications of their actions or inactions. They certainly are not alone in their beliefs and responses. William Butler Yeats, Thomas Edison and Alfred, Lord Tennyson were all great proponents of reincarnation. Basically reincarnation and karma teach that the past affects the present, and the present affects the future – no matter what life cycle you are talking about.

Living and Thinking Globally

The world view of most Witches bears striking similarity to those walking a Shamanic Path. As do shamans, they see the earth as a living, breathing classroom to be honoured and protected, not a place to conquer and control. Every living thing in this world has a spirit, a unique energy pattern, including the planet itself. As a result, Witches tend to think globally, mindful of nature and the cosmic universe.

The word *shaman* comes from one of two sources. In Tunguso-Manchurian, the word *saman* means quite simply 'one who knows'. In Sanskrit, the term *sranaba* was used to describe an ascetic who depended on spirits for information, knowledge and guidance.

Earth as a Classroom

The Witch's body houses his or her soul. Since most Witches believe in reincarnation, their time on this planet is spent gaining and applying spiritual principles to eventually stop the cycle of reincarnation and return to the source. Witches regard the earth, its creatures and its elements as their teachers, which have the power to reflect the divine plan and pattern that extends throughout the universe.

With this in mind, most Witches strive to weave their magick and live their lives within natural laws, working in partnership with the planet instead of fighting it. Many Witches are strong proponents of protecting endangered lands and wildlife, feeling that the loss of either not only eliminates a wonderful learning opportunity but also is a crime against Gaia (one name for the earth's spirit; in Greek mythology, goddess of the earth). In addition, many Witches donate their money or time to ecological causes in the hopes of educating and inspiring others to do likewise. They do not wish to see humans (or anything else) on the endangered species list!

Stewardship of this planet doesn't end with donations or recycling efforts; it also extends into magickal practices. Witches often send out positive energy from spells and rituals. The energy may be aimed at protecting a particular environment or species, or directed, like a healing balm, at the whole world. Perhaps that sounds rather grand, but magick is only limited by the practitioner's perception of what it can and cannot do and what it can and cannot reach. There is no reason magickal energy cannot encompass the whole globe, like a giant hug.

'It's sacred ground we walk upon with every step we take', many Witches sing. The meaning in that verse should not be lost in the way a Witch moves through every moment of every day. We need to move gently, to respect all life and to respect the sacredness in all things and in each other; otherwise we are not truly honouring our magick.

The World Through a Witch's Eye

Above and beyond caring for the environment, how else does this kind of global thinking affect Witches? Mostly in the way they perceive things. A rock, a flower, a herb, a tree, a stray animal may all hold special meaning, depending on when and where it appears and what's going on in the life of that person. For example, if a wild rose suddenly grows in a Witch's yard, he or she might take it as a positive omen of love growing in the home. Taking this one step further, the clever Witch would thank nature for its gift, dry some of those petals and turn this little treasure into love-inspiring incense! In this manner, a Witch will often discover that walking a magickal Path reinspires a childlike wonder towards the planet and the small things that are often overlooked in our busy lives.

'Nature is a temple in which living columns sometimes emit confused words. Man approaches it through forests of symbols, which observe him with familiar glances.'

Charles-Pierre Baudelaire (1821–67), poet

The Next Generation

'Teach your children in the way they should go' instructs a biblical writer. Does this idea apply to Wicca and Witchcraft, where the idea of proselytization is abhorrent? What are the karmic implications of 'teaching' a child magickal methods and ideology? These are the types of questions the magickal community continues to struggle with. In part, a Neo-Pagan parent doesn't want to close off the world of magick to his or her child – it's such a wonder, and something to which children are naturally drawn. In addition, because younger children have a high capacity for belief, they can achieve amazing results from their Craft. On the other hand, does teaching children magick and nothing else hinder their free will?

One school of thought maintains that since many Witches have been brought up as Christians, the option to change direction and choose their own way still exists. In addition, if a child shows talent and interest, it seems wrong not to foster both. Magick was often a family-trained Craft, so learning at the foot of a parent or grandparent is part of the Witch's legacy.

According to a second school of thought, children should find their own way, and parents should not influence their search for a personal Path. Many Witches have difficulty comprehending this approach because a good parent teaches by example. How can a child *not* be influenced by a Witch truly walking the walk?

The answer for most parents seems to lie somewhere between these two extremes. The primary consideration seems to be teaching children tolerance, respect, earth-awareness and self-confidence – in effect, teaching them to be good and sensitive human beings. Nothing too much like hocus-pocus there.

A secondary focus may be on spirituality, which need not be coloured by specific beliefs and practices. Finally, parents should focus on something that children take to quite naturally – joyful, expressive living. There is a passion to Wicca and Witchcraft, a zest for life and an appreciation for it that's refreshing. In fact, I've often heard magickal parents commenting on how their child has taught them much about true magick and true happiness. In any case, isn't that true for many parents?

The fourth point of focus is welcoming children into magickal celebrations. At a variety of gatherings and observances, there are special games and activities for various age groups. Many Bardic Circles invite children to sing, tell stories or recount jokes. There are also ritual circles where each child present stands hand-in-hand with adults as an important part of the whole. Although children are not required to do any of these things, they seem to truly love to participate when they are given the opportunity.

These four points are like spokes on a wheel, rounding out a child's experiences with his or her magickal parents. In observing the results in the Neo-Pagan community, the process appears to be working: the youth are confident, feel as if their voices matter, have some semblance of manners and generally exhibit a level of sensitivity that surprises many adults. Considering that apathy, doubt, uncertainty and insecurity are some of the greatest problems among today's young, the four-point focus seems to be working.

CHAPTER 2

A History of Magick, Wicca and Witchcraft

Witches have a rich cultural heritage that they continue to celebrate today. In the pages that follow, you'll get a glimpse of the ancient roots of Witchcraft in all its forms and learn about the modern reincarnation of Witchcraft, which has a whole new face and a relatively young presence in the public eye.

The Earliest Seeds

The history of magick and Witchcraft are impossible to separate. Although not all magick comes under the broad title of Witchcraft, all Witches practise magick in one form or another. At the dawn of the human race, when people first began to understand the idea of cause and effect, they began their ongoing search for reasons behind everything that takes place in the world. So if a wind brought down a tree and hurt someone, the wind might be characterized as 'angry' and then considered a spirit worthy of appeasement. In this manner, nearly all aspects of nature were anthropomorphized and the first vestiges of magickal thinking were born.

As civilizations developed, each brought a new flavour and tone to magickal ideas. The most common of these ideas was that the universe is like a web made up of all kinds of invisible strands or connections. If humans could learn to influence one of these connections, they could affect the whole web.

At first, these attempts to influence the world were very simple: one action for one result. For example, to bind an angry spirit, a person might tie a knot in a piece of yarn or rope. If the action worked, it was used again, and eventually a tradition was born.

Modern Wicca and Witchcraft have departed from the custom of delegating magickal authority to a select few. Today, everyone is welcome to explore these Paths and processes, not just an elite few.

Very often, people delegated the tasks of influencing the universe to a few select individuals, who were elevated to a position of authority in their community. We find these people in various cultures and under various names – shaman, priest, magus or Witch – yet they are all performing the same basic functions, although the symbolic meaning of their actions generally depends on their particular culture and time frame. Secondary attempts at influencing fate became more elaborate and included ritualistic attempts to coerce the ancestors, powerful spirits or gods into action. Again, the community would place a few venerated people in charge of such sacred duties. Here are some titles of magickal practitioners from around the world:

A BA'ALATH OB: Mistress of talismans (Hebrew)
CYRABDERIS: Witchdoctor (Mexican Spanish)
KASHAPH: Magus and sorcerer (Hebrew)
MAGOS: Wise person (Greek)
MALEFICUS: Diabolical Witch (Latin)
STREGA: Witch, originally with negative overtones (Italian)
VOLVAS: Sorceress (Norse)

Witchcraft in Europe

History is imperfect and is often clouded by societal, personal or political agendas; for these reasons, the study of magickal history is no easy task. To trace the course of events that led to modern Wicca and Witchcraft, let's begin by examining the first manifestations of Witchcraft in Europe.

f@ct

'History is the witness that testifies to the passing of time; it illumines reality, vitalizes memory, provides guidance in daily life and brings us tidings of antiquity.'

Marcus Tullius Cicero (106–43 BCE),
Roman orator, statesman and philosopher

There are four competing interpretations of how Witchcraft took root in Europe. The first view, which most in the magickal community have rejected, is that Witches never really existed and that Witchcraft was simply an invention of the Church authorities, used specifically to gain power and wealth.

The second view is that Witchcraft developed out of European fertility cults that emphasized a goddess as a central deity. Although this concept has some merit, historians have yet to substantiate it with written chronicles.

fact

It was not until the 3rd century, the period of Rome's conversion to Christianity, that any substantial writings on witchery can be found. The vast majority of these writings, the most recent of which date to the 1700s, portray Witches in a very negative light.

The third view is that the idea of Witchcraft was a social convention: when people could not explain an event, they blamed a Witch. This perspective traditionally does not allow for the real existence of Witches, but instead sees them as part of superstition.

Finally, and most accurately, there is a theory that describes how Witchcraft developed gradually from a wide variety of practices and customs. Many of these customs have their roots in Paganism, Hebrew mysticism and Greek folklore surrounding sorcery, and many of them carried into Christianity – vestiges of magickal and Pagan traditions were seen in the early Church, and some remain even to this day.

Saint Brigid was originally a European goddess figure so beloved by the common people that the Church adapted her story and canonized her. This is an excellent example of Pagan beliefs and symbolism that the early Church 'borrowed' and incorporated into its tradition.

Despite (or because of) the Church's obvious connection to Paganism, early Christians did everything in their power to discourage the old ways. Books of penance from the Middle Ages often speak of appropriate punishments for people caught practising magick: for example, a mother caught putting her daughter on the roof to cure sickness was commanded to do penance for seven years (penance generally consisted of some type of fasting or other restriction).

Witchcraft was also influenced by the myths that travelled from one culture to the next. The legends of Diana, the Roman goddess honoured by many Witches as a patroness, for example, integrated a blend of Celtic and Teutonic lore. What is most important here is not so much the blending of customs but the communication involved – a great number of magickal traditions have been handed down through successive generations by oral teaching.

Witchcraft Made Illegal

Sometime around the 8th and 9th centuries, laws regarding Witchcraft became much more prevalent. Some of these laws actually made sense: for example, Charlemagne made human sacrifice a crime punishable by death. Other laws, however, began to undermine the customs and traditions of the common people. For example, in 743 the Synod of Rome declared it a crime to leave offerings to spirits; and in 829 the Synod of Paris passed a decree proclaiming that the Church no longer tolerated incantations and idolatry. By 900 Christian scholars had dedicated much time and effort to writing about how women were supposedly being led astray by the devil. These events helped prepare the scene for the fires of the Inquisition.

> The modern Wiccan community's insistence on the Goddess aspect of deity is a reaction to the 2,000 years of Christian presence, when only the male aspect of the Divine was recognized in Europe.

The Inquisition

Between the 1100s and 1300s, the image of a Witch continued to be transformed into a devilish creature who despised all things sacred, ate children and held wild orgies to seduce innocents. Stories of sorcerers who required that supplicants renounce the Church or Christ as payment for their services ran rampant. Christopher Marlowe's *The Tragicall History of Dr. Faustus*, published in 1604, recounted a story about a philosopher who sold his soul to the devil and used magick in his quest to find sensual delight.

The tales and heinous charges ascribed to Witches were nothing new. Similar accusations happened when the Romans and the Christians first clashed, and when the Syrians fought against the Jews. In effect, every group wanted its beliefs to be the one 'true' religion.

Members of the learned community railed against the evils of Witchcraft in flowery, educated language, and the preachers disseminated these ideas among the common folk. In effect, the Church labelled everything magickal as heresy. Witchery became a crime against God and the Church, with the exception of England, where it was regarded as a civil violation.

From the 12th century onward, both clerical and mundane law grew harsher towards witchery. Punishments included burning and excommunication, as well as hanging. Worse still was the entire Inquisition process, which resorted to torturing people to get the 'truth' from them; that is, to 'encourage' them admit to whatever the inquisitor wished. In the process, accusing someone of Witchcraft became a bureaucratic convenience, conviction rates soared and the scene was set for the Witch hunts.

'It is the customary fate of new truths to begin as heresies and to end as superstitions.'

Thomas Henry Huxley (1825–95), biologist

The Witch Craze

The Witch craze picked up pace during the Reformation period. The intellectual leaders of this religious movement, which sought to reform the Christian practices of Europe and reject the Catholic Church as being the only true Christianity, felt no need for what they saw as Witchcraft's superstitious prattle and offered no protection to the accused. Meanwhile, the public struggled with the new religious ideas and in its confusion was only too willing to project desires and blame onto anyone who differed in their opinions and traditions. It was the perfect environment for mass persecution – Catholics were killing Protestants, Protestants were killing Catholics, and both were killing Witches. The legal sanctions against witchery became even harsher than before, and the lengths to which authorities would go to secure a confession became even more malevolent.

The simple folkloric face of the wise person or healer was now concealed behind a veil of evil and secrecy. Most practitioners of the old ways hid their thoughts and practices until the atmosphere changed (not necessarily in their lifetime). Meanwhile, the notion of Witchcraft as a 'diabolical' practice spread from central Europe into Scotland, Spain, France, Germany, Switzerland and Italy, finally reaching as far as Scandinavia by the 17th century.

fact

Between 1317 and 1319, Pope John XXII authorized a religious court, known as the Inquisition, to proceed against sorcerers and all persons who had made a pact with the devil.

The Witch craze abated briefly in the 14th century, only to increase again with secular courts adopting the processes of the Inquisition. Thousands of trials proceeded, and the infamous *Malleus Maleficarum* (*Hammer of Witches*), published in 1486 by Heinrich Institoris as a guidebook for inquisitors, added fuel to the fires of Christian righteousness. The godly people who tortured innocent individuals believed that if the person was not guilty, God would certainly intervene. Of course, he never did, and each confession and death gave the inquisitor more power.

The atmosphere in England was different, however. Because Henry VIII had separated from the Catholic Church to form the Church of England, the Inquisition never took place. Witchcraft trials were strictly a civil matter, and there were far fewer instances of death sentences. In part, this may have been the influence of Mr John Dee, a Wizard of some renown, who, having been imprisoned for treason by Queen Mary, was regularly consulted by Elizabeth I.

It wasn't really until James VI of Scotland became king of England in 1603 that we see strong strictures against cunning folk and any type of Witch hunt occurring. The hunts then continued until the early 1700s, when the Witch statute was finally repealed.

It's hard to know for certain exactly what caused the fever to subside. In part, public opinion certainly helped: people had grown weary of the violence. The number of individuals accused and sentenced as Witches throughout Europe declined steadily, much to everyone's relief. The last execution on record occurred in Germany in 1775.

Witchcraft in America

The Witchcraft mania didn't seem to reach the American shore until the mid-1600s, reaching its height with the Salem Witch Trials. This was a marvellous example of how an innocent moment can turn to tragedy. After some girls tried divination methods, they got frightened and began to feign having been bewitched. They accused specific women (whom they disliked) of harming them through witchery. Confessing to the accusations often spared the person's life, but those who did not admit to being Witches were executed.

Eighteen people were hanged alongside a couple of cats and dogs. In addition one man was crushed to death by stones, although apparently the intention was not to kill him but to scare him into confession. Between four and seventeen people died in prison (sources on this point are unreliable). Historians believe that while a few of those accused may have been part of a secret society, there is no evidence to suggest that the majority had any associations with diabolical Witchcraft.

Witches in Hiding

Over the centuries, Witches gradually lost their status as village helpmates and were banished to the fringes of society. Still, Witchcraft as a community service remained an unspoken, unacknowledged truth. Were cunning folk still practising their arts? Yes, but they practised very quietly and very carefully in the shadow of the new world view that witchery was nothing more than superstition. This status quo continued until the 19th century, when the intellectual community began to consider Witchcraft in a different light.

The Modern Rebirth of Witchcraft

Intellectuals began to see Witchcraft as a natural religion, which had nothing to do with Satan. This romantic portrait, complete with a deep respect for nature, revived interest in the Craft. Witches had been misunderstood, maligned and harmed, but now they were elevated to a new type of mythology. Well-known people such as Sir Walter Scott argued that Witchcraft was real and that it owed its origins to the pre-Christian traditions of the common people. Public interest in the occult once again began to grow.

Groups like the Rosicrucian Order, the Order of the Temple of the Orient (OTO) and the Hermetic Order of the Golden Dawn sprang up, all focused on the occult arts, their ranks including such notables as W. B. Yeats and Bram Stoker. These groups, and others like them, translated Kabbalistic texts filled with spells, herbals and other magickal processes. In the midst of this revival, Aleister Crowley and Gerald Gardner came to the forefront with their new ideas, and the new breed of Witchcraft was born.

Although some of Aleister Crowley's practices have been criticized as unnecessarily gruesome or aimed at creating a public stir, his definition of magick still stands as one of the best ever given. Crowley said, 'Magick is the Science and Art of causing change to occur in conformity with the will'.

Magick Today

Imagine that it is the 1970s. Magickal practices, especially folk magick, are still found all around the world. (In fact, it is fairly safe to say that folk traditions never suffered the same fate as Witchcraft and sorcery.) The Western world has experienced the hippie movement and the rise of a whole new type of individualism. It is time for a new breed of Witches to come out of the broom closet.

While many people still associate Witchcraft with diabolical deeds or mistake it for Satanism, more people are seeing witchery in the light cast by the romantic revival. Practitioners of witchery or Wicca believe that magick and psychic abilities are available to anyone with the time and inclination to learn.

It is impossible for a Witch to be a Satanist. Satanism is based in Christian mythology and focuses on a being called Satan. Witchcraft (and Wicca, in particular) is based on the history outlined in this chapter and has no such diabolical deity.

By this point Gerald Gardner's book *Witchcraft Today* is widely known and discussed; Alex Sanders has established the Alexandrian tradition of Wicca; Dianic Witches, who are tied into the feminist movement, are on the scene; and the Covenant of the Goddess is active. Dozens of small covens and study groups are forming throughout the country.

In 1979, Starhawk writes *Spiral Dance*, which is now on most Witches' lists of essential readings. More and more magickal organizations from varying traditions begin to form worldwide. Although there are no official numbers that we can gather, estimates based on periodical subscriptions and word-of-mouth networking show as many as 10,000 practising Witches in the world by 1980.

On the heels of such growth, a whole new group of leaders emerges. These leaders are people just like you – bright, friendly people like Marion Weinstein, who starts teaching positive magick and performing stand-up comedy about Witches; Isaac Bonewits, who comes forward to teach us about our heritage and provide us with practical guidance to living the magick; and Scott Cunningham, who shares the down-to-earth methods of Witchcraft with the public. (Appendix A contains a more complete list of contemporary Witchcraft and Wiccan leaders.) Mail-order courses are also easily available for those who want to learn serious magick outside a coven setting.

Today, if you were to visit *www.Amazon.co.uk* and search for titles on magickal practices, including Wicca, Witchcraft, Paganism and the occult, you would have to wade through more than 500 listings – and that's just books! Yet one of the most significant indicators of the surging popularity of these subjects is the phenomenal success of Harry Potter, J. K. Rowling's schoolboy wizard, whose adventures have captured the imagination of over a quarter of a billion readers in 200 countries. As the saying goes, we've come a long way, baby!

The Contemporary Outlook

Having examined the history of Witchcraft, you can now better understand the diversity of beliefs and traditions in modern Wicca and Witchcraft. Some Witches, for example, meet in covens of 13; others have larger and smaller groups. Some specify that meetings have to take place in 3m (9ft) circles; others simply gather around a fire or an altar. Some Witches are Pagan (honouring many gods and goddesses); some are monotheistic (believing in the existence of one deity); and some are agnostic (not believing in any god figure).

This diversity of beliefs and practices is what makes describing modern Wicca and Witchcraft very difficult. Who can say what *all* Witches do or believe in?

Nevertheless, there are some general tenets that can be applied to most practitioners of Wicca and Witchcraft. Perhaps the most universal connection between all modern Witches is an appreciation of nature. The natural world is an unending source of metaphors and symbols that relate to our daily lives in a variety of ways; as did their ancestors, Witches look to those symbols for guidance (and as a source of power, since all life contains energy that can be acted upon with magick).

A second, semi-universal outlook in modern Wicca and Witchcraft is the quest for self-improvement. Modern Witches hope to improve the quality of their lives and the lives of those they touch through their studies and arts. They regard each person as sacred, so their practices uplift the human potential and provide psychological support. The power of positive thinking is something that shouldn't be underestimated.

A third common factor is the overall atmosphere of witchery. Witchcraft is not a grim practice – Witches celebrate life and laughter, and generally consider humour as good food for the soul.

Fourth, modern Witches do not see their arts or abilities as 'supernatural'. In fact, their Craft is a wholly natural way of directing energy within and around the self. The tools they use are simply a means to an end. The only difference between people in terms of the way magick manifests is exactly what type of magick they choose to practise and how adept they become through their own willpower and focus.

The final, and perhaps most important, universal connection between Witches and Wiccans is that they recognize their responsibility for their life and magick. Rarely will a Witch or Wiccan blame the spirit or fate for his or her woes. Wiccans consider themselves co-creators with the Divine. They see the latent potential in all things and put that potential to work to transform reality.

No, this isn't exactly the Witchcraft or Paganism of our ancestors. It isn't the Witchcraft of storybooks or films either. Instead, this Witchcraft is something very new, but with long and tangled roots. It is a responsible, socially aware, ecologically mindful way of living that is rapidly attracting people from all walks of life and all age groups. Now, finally, Witches no longer need to hide in the shadows of the past.

The New Millennium and Looking Forward

Every day, people are discovering the wonders of magickal living in new, personally enhancing ways. The results from all this shifting and changing will resonate in the spiritual community for many generations to come. Wicca specifically teaches that spirituality should grow and adapt with the times; in other words, it should remain proactive. So we can expect ongoing transformations within the Witchcraft and Wicca movements – who can predict how different Witches 200 years from now will be?

What is happening now, and what does the future of Witchcraft and Wicca look like? Well, if the East Coast of the USA is any indication, the future seems very bright indeed. Recently, two well-established, successful magickal gathering coordinators, Out of the Dark, Inc. (*www.outofthedark.com*) and Phoenix Festivals (*www.phoenixfestivals.com*) purchased land on which to hold ongoing Neo-Pagan festivals and activities. This trend is not new, and is likely to continue – in fact, it is very similar to the way in which Christian churches grew in their heyday.

On a broader level, looking to the Internet, we see thousands of websites dedicated to Wicca and Witchcraft. Internet groups such as Wiccans and Witches in London (see Appendix B) attract over 1,000 members; and *www.witchvox.com* receives thousands of hits per week. Containing over 40,000 listings of Witches from around the world and 5,000 website links, *witchvox.com* also receives 1,000 submissions each week for networking. The people who run this site are very proud of its success – and rightfully so, as this is a noncommercial community-supported website and is run on a voluntary basis.

As you can see, Wicca and Witchcraft are definitely on the rise. At this juncture, it would take something major to quell the wave that is already washing out in all directions. As long as freedom of religion remains an important tenet of humankind, there will be Witches celebrating their beliefs and practices alongside others of alternative faiths.

CHAPTER 3
Folklore
and Superstitions

As we have seen, the historical roots of Witchcraft and Wicca reach back to the origins of humanity. The magickal heritage carefully preserved by Witches throughout the ages includes splendid folkloric tales of divine legendary figures, memories of ancient rituals and practices, and various superstitions.

Witchy Lore and Superstition

Fantastical tales and superstitions, an inherent part of Wicca and Witchcraft, come from various sources. Some beliefs developed from simple misunderstandings: for example, an ancient Witch would leap or jump about with a broom to encourage crop fertility and growth, hoping that the crops would follow the example and also strain upwards. Observers of such a magickal rite, not realizing what they were seeing, probably thought the Witch was trying to fly on her broom, and so the idea that all Witches fly on their broomsticks was born.

Other beliefs about Witches developed in mainstream religions that intentionally wished to demonize the old gods. Still other ideas grew directly out of magickal customs, many of which have roots in country sayings and conventions.

Although some superstitions are rooted in truth, many are simply misrepresentations of Witches and what they stand for. A good illustration is the celebration of Halloween: pointy hats, warts and black cats – the symbols of this celebration – are all products of unfounded superstition. Although most modern Witches wouldn't be caught dead in these accoutrements, it's really difficult to get away from the stereotype. So, rather than trying to reinvent the wheel, modern Witches have made light of the nonsensical portraits – for example, as you drive to work one day, you may see a Witch's car bearing a tongue-in-cheek bumper sticker that reads 'My other car is a broom'.

On another level, however, clever modern Witches embrace folklore and superstition as a treasure chest filled with magickal potential. For example, while modern Witches don't ride brooms through the night, they do use brooms to sweep the magick Circle clean of negativity, or to gather good luck at certain times of the year. It's also not uncommon to see Witches wearing dramatically styled robes to help them make a mental shift from the mundane to magickal workings.

Old Is New Again

As you read, you will find that some of the ideas presented here reappear later in this book: for example, many herbs that people used to safeguard themselves from magick still belong in the Witch's kit; they have been saved for protective spells and rituals. Similarly, today's Witches often continue to employ the stones and plants used hundreds of years ago to improve the effect of a magickal working.

Why does this happen? In part, it's thanks to the diligent efforts of scribes and other learned people who recorded the correspondences and uses of herbs, stones, plants and animal parts according to their culture and time. Modern Witches can look at those notes and consider how and where to best apply them (especially if they're practising a culturally influenced methodology).

If our ancestors repeatedly used a specific component for a magickal process, it must have been working. As the saying goes, if it ain't broke, don't fix it!

Witching Powers

Modern Witches are pretty familiar with the processes involved in all the abilities traditionally ascribed to Witches, but the general public is not. Since lore comes from the common people, the confusion and uncertainty about such powers have become the fodder for all kinds of tall tales – everyone likes a good story! Sadly, these tales also made Witches easy prey for people who wanted someone to blame for nearly any unfortunate event.

Consider for a moment the young married man whose eye strays to another woman. He, or his wife, might blame that woman of bewitching the man. Exactly how she would be punished for her crime depended on the culture and the time in which she lived, but it's interesting that the gentleman involved was rarely held accountable for his indiscretion.

What Powers Do Witches Possess?

Old stories endow the Witch with a variety of talents; some talents came naturally and some were learned from a respected teacher (parent or otherwise). These abilities include divining the future, transforming into animals, flying, raising winds or thunder and lightning, becoming invisible, animating inanimate objects, casting spells, raising spirits and understanding herbal medicines and poisons. You might translate this list for the modern Witch as fortunetelling, glamoury, shapeshifting, astral projection, weather working, the making of elementaries, charm making, invocation (or mediumship) and herbcraft or cunning craft.

Besides what the Witch knew by instinct or learned from her mentor, there were a variety of natural objects, such as plants or rocks or even animals, that were said to improve or support the Witch's powers. For example, to bring good luck, a Witch would have bound swallow feathers with a red ribbon and placed them in her bed. A Witch who wished to protect himself from an invoked spirit would have carried angelica into the sacred space. A Witch wishing to improve her rapport with a cat familiar would have used catnip in her spell. Other examples of the traditional use of herbs or plants to enhance powers include:

- ☾ Sowing chamomile or coriander in the garden to increase the plants' magickal powers.
- ☾ Adding a pinch of dragon's blood (a resin from the red berries of the tree *Calanus draco*) to incense or spell components to increase the power.
- ☾ Invoking a helpful spirit with echinacea or vervain.
- ☾ Putting figs into love foods or potions to improve the results.
- ☾ Carrying juniper or mugwort to improve psychic sense.
- ☾ Placing a sprig of mulberry in a spellbook to keep it safe from prying eyes.
- ☾ Using periwinkle in nearly any magickal process (this herb increases overall magickal power).
- ☾ Holding a Y-shaped piece of poplar wood for divining (especially water witching).
- ☾ Dabbing rose water to create favourable, hospitable responses from others.
- ☾ Gathering sage leaves at dawn and burying them to encourage rain that day.

Witches also carried or wore rocks or minerals for protection or to improve their powers. For example, if a Witch kept a holey stone (any stone with a hole all the way through it) or Witch stone with her other magickal tools and components, it would both improve the power in these items and protect her house. Here are a few more uses:

☾ Wearing amber and/or jet (to signal one's status as a priest or priestess).

☾ Placing a moonstone over the third eye to improve psychic 'sight'.

☾ Using a bloodstone in spells, specifically those to secure victory.

☾ Placing a quartz crystal on the altar to honour the Goddess (or wearing it to invoke and welcome her energies).

☾ Donning malachite to warn off forthcoming peril (this stone is said to shatter if the Witch is in danger).

☾ Binding an opal to one's arm or gathering fern on Midsummer Eve as part of an invisibility spell.

☾ Watching to see if a ruby glows to know if trouble is afoot.

☾ Rubbing a piece of jasper to improve mental focus.

As you can see from this list, Witches had (and continue to have) similar goals to everyday folk. They worked towards self-improvement, luck, happiness, health and safety, towards refining their arts – by doing so, they also protected their position in the community. And at some points in history, Witches who made promises they didn't keep often were killed for their error.

Traditionally, Witches have been endowed with some amazing abilities. For example, Witches were supposedly able to:

☾ *Twist a person's mouth if he breaks a promise.* A modern Witch would consider this ability the power of true seeing (or the ability to discern the truth from a lie) or some type of a curse.

☾ *Walk between two people, or a person and an animal, to separate the connection between them.* This activity might be considered a kind of cleansing or banishing of astral energy ties that we attach to people and pets when we're close to them for a long time.

These two examples show that even the strangest ideas may have some root in a very real experience, some glimmer of truth. The trick for historians is to discern the truth from the traditional story so that we can better understand the spirit of the times.

A Witch's Weak Spot

As if to balance all these amazing talents, popular legends and beliefs teach that a Witch cannot weep, has an ugly birthmark in her armpit, must stop and count the straws on every broom he sees, often bears a large wart on her nose, floats in water, can have spells beaten out of him and cannot stand holy water. It is also said that you can take away a Witch's power by scratching her forehead (called 'scoring the breath' in the mid-1500s).

Now, it's pretty obvious that these beliefs are silly, but how did they begin and why have they been perpetuated? For one thing, the power of the Witch in the local community shouldn't be underestimated. Witches were important figures and had considerable influence. The early Church saw cunning folk as a hindrance to new converts, and looked for an easy way to appropriate their lands and money. So a good number of the ugly rumours about Witches can be traced to this source (especially during the Witch hunts).

Second, common people needed to feel as if they understood something about the often mysterious world around them, even if that 'something' was only to explain wonders as being 'magick'. In turn, they also needed to feel that, if need be, they could overcome this awesome magickal power, so the idea that all Witches must have fatal flaws and characteristics that expose their true identities makes perfect sense. This also explains why the predominant amount of superstition surrounding Witches and Witchcraft focuses on how to protect yourself from both.

Signs of Witches and Witchcraft

Weaknesses weren't the only factors used in trying to work out whether someone was a true Witch. Folklore and a good number of pages in the

Witch-finder books of the Witch hunts were dedicated to this 'science'. Some supposedly tried-and-true signs included:

☾ An elderly woman who has several animals (cats, certain breeds of dog, black birds, frogs, black sheep and horses were all said to have a special affinity for Witches). A creature that forms a special bond with a Witch is called a familiar. This familiar was believed to have a variety of powers, including the ability to gather information about unsuspecting humans . And if this creature bore the name Makeshift, Swein, Greedigut, Rapha, Littleman, Volon, Rory or Tissy, it served as even more potent proof that its master was a Witch.

☾ A smoky fire or a fire that burns only on one side (This sign means that a Witch has taken up residence nearby. The solution: place a poker at your gate to keep the Witch away.)

fact

The interpretation of fire signs is called pyromancy. If you observe something tossed in the fire (the way it burns) rather than the fire itself, this is called causimomancy.

☾ Possessions such as a broom with an ash handle (thought to be indispensable), a cauldron, a crystal ball or other witchy tools such as candles, scarabs, coloured thread, bells, ashes, bones, mirrors, coral, a drum, herb bundles, feathers and so forth.

☾ A hawthorn hedge around the garden (said to keep the Witch's power within).

☾ Hex marks painted or engraved on doors, windows, floorboards or other parts of the home.

☾ Living in forsaken ruins, a lonely forest or a mountaintop cave.

☾ Eyebrows that grow close together or that meet over the nose.

☾ Turning a churn to no purpose (the motion of churning was regarded as a kind of spellcraft).

☾ Two pupils in one eye, squint eyes, crossed eyes, one eye set lower than the other, or the ability to wink with one eye and look with the other.

Sounds as if at least one of these things could pertain to anyone? Of course. The Witch-finder books were written to enable the Witch-finder to accuse anyone he chose of Witchcraft. Sadly, these kinds of broad generalizations cost hundreds of innocent people and animals their lives.

The kind of injustice that occurred when people were accused of Witchcraft is why, to this day, one of the favourite mottoes among witches is 'Never again the burning'.

Protection from Witches

OK, the woman just outside town has been deemed a 'bad' Witch (or, at the very least, one with an axe to grind with you). What do you do?

Here is what people in the past did to protect themselves. Since they believed that personal belongings could be used in spells, they made sure to pick up and dispose of pins, metal, hair and fingernail clippings. They would never allow a Witch to measure them (or any part of their body) unless it was for curative purposes, because such measures could be used for curses. And if a Witch did measure them, they got the measure back or saw that it was destroyed. Mostly, however, our ancestors used what they found in nature – plants, herbs, rocks, minerals: for instance, placing rowan wood, communion bread, bits of coral or iron near a child's cradle would keep the infant from harm.

Here are a few examples of the way plants were used for protection:

- ☾ Drinking angelica tea to cure bewitchment and banish curses.
- ☾ Dabbing elderberry juice on your eyes to see Witches.
- ☾ Carrying elder wood to recognize a Witch when you see one.
- ☾ Hanging fennel in doorways and windows to keep bad magick away.
- ☾ Putting a fern frond over the ear of a horse to baffle Witches.
- ☾ Planting a holly bush, bay laurel, ash or elder tree outside the front door.
- ☾ Carrying marjoram, chamomile, cinquefoil, garlic or mistletoe to turn away unwanted spells.

☾ Eating nettles to dispel a curse.

☾ Keeping nuts and apples in the house on Halloween.

☾ Carrying a double nut, especially a double hazelnut.

☾ Feeding farm animals oats to keep them safe from witchery.

☾ Tying rowan wood with red thread as a powerful anti-magick charm.

☾ Binding and carrying vervain and dill as an anti-Witchcraft charm.

Our ancestors also used certain minerals or rocks to protect themselves from Witches. Holding carnelian would keep a Witch from reading your mind and protect you from spells. If you carried a piece of coal for luck, turning it over would turn away bad magick. Another way to safeguard against magickal misfortune was to keep a piece of jade in the house.

Certain activities also claimed to offer protection from witchery. Sometimes it was as easy as leaving out bread or small sweets overnight: the food would so tempt a visiting Witch that she would forget to do any mischief. Showing kindness to a black cat (thought to be a Witch in disguise) would bring magickal favour instead of a curse. However, some of these activities required some effort, such as staying home for the entire month of May or only going out briefly, because Witches were said to have more influence in May. To protect livestock from witchery, people would hang the carcass of a cow or lamb in the chimney or in a thorn tree; this custom probably grew out of the superstitions surrounding the power of blood. Other examples include:

☾ Carrying a blessed candle.

☾ Laying a broom across the threshold (supposedly the Witch would make an excuse and turn back).

☾ Chalking elaborate patterns across the stone or wood of the doorstep so the doorposts are joined (the more detailed the pattern, the greater the protective power).

☾ Putting cow dung in the mouth of a newly born calf to keep it safe from witchery. (A lot of similarly gruesome practices are discussed in collections of folklore, based on the idea that the more disgusting something is, the more likely it is to keep away foul things.)

☾ Breaking an egg to break the influence of a curse or spell.

☾ Carrying a rabbit's foot (perhaps this is why a rabbit's foot is still considered lucky).

☾ Sprinkling salt around the home to keep away Witches, sorcerers and evil spirits.

Warding Off the Evil Eye

Of all types of magick, however, the most feared was the infamous 'evil eye'. (In Greek, the expression for *evil eye* literally means 'to kill with a glance'.) Not surprisingly, people took literally hundreds of protective measures against something that could harm from a distance without anyone ever knowing. These measures included:

☾ Donning a carnelian ring (Turkey and Greece).

☾ Wearing a silver crescent moon amulet (Middle East/Asia).

☾ Carrying an eye agate (Europe).

☾ Sprinkling gold and silver water over a child who was given the evil eye.

☾ Burying a phallus-shaped stone near one's home to turn away the evil eye (predominately Greece and Rome).

Every item on this planet has been credited with having some spiritual or magickal attributes. Exactly how each item got its reputation is open to debate, but more than likely it was a blend of coincidence, observation and repetition. Over time, the oral tradition was written down and committed into customary actions, where it remains to this very day, often without us being the wiser.

Although people from long ago feared and ostracized Witches, they nevertheless depended on magick for protection from Witchcraft! Did these people consider their actions remotely magickal? Probably not. They acted out their superstitions and folkloric beliefs, which were far more acceptable than they are today.

CHAPTER 4

The Witch's Kit: Tools and Symbolism

The tools of the Craft speak to our subconscious mind in forms that help support magickal workings. The purpose of this chapter is to delineate what tools and symbols are commonly found in Wicca and Witchcraft, how they're used and what they represent.

The Role of Tools in Witchcraft

Witches and Wiccans will tell you that tools are good helpmates to magick, but they are not necessary to the success of any spell or ritual. A tool is only a focus, something to distract you from yourself. Without the Witch's will and directed energy, the potential in any tool remains dormant. For example, a Witch might talk about quartz crystals as having energy-enhancing power, but until a crystal is charged and activated, that ability 'sleeps' within. In magick, the Witch is the enabler. A focused will is all that any effective Witch needs for magick. Everything else just makes the job easier.

What happens if a specific tool isn't available?
Find something else with appropriate symbolic value. Some alternatives for an athame include a butter knife or wooden spoon (especially for a kitchen Witch), a dirk (Scottish Witchcraft), a sword (commonly seen in High Magick) or even a finger!

Athame

The origins of the word *athame* have been lost to history. Some speculate that it may have come from *The Clavicle of Solomon* (published in 1572), which refers to the knife as the *Arthana* (*athame* may be a subverted form of this term). Another theory is that *athame* comes from the Arabic word *al-dhamme* (bloodletter), a sacred knife in the Moorish tradition. In either case, there are magickal manuscripts dating to the 1200s that imply the use of ritual knives in magick (and special knives were certainly used in ancient offerings).

Modern Wiccans use the knife to represent the male aspect of the Divine and as a symbol of the will (both good and ill). Some Wiccans do not use their knives for anything other than spellcraft and ritual, while others feel that the more they use the tool, the more potent it becomes. There is also a strong belief that an athame used to physically harm another will never again be functional in magick, although in ancient times Witches often 'fed' special knives with blood.

Some Alternatives

The following short list includes tools Witches might use instead of, or together with, an athame.

LABRYS: A double-headed axe that serves as a holy symbol for some Witches, particularly those who choose to follow Artemis or Rhea. The image of a labrys has strong connections with the Greek oracle at Delphi and, as such, is also suitable for anyone following Greek magickal traditions, in combination with or as a substitute for the pentagram (see pp 45–46).
STAFF: An alternative to an athame or wand, used for directing energy. A staff may also be used like a sword in opening energy pathways.
SWORD: A High-Magick alternative to an athame. Witches sometimes use swords to cut an energy pathway into and out of the sacred space once a Circle has been cast.
WAND OR ROD: These tools have all the functions of an athame. The only difference is that sometimes wands and rods become divinatory tools when carved or painted symbolically and then tossed or cast onto a surface. Some wands, such as witching wands (Y-shaped branches), are used to locate lost items or sources of water.

Beyond its symbolic value, Witches may use an athame to draw magickal emblems in the air, indicate the perimeter of the sacred space, and as an alternative wand for directing energy.

Broom and Cauldron

Modern Witches do not rely on their brooms for flying, nor do they use their cauldrons to make slimy, noxious concoctions. But they do incorporate these tools into their magickal spells and rituals.

Broom (Besom)

The besom is a long-handled tool with a bundle at one end that was once made from the broom plant, which grows plentifully on European heaths and sandy pastures. Broom is characterized by yellow flowers and angular branches, ideal for bundling. Thus the instrument made of the broom plant and a stick also came to be known as a broom.

Since Roman times, the broom has been associated with feminine power and magick. Prior to childbirth, women used a broom to sweep the threshold of a house, both for protection and to prepare the way for the new spirit to enter. Gypsy marriage rituals included jumping over a broomstick to ensure the couple's fertility; this ritual neatly marked the line between single and married life.

The broom is present in the folkloric lore of various countries and cultures. Here are some interesting details:

☽ In some parts of the Western world, a broom propped up outside a house identified it as a house of prostitution.
☽ In Madagascar, women danced with brooms while their men were at war, in order to sweep away the enemy.
☽ In China, the broom represents wisdom and insight because it brushes away worries.
☽ In Japan, brooms are used during spring rituals to purify the ceremonial space.
☽ In 19th-century America, a new broom would never be bought in May, 'lest you sweep the family away'.

Cauldron

The cauldron performs numerous symbolic functions for Wiccans, as well as some very practical ones. Cauldrons appear in mythological accounts: Odin received wisdom and intuitiveness from a cauldron; Celtic legend mentions a cauldron of regeneration for the gods. These types of stories are global in nature and give us clues as to where our modern symbolic value for the cauldron originates. Specifically, Witches see the cauldron as an emblem of the womb from which all life, and many other gifts, flows. The three-legged cauldron represents the threefold human and divine nature.

A good alternative for a cauldron is a brazier, which word comes from a French term meaning 'live coals'. A brazier is a fire-safe container that can hold a small fire source or burning incense. A small brazier safe for indoor use is ideal for indoor rituals and spells where fire is a key component of the process.

Witches have many practical uses for cauldrons. For example, they may use a cauldron to cook magickal foods and hold beverages. In addition, the cauldron can be filled with fire, water, flowers or other items at specific times of the year to honour the point in the Wheel of the Year (see p 129) that a festival or altar commemorates.

Other Ritualistic Tools

Additional ritualistic tools commonly used by Witches include aspergers, chalices, goblets, horns, knots and mirrors.

ASPERGER: Any item used to sprinkle water in and around the sacred space. In Scotland, a freshly picked branch of heather, which has the benefit of adding a lovely aroma to the water, is often used. Feathers, flowers, leaves and brooms are all items used for asperging, along with the Witch's handy fingertips.

CHALICE OR GOBLET: A symbol of the feminine aspect of the Goddess (and sometimes used to represent the water element). The chalice can be used to make libations. For a symbolic enactment of libations, the Witch places the athame point down in the cup to represent the power of creation that comes from uniting male and female energies.

In many magickal observances (including handfastings, which are marriage-like rituals), drinking from one cup represents the linking of destiny and unity of purpose.

HORN: An alternative to a cup or goblet, often used among Witches who practise a Norse or Germanic tradition. In addition, a horn can be used as a symbolic item. Place it on the altar during times of need to invoke the spirits of plenty. Musical horns can also be used to call the quarters (see p 54) or to mark the release of a spell (announcing the way for magick).

KNOTS: Often used in spellcraft to represent the binding or loosening of energy. A Witch may choose to create lines of knots (akin to a rosary) for specific functions and keep them in a safe place (such as on the altar) for use as needed; these lines are sometimes called a Witch's Ladder. Untying one knot represents the release of the energy bound therein and the beginning of that particular spell. Alternatively, if a Witch or Wiccan notices that there is a problem with unwanted energies in a space, he or she may quickly tie a knot in a piece of clothing or the altar cloth to constrain that problem until after the magickal working.

Mirrors are sacred symbols for a variety of gods and goddesses, including Tezcatlipoca (Aztec), Amaterasu (Japanese), Isdustaya (Hattic), Kubaba (Mesopotamian) and Kybele (Phrygian).

MIRROR: Another multifaceted tool that can function as a component for spellcraft (usually to reflect away negativity or as part of improving self-image). Mirrors also make wonderful (and handy) scrying surfaces, and are a common tool for Witches who blend feng shui (the Chinese art of managing *chi*, or energy) with their arts.

Emblems and Regalia

In addition to the basic tools, many a Witch has certain personalized emblems and regalia kept for specific spells and rituals. A good example is a poppet; typically, poppets are created in the image of a specific person so they can direct sympathetic magick from a distance at the person represented.

What is Sympathetic magick?
Sympathetic magick means that a symbolic action with one item can affect another item over long distances. So a voodoo doll works based on a sympathetic connection with the person it represents.

Poppets may also be created to represent a creature or situation, and actions done to the poppet symbolize the actions done to whatever or whomever the poppet represents. For instance, if you were to make a poppet of a beloved pet and carefully wrap it in white cloth to protect it, the animal would then receive the benefit of that protection.

Witches may also create poppets for protection – specifically, they use corn or wheat to make poppets that represent the 'spirit' of the grain, and keep them at home to ensure luck, a good harvest and ongoing protection.

Other emblems and regalia might include the following:

AMULETS, CHARMS, FETISHES AND TALISMANS. A Witch can take these magickal tools with her, wherever she may be. Although these terms have frequently been misused and mixed up in modern vernacular, each has a specific definition and function in the Witch's kit; specifics on each tool can be found in Chapter 10. But, in brief, the main differences are derived from the way the energy in each is eventually applied, whether the tokens are active or passive in nature, and the manner in which each was created.

CRYSTALS, METALS, MINERALS AND SHELLS. Nearly all types of crystals, gems, metals, minerals and shells have been categorized for their elemental and magickal correspondences. Many Witches keep crystals on their altars to generate or collect specific types of energy, carry stones as amulets and charms, and make crystal elixirs to internalize a specific stone's attributes.

tips

A crystal elixir is made quite simply by steeping the stone in water for a predesignated period, often in sunlight or moonlight (to improve the effect). Afterwards, the Witch would remove the stone and consume the beverage.

Sigils and Emblems

Be they astrological emblems or symbols for the gods and goddesses, sigils play a very similar role in Witchcraft to that of runes. Other common emblems and symbols in Witchcraft and Wicca include a cross and a pentagram.

An equidistant cross represents crossroads (an in-between place), the four corners of creation, the elemental powers and the four quarters of the Sacred Circle. Some Witches prefer to wear the cross in lieu of a pentagram, a symbol worn by many Witches to represent the harmony of the elements, Spirit and the self working together to create magick.

The pentagram is also sometimes employed as a protective ward in written form either on paper or on the floor of a ritual space. Without the Circle around it, the pentagram is known as a pentacle, Solomon's Seal and the Witch's cross.

Witch's Helpers

Gifts from nature are among the most highly prized tools in Wicca and Witchcraft. Many Witches see nature as a shadowy blueprint for universal laws and principles. In other words, Witches believe that through creation they can eventually come to better know the Creator. So it's not surprising that they would study nature and apply its symbolic value to their Craft. Witches record their observations and experiences in the Book of Shadows, a Witch's guide and magickal diary.

Animals

Although the days of animal sacrifice are long over for the majority of Witches, animals have not disappeared from rituals and spells altogether. Cat whiskers, for example, are still used in wishcraft (magick that's based in wishing customs). If your pet is a familiar, a cutting from its fur might be used in spells to improve the rapport between you. A found bird feather might be used on the altar to represent the air element or to disperse incense around the sacred space.

Beyond these kinds of applications, small statues or images of animals sometimes become markers for the sacred space, depending on the creature's elemental association. For example, a fish image might be placed in the west to represent the energies of water, whereas a lizard might be placed in the south for 'fire' energies.

Additionally, some witches will carry the image of a creature as part of spells or charms with specific goals in mind: carrying a lion carving might be part of a spell for courage. If the carving is made from bloodstone, carnelian or tiger's eye, all the better, because these stones have strong metaphysical associations with bravery. For more information on animal symbolism and applications, see Chapter 18.

Herbs and Other Plants

In Chapter 17, we will discuss in great detail the ways in which herbs and plants figure into Witchcraft and Wicca. One of the major talents noted for cunning people of old was a knowledge of herbs and how to use them. The wise country folk would carefully gather herbs at a certain time and prepare them with similar tenacity. Be they in a potion or poultice, herbs and other plants were used for nearly every daily need – from healing and fertility to giving star-crossed lovers a nudge.

Why call it a Book of Shadows?
Because magick, by definition, works outside space and time – between the light and darkness, between sounds and silences. Shadows are such an in-between space. Historically, Witches often had to meet in the shadows to exchange information, or to gather for celebrations.

Book of Shadows (Grimoire)

Not so much a tool as a very handy reference item, a Book of Shadows can include everything from successful spellcraft formulas to the proper preparation of potions and timing for talismans. The Book of Shadows is akin to a bible for the Witch, who will turn to it again and again for insights, ideas and tried-and-tested recipes.

Setting the Mood

The right mood can make or break a magickal undertaking. Paying attention to clothing, candles, incense and even the timing of spells are all 'tools' in Witchcraft because they help the Witch set the right atmosphere for making magick.

Robes, Masks and Costumes

While some Witches practise skyclad (naked), others prefer to wear robes, masks and other accoutrements. These items have several functions. First, 'dressing for the occasion' separates that particular time from everyday-life events and sets the tone for magickal workings (much like the different tones set by candlelight and electric light). Second, many covens use special markings or colours to indicate different things, such as the season or a person's level of achievement in that group.

Other costuming items such as masks usually play a role in sympathetic magick, whereby a person 'becomes' what the item represents in the sacred space. The psychological effect this has on participants shouldn't be underestimated either: consider the medicine man who puts on the mask of an honoured tribal spirit before going out to a healing ritual. Participants no longer see a friend or family member; they see the face of a spirit. In this manner, robes and costumes provide an extra sensory dimension in ritual and help improve the overall result.

Cords

In addition to being a utilitarian item for holding robes in place, cords can indicate a Witch's level of skill in a specific tradition or group. Exactly how this custom came into being is uncertain – it may connect with the umbilical cord, thereby symbolizing a Witch's connection to the Sacred Parent, or perhaps even the myth of Ariadne's thread leading Theseus safely out of the labyrinth (which is a metaphor for life). Historically, cords were used in spellcraft, especially knot magick in Egypt, Arabia and Europe, and they continue to carry that role today.

Candles

Lighting candles also helps to set the scene and provide meaningful symbols for magickal workings. In various ritual constructs, candles represent the individual's soul, the presence of Spirit or any one of the elemental powers. Candles may also be used for scrying (see Chapter 12), as a spell focus or component and as a way of shifting the overall ambiance of an area to something more magickal. No matter the application, however, Witches will often choose the candle's colour and aroma to match the theme of the magick being created: for example, red or pink candles might be used in love spells, while a simple white candle adorns the altar to represent purity of Spirit.

Incense

Incense has numerous functions. First, specially prepared blends like cedar and myrrh clear the air of any unwanted energies. Second, the smoke carries wishes and prayers to the winds (in this case, the aromatic base should match the intention of the wish). Third, burning incense can represent either the fire or air element in the sacred space.

It isn't that difficult to make your own incense. Grind up some small twigs or sticks of aromatic wood using a pencil sharpener that's been cleaned out; add some finely powdered kitchen herbs or dried flowers, and cast onto hot coals or a wood fire.

Timing

Timing is an odd tool in that it's not something you can hold in your hand, but it's certainly available! Every moment of every day is propitious for specific types of magick. Similarly, every phase of the moon, dawn and dusk, and specific dates throughout the year also have energy patterns that the Witch can tap into to support his or her magick. Dawn, for example, represents hope and new beginnings. Dusk is a perfect time for working closure-oriented magick, and so forth.

CHAPTER 5

Going in Circles: Creating Sacred Space

In Wicca and Witchcraft, rituals are often called 'circles', and group work (especially gatherings in which there are public rituals) frequently takes place in 'sacred space', which has a circular format for its creation. This chapter will explore how Witches create and then release sacred space.

The Circle

Traditionally, many rituals and even spells are performed in a circle. In a group setting, a circle shows that each person present is important to the success of the overall working. The Circle also represents unity, accord, wholeness and a safe psychic sphere within which all can find comfort and protection.

What Makes a Circle Sacred?

Buddha once said, 'Wherever you live is your temple if you treat it like one'; most Witches and Wiccans would agree. Sacredness is more a matter of attitude and behaviour than it is of trappings, and it certainly requires no building or props. Nonetheless, there are tools and processes that Wiccans have used successfully for decades to create magickally safe havens for their efforts. It is this process that we'll examine.

The Circle may or may not be actually visible in any magickal working. Sometimes the wards are set directionally by words and actions alone. Other times there are functional altars set up at the four quarters to honour the powers there. In ritual magick, the Circle may actually be drawn on the floor along with various magickal sigils. It all depends on the practitioner and the overall goal of the working.

Ambiance

So, why is a special ambiance important to specific types of magickal practices? There are actually several reasons. First, a protected space keeps out unwanted spiritual influences: the casting of the sacred space purges the air of negative vibrations and instills a sense of positive purity. Second, the sphere of energy around a space holds any magick created within it firmly in place until the practitioners are ready to release and guide the magick outwards. Finally, and perhaps most important, the time spent in creating sacred space is an important psychological ally for the participants, giving them time to adjust their thoughts and attune them to matters of Spirit rather than flesh. This attitude is highly important to the success of even the simplest magickal process.

The overall sensuous atmosphere of the sacred space plays an important role in how deeply focused each individual will be. Only a focused Witch can harness the energy to enact the intended effects, so creating a successful sacred space means having the right overall surroundings for whatever is going to take place. The following guidelines will help you set the right ambiance for your sacred space:

1. Ensure you (or the group) won't be interrupted.
2. Choose the right space for your task, taking into account weather, personal time or physical constraints, and what's going to take place in the sacred space once it's created.
3. Make sure the area is safe and tidy; get rid of anything that will distract you from the task at hand.
4. Set up your tools so they're readily accessible.
5. If you light candles, make sure they are not a fire hazard. Keep them away from flammable materials (such as cloths or curtains).

This list may seem simple; but in magick, simple things count, especially if they carry important meaning. You do not need to follow all five guidelines; just consider those that will help you awake your spiritual nature, which has the power to make magick!

Think of ways to appeal to all your senses: play music (hearing), serve specially prepared foods or beverages (taste), wear robes or other unique items of clothing (touch), burn incense (smell) and put up thematic decorations or altars (sight).

Altars and Other Tools

Generally, there is at least one central altar in a sacred space. Some Witches believe it's important to place their altars in the east (although there seems to be no explanation for this preference). For practical purposes, placing the altar in the middle of your Circle makes more sense:

participants can gather around it, and a central candle can symbolize Spirit as the guiding force and nucleus of all assembled.

The tools and symbols you bring to the altar largely depends on the function of the magick you will be working in your sacred space. For example, for a ritual to honour your ancestors, you might want to include their photographs or personal effects. No matter what the goal, it's a good idea to cleanse all the tools beforehand. Several cleansing rituals are available: in one, you simply pass objects through the smoke of purifying incense such as cedar or sandalwood. It's also good to work regularly with your tools, both inside and outside the sacred space, so they resonate with your personal energy imprint.

An altar is not a necessity to creating sacred space. It is helpful to have one, and it certainly evokes a greater sense that something special is happening.

A Circle Within a Circle

To honour the elemental powers and the four corners of creation, some magick circles have four mini-altars, one at each of the four main compass points of the working space, known as the quarters. Wiccans frequently place items that represent the elements of each quarter in the corresponding corners of the sacred space. This honours the energies of that quarter. Each altar may hold any number of objects, which represent the direction/element of that altar:

DIRECTION	ELEMENT
East	Air
South	Fire
West	Water
North	Earth

In the east corner, you might find a piece of aventurine or tin, a yellow candle, a feather or frankincense and myrrh. Going clockwise around the outside of The Circle to the south corner is the fire altar, which might house a piece of amber, a red candle, marigolds or juniper incense. In the west corner, suitable altar decorations might include a seashell, a blue or green candle, coral, vanilla incense and a bunch of chamomile flowers. And in the north corner, you might use a potted plant, a green or brown candle, a piece of moss agate and some patchouli incense.

Obviously these are only examples; there are dozens of possible variations. More information on elemental correspondences can be found in Chapters 16, 17 and 18. Some contemporary Witches change this correspondence to better reflect their living space (for example, if they have a lake to the east, the east corner will represent the water element).

So now you have the four points of a circle set up and possibly a central altar. What about defining the boundary of the sacred space and connecting these items?

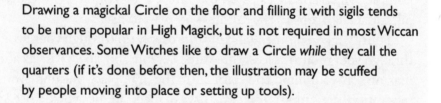

Drawing a magickal Circle on the floor and filling it with sigils tends to be more popular in High Magick, but is not required in most Wiccan observances. Some Witches like to draw a Circle *while* they call the quarters (if it's done before then, the illustration may be scuffed by people moving into place or setting up tools).

The medium for accomplishing this connection varies. For example, in creating the sacred space for an autumn festival, corn meal might be sprinkled on the floor. For spring, asperging with water would be appropriate. A Witch working a love-oriented spell or ritual might release flower petals (particularly rose petals) between each altar point. In this manner, the item used to physically create the perimeter of the sacred space matches the theme or goal of the magick being worked. Other potential media include dry beans, breadcrumbs, chalk, Christmas tree lights (laid out around the edge of the Circle), flour, leaves, macaroni, oats and rice.

Personal or Group Preparations

In addition to reviewing your materials, gathering tools and creating a suitable ambiance, there are a variety of ways you can prepare yourself for invoking the quarters and all the magick to follow. First, make sure you're well rested and mentally and physically healthy – negative feelings undermine the success of any magickal effort.

Second, you might want to take a ritual bath or shower before entering the Circle. This cleansing symbolizes washing away unwanted thoughts, tension and energies. If this isn't possible, just taking a moment to rinse your hands in rose water (for perfect love) is a good alternative. A bowl and towel for this purpose can be left near the entryway to the Circle.

Third, dab your pulse points and third eye (located in the middle of your forehead) with a dilute essential oil that represents the purpose of your ritual or spell – add one or two drops of essential oil to 1 teaspoon of almond oil. This anointing acts as a kind of magickal aromatherapy both through the scent of the oil and the vibrations it carries. For example, if you're raising energy to improve a divinatory effort, choose an oil such as jasmine, which enhances psychic abilities. If you don't wish to wear the oil, add a few drops to the candles you plan to use.

Fourth, take a moment and breathe deeply (in through your nose and out through your mouth at least three times, evenly and slowly). Relax and release, making sure your mind and spirit are in the right place (meaning your motivations are sound). You don't have to meditate, but you do need to be focused and centred before working any type of magick, especially when you're calling on elemental powers. In fact, do this deep breathing exercise before setting up your working space because then you won't be handling magickal tools and symbols with any lingering 'bad' vibrations in your aura.

Finally, say a prayer. If you're working with a group, ask everyone to breathe together and join hands to unite wills and spirits before praying. The prayer simply welcomes Spirit as a helpmate to the magick you're about to create. The prayer doesn't need to be fancy, just sincere.

An Example of a Preritual Prayer

Great Spirit, I/we take this moment to say welcome. While you are always part of every breath I/we take and the beating of life's blood, in this moment I/we stop to honour you. Please come and share these magickal moments with me/us so that the power raised is directed to the good of all, and so that blessings flow abundantly. So mote it be.

Preparing to Work the Magick

Before actually trying a precontrived spell or ritual that includes creating sacred space, consider the following:

☾ Do you want/need costumes to help set the tone and get yourself in a good 'head' space?

☾ Does anything about the invocation or the ritual/spell need to be changed or personalized before you begin? If so, change it before you start. If you're working with a group, everyone should review the process and discuss possible changes or adaptations.

☾ Do you have all the tools and components you need to complete the ritual without breaking the Circle? Bring everything into sacred space.

☾ Do you want to wait for a significantly beneficial astrological time to enact this rite?

☾ Do you want to further personalize things by adding decorations or anything else not already specified in the format you're working with? Set these up before you call the quarters.

More specifics can be found in Chapter 11.

Calling the Quarters

OK, now we get to the heart and soul of creating sacred space, which is calling the quarters. Every magickal tradition (and individuals within those traditions) has different words and gestures for performing this function; as a consequence, the following description is eclectic and generic but nonetheless quite functional.

Calling the quarters creates an invisible line of force that marks the space between two worlds – the mundane and the spiritual, the temporal and the magickal. This boundary usually begins in the east (where the sun rises) and ends in the west, creating a complete circle around, above and below the practitioner. The only time calling the quarters begins elsewhere is during banishing (when it often starts in the north and progresses anticlockwise to decrease negative energy), or when another quarter is more important or significant to the working. For example, if the Witch is planning to commune with water devas to improve his knowledge of them (see Chapter 13), he should honour the water quarter of the space in a unique way: he could invoke (invite) that elemental power into the space first and then go clockwise around the space.

If you're working in a group, the high priest or priestess may invoke the quarters, but if you're alone, it's up to you! Get used to being your own guru and guide right now; that is a big part of progressing as a Witch.

For the sake of simplicity, let's stick with convention and begin in the east. Walk from the altar to the eastern part of the Circle (or where you've placed the altar for that direction). As you stand there, visualize a pure white light filling that space. As you walk the perimeter clockwise, continue visualizing this light shimmering outwards, creating a three-dimensional boundary in your mind's eye. Some Witches find it helpful to trace this line with a wand or athame to better direct the energy.

As you arrive at each of the four directional points, recite an invocation, welcoming the elemental powers and asking them for protection and support of your magick.

Sample Invocation

This invocation begins in the east and proceeds clockwise around the space; it ends at the centre altar with an invocation for Spirit. Note that the elemental energies of each quarter are honoured in the words. If symbolic elemental items have been left at these four spots, they're somehow used during the invocation (like lighting a candle to symbolize the presence of that power and honour it).

EAST: Beings of Air, Guardians of the East, Breath of Transformation – Come! Be welcome in this sacred space. I/we ask that you stand firm to guard and protect, refresh and motivate. Support the magick created here by conveying my/our wishes on every wind as it reaches across the earth.

SOUTH: Beings of Fire, Guardians of the South, Spark of Creation that banishes the darkness – Come! Be welcome in this sacred space. I/we ask that you stand firm to guard and protect, activate and fulfill. Support the magick created here by conveying my/our wishes to the sun, the stars and every beam of light as it embraces the earth.

WEST: Beings of Water, Guardians of the West, Rain of Inspiration – Come! Be welcome in this sacred space. I/we ask that you stand firm to guard and protect, heal and nurture. Support the magick created here by conveying my/our wishes to dewdrops and waves as they wash across the world.

NORTH: Beings of Earth, Guardians of the North, Soils of Foundation – Come! Be welcome in this sacred space. I/we ask that you stand firm to guard and protect, mature and provide. Support the magick created here by conveying my/our wishes to every grain of sand, every bit of loam that is our world.

CENTRE: Ancient One... the power that binds all the elements into oneness and source of my/our magick – Come! Be welcome in this sacred space. I/we ask that you stand firm to guard and protect, guide and fill all the energy created here. May it be for the good of all. So mote it be.

Within the Sanctuary

What can you do inside this sacred space once it's created? Anything you wish. Read a spiritually inspiring book. Meditate. Pray or hold a ritual. Weave a spell or work on your Book of Shadows. There is nothing inappropriate to do here, so trust your heart. Within this space, your soul can find a moment of calm and a sense of timelessness. All things are possible. There is no distance between you and the stars but a thought. Enjoy it!

Releasing the Space

The more you work magick in an area, the more saturated with energy it becomes. Similarly, the more you invoke the quarters in that space, the more protective energy lingers therein. However, it's generally considered rude to ask the elemental powers to tarry. So at the end of your workings, release the sphere you've created, thank the powers, ask them to keep guiding the energy you've raised and bid them farewell until the next time.

Bear in mind that working with the quarters and the elementals is a lot like a relationship with someone you respect and admire. If you treat them accordingly, you will rarely be disappointed.

Releasing the sacred space is effectively the reverse of erecting it. This time, begin in the north quarter and move anticlockwise (as if you're unwinding something). Instead of envisioning the lines of force forming, see them slowly evaporating back into the Void. Just because they leave your sacred space, it doesn't mean they're gone (energy can't be destroyed – it only changes form). They simply return to their source at the four corners of creation and attend to the tasks for which they were made.

As when casting the Circle, it's nice to add a verbal element to the process. In either a solitary or group setting this helps to create the 'group mind' and provides closure. Words also have very real power: the vibrations they put into the air clarify your understanding of what's happened in the sacred space and provide evocative images that can dramatically change the outcome of your efforts.

Sample Invocation for Releasing the Circle

NORTH: Guardians, Guides and Ancestors of the North and Earth, I/we thank you for your presence and protection. Keep me/us rooted in your rich soil so my/our spirits grow steadily until I/we return to your protection again. Hail and farewell!

WEST: Guardians, Guides and Ancestors of the West and Water, I/we thank you for your presence and protection. Keep me/us flowing ever towards wholeness in body, mind and spirit until I/we return to your protection again. Hail and farewell!

SOUTH: Guardians, Guides and Ancestors of the South and Fire, I/we thank you for your presence and protection. Keep your fires ever burning within my/our soul to light up any darkness and drive it away until I/we return to your protection again. Hail and farewell!

EAST: Guardians, Guides and Ancestors of the East and Air. I/we thank you for your presence and protection. Keep your winds blowing fresh with ideas and hopefulness until I/we return to your protection. Hail and farewell!

CENTRE: Great Spirit, thank you for blessing this space. I/we know that a part of you is always with us, as a still small voice that guides and nurtures. Help me/us to listen to that voice, to trust it, and trust in my/our magick. Merry meet, merry part and merry meet again.

f@ct

The phrases 'hail and farewell' and 'merry meet, merry part, merry meet again' reflect an ongoing wish that Witches have to share with others of a like mind and commune with positive energies for spiritual enrichment. These words also honour the Circle (a beginning, ending and beginning is a circular path).

The Sacred Space of Self

There are many moments in everyone's life (even in the life of the most dedicated Witch) when there isn't time to create formalized sacred space. Many Witches overcome this temporal challenge by accepting the idea that each person is a sacred space unto himself or herself; so when time is lacking, the clever Witch simply uses visualization (often that of a white-light bubble) to provide herself with sacred sanctuary.

Another alternative is to have four items that symbolize the four elements. Each of these items is cleansed, blessed, designated for its function, charged and then placed near its directional point. This alternative creates all the potential for a quickly activated sacred space, simply by envisioning the four objects connected by a line of energy, or by offering a shortened invocation during which the Witch may just point to those spots in the room. It could be as simple as the following phrase:

> Earth, Air, Fire and Water—
> hear the words of my heart;
> protection and power impart!

Bear in mind that abbreviated castings of this kind can be just as powerful and functional as the long versions, so long as the Witch maintains a respectful demeanour, focus and intention. She must have faith in the process used, trusting in not only personal ability but in that process, to yield the desired results.

Natural Sacred Spaces

All around the world there are special sites (both famous and not) that seem to radiate with remarkable energy. Exactly how these places came by that energy is unknown. Some people believe it comes from the ley lines that network themselves around the planet and create an energy grid; some of these lines are more powerful than others. Other people believe that an energy vortex or even a localized spirit may help engender that sensation. In any case, there are certainly both natural and manmade sacred sites you can visit to experience this energy. Experiencing a natural sacred space firsthand will help you know when you've created your sacred space.

What are ley lines?
They are invisible lines of force said to network throughout the earth in geometric patterns. When these lines are disrupted or injured, the associated land may suffer. (See Chapter 21.)

If you're close to a space that has this kind of natural holiness, you need not create a sacred space – it *is* one! So it's the perfect spot for working magick – if permissible by local law. I mention this because not everyone wants wilderness Witches tramping across private property to hug a tree or enact a spell! We must respect the land (and its owners).

CHAPTER 6

Meditation and Visualization

Meditation and visualization, common methods in Wicca and Witchcraft, help a person direct, ground and centre energy, and manifest goals. This method is recognized by many spiritual seekers as a great gift to the self because it allows the practitioner to touch parts of his or her inner reality in new and different ways.

What Is Meditation?

To meditate means to think, to reflect on or review in one's mind. It is a method aimed at heightening the mind's functionality while letting the body rest. Unfortunately, that definition alone doesn't adequately explain modern meditative methods or goals.

According to Jeremy Taylor, the 17th-century prelate and author, 'Meditation is the tongue of the soul and the language of our spirit.' Perhaps that sounds somewhat lofty, but meditation isn't a high-and-mighty process, and you don't need to be a monk to learn it. Even those who have never officially meditated before will find it's something they can learn with a little time and tenacity.

For those who practise transcendental meditation, the goal is inner connection and focus. Taoists strive for nonthought – to find total stillness within. Other esoteric traditions seek a clarified vision of the universe and Spirit. The definition of meditation depends heavily on the cultural, religious, spiritual or philosophical approach in question.

Meditation in Wicca and Witchcraft

For Witches and Wiccans, meditation represents a way to bring ideas and beliefs together, better comprehend them and then express them outwardly. It's a method of pondering deeply, clarifying singular thoughts, bringing symmetry to the inner and outer worlds, dispersing tension, centring the spirit and creating an aural atmosphere wholly ready for the magick we're about to create. From this hushed state of the body and soul, it's much easier to become a channel for energy, and it's also much easier to explore the 'mysteries' that have consumed human hearts and minds for aeons.

'Meditation is the dissolution of thoughts in Eternal awareness or Pure consciousness without objectification, knowing without thinking, merging finitude in infinity.'

Sivananda (1887–1963), Hindu religious leader

Historical Background

The roots of meditation are very hard to trace. The first time a human being looked thoughtfully into the sky or savoured other sensuous cues and really experienced the moment, he was meditating! In this manner, at least at first, meditation was something discovered by individuals who were just doing their daily jobs. The dancer twirling near a tribal fire who suddenly felt outside herself, the bard who gave himself over fully to the song and the muse – these people and others like them moved into a meditative state without trying and without anyone knowing it. It follows, then, that meditation is a natural aptitude that anyone can learn.

In terms of written history, the first texts that link meditation (as an altered state of consciousness) to various therapeutic benefits appear around 3,000 years ago among Indian yogis. The early Church was also aware of meditation's benefits to mystical efforts. Among Buddhists, meditation is essential for maintaining the body-mind-spirit balance.

Nevertheless, in the Western world, meditation became a silent practice, with little in the way of public awareness until the 1960s and 1970s, when medical institutions began studying it more seriously. Those studies, combined with the popularity of the New Age movement, brought meditation to the mainstream – and to Witches.

Benefits of Meditation

Medically speaking, meditation has been shown to help moderate high blood pressure and other stress-oriented problems. Every day we are bombarded with sights, sounds and hundreds of pieces of information that keep our minds humming at warp speed. When we meditate, that pace decreases and we are left to pay attention to ourselves and to truly exist in that moment. It's like being able to take a short holiday or break without ever leaving home.

Regular meditation affects and improves:

☾ Self-comprehension (thoughts, perceptions and experiences)
☾ Detachment and impartiality

☾ Awareness of the body-mind-spirit connection
☾ Inner peace and harmony
☾ Creativity and intuition
☾ Instincts (and control over those instincts)
☾ Sports performance
☾ Balance between heart and mind
☾ Work proficiency
☾ Well-being and connection
☾ Relationships with others, the environment and the world

Although Witches use meditation for specific purposes, you don't need to subscribe to a particular religious or philosophical belief system to benefit from it. The same techniques that promote personal or spiritual growth also improve the overall quality of life. In other words, meditation is good for you. It will strengthen the mind, improve the body's involvement in spiritual pursuits and provide great food for the soul because you stop rushing about and internalize all the lessons life has been giving you.

Preparing to Meditate

So exactly where should you begin? Do you have to sit in a lotus position, like a human pretzel? Do you have to hold your hands in front of you and say *Om*? Well, first of all, just relax. If you can do that much, you're well on your way. Then read the following directions. You don't have to follow them exactly. Trust your instincts; if something feels awkward, it's going to make meditating harder. And remember, meditation isn't something you'll master overnight.

Your mind is used to thinking of dozens of things at once, and now you're asking it to stop — and to hone in on one particular task and goal. That's why Buddha recommended three things for successful meditation (and, indeed, any spiritual pursuit): practice, practice, practice!

Before beginning, release any ideas about how quickly you should be learning meditation, or what kind of magickal experiences might result. If you set lofty expectations for yourself, you're likely to be disappointed and to make learning more difficult. Meditation is a subtle art and isn't susceptible to the flash and fanfare of TV. When you can let go and simply *be*, you're halfway to success.

Second, commit yourself to at least five minutes of meditation a day and then slowly increase the amount of time. At first five minutes may seem like an eternity, but with practice you'll stop glancing at your watch and direct your attention to what you're trying to accomplish.

Third, 'shake your sillies out'. What this boils down to is shaking out your arms and legs, stretching a bit and generally getting rid of all those little itches and kinks. If you don't do it now, you'll notice every last one of them when you begin to meditate!

Fourth, find a way of sitting or lying down that is comfortable (AKA not distracting). The more comfortable your body is, the easier it becomes for your mind to direct its attention towards the purpose you've intended. At first, your mind is going to be looking for little things to grab on to, rather than the focused subject you've given it. Everything from a little twitch in your leg to a dog barking down the road can potentially break your concentration. That's why meditation is considered a discipline.

Take it from the Monks

Buddhist monks believe that, with the right mindfulness and intention, any daily activity can become a kind of meditation unto itself. In the Far East, many teachers advocate standing, walking and dancing as good 'postures' for meditation, because they require motion – like life itself. The standing meditation presents an air of readiness; the walking meditation moves out to meet life and embrace the moment; and the dancing meditation celebrates the joy of the moment.

Once you're comfortable, close your eyes and let the world around you fade away. When you are alone with nothing more than your breath and your heartbeat, you're well on your way.

What to Expect

It's not easy to gauge success or failure in meditation without having some idea of what to expect. First, as seems to be the case with a lot of things in Witchcraft, the results for each individual will vary not only according to personality and concentration level but also according to the goal of the meditation. Minimally, if all you experience is a deep sense of calm and inner resolve, that is certainly worthwhile.

Physically, the deeper levels of meditation often leave you uncertain of how much time has passed and can make you feel warm or tingly. You may also hear a buzzing sound. Exactly why these physical reactions occur is the subject of some conjecture; the main theory is that our body is interpreting a spiritual experience in a way we can easily recognize.

At deeper levels, you may sense a deeper connection with Spirit (however you interpret that connection). You may also experience dreamlike visions, be able to release old wounds and comprehend life's network better. This is a kind of inner knowingness that can't easily be described by words – it simply *is*.

Meditation aimed at resolving issues or changing personal patterns takes time to manifest in reality. Lifelong habits won't change overnight, and long-lived perspectives are hard to adjust, no matter how unhealthy they may be. Stick with it! Commit yourself to this path of transformation with diligence. In time, you will experience success.

Effective Meditation

OK, you're finding that just sitting in your room breathing isn't quite giving you enough input to transport your mind to another space. That's normal, but there are other things you can add to the process to help out.

Metered breathing is the most universally suggested meditation aid. Here's how it goes. Take three cleansing breaths in through your nose and out through your mouth; then continue to breathe slowly. Let one breath naturally lead to the next, so there's no end and the cycle is whole and complete.

Now, just for the fun of it, breathe a little more quickly than normal for about 10 seconds and see if your senses heighten or diminish. Inhale, hold that breath for a beat or two, then exhale normally. Repeat this for about five minutes and note the results. Now mix and match the breathing: inhale slowly, exhale quickly; exhale slowly, inhale quickly. Finally, try the slowed breathing and note the results again. Whichever seems to work better for focusing your attention and improving overall insight is the direction to take at the outset of meditation.

Another option is trying mantras or chants. These words and phrases have a songlike quality; in some ways, you can think of them as spiritual lullabies that sway and nudge your mind and soul into another state of awareness. Combined with breathing techniques, the results can be quite impressive. With repeated use, you'll find that a mantra or chant will evoke a heightened spiritual experience simply because it 'cues' your subconscious into reacting just from repeated use. By the way, if you're not comfortable saying phrases out loud, think them; or if you like to sing, sing them – that will give your mind something specific on which to focus, something that also has the right energy.

When is the best time to meditate?
Experts on meditation recommend meditating either first thing in the morning, when you're fresh, or just before your main meal of the day.

A third option is trying aromatherapy. You can use a perfume, incense, pot-pourri or anointing oil (a dilute essential oil; see p 56) placed on your pulse points. You'll want an aroma that calms and centres you. Witches often use sandalwood or lotus to these ends, but choose a scent that has personal meaning and inspires an immediate emotional response.

Fourth, try drumming. From Lapland to Africa, spiritual leaders use the sound of the drum to encourage deep meditative states and even manifest astral travel. The vibrations and resonance of drum-song mirror those of our own hearts and house tremendous potential for meditation and many other witchy endeavours. Anything you can use to sound out a beat can become a makeshift drum. Start out with slow, sturdy beats – try mirroring the pace of your breath or your heart – then let the sensations guide you.

Here are some additional pointers for successful meditation:

☾ Make a daily date with yourself for meditation.
☾ Make sure you can meditate in a peaceful, safe and uninterrupted area. Turn off the phone. Put a 'Do Not Disturb' sign on your door. Get rid of all the distractions. If the only private space you have is the bathroom, then use it.
☾ Add any sensuous cues that you find helpful: soft music, drumming, candlelight or incense.
☾ Breathe deeply and slowly. Let your breath become all-connected and no longer an object of focus.
☾ Listen to your heartbeat. This natural rhythm that each person has acts as a guide for many metaphysical processes.
☾ Release stress, worries and expectations.
☾ Practise visualization if you find it helps you.
☾ Allow the meditation to grow and transform; don't restrict what happens as you meditate.
☾ Regularly increase the amount of time you spend meditating (within the realistic bounds of your personal life and responsibilities).
☾ Keep a journal to record your experiences.

A final suggestion is to turn meditation into a ritual. Pray or create sacred space at the outset. This not only saturates your area with protective, positive energy, but also sets a pattern that you can recognize. As you repeat the pattern, the results will improve.

This is a good time to declare your purpose to the Sacred and to your higher self. Even if the meditation takes a different direction, having clarity at the outset is always beneficial.

Overcoming Barriers

Everyone experiences problems with meditation from time to time. When you find that small parts of your body are distracting you (by itching or being uncomfortable) or that your mind is wandering, try taking a long, hot bath, and then go back to meditation. Your body will be more relaxed and your mind more alert, a state beneficial for meditating. Another alternative is fasting for a few hours beforehand: if you're digesting food and hearing all kinds of stomach noises, it's bound to be distracting.

Be patient with yourself, and keep practising. It's not unusual to fall asleep during meditation (in fact, meditation is frequently prescribed for people with sleep disorders), and it will take you some time to get used to being this mentally focused.

Closing the Meditation

In much the same way that closure is important to ritual, it's similarly important to meditation. You need to get your feet back on the ground, and come back to normal levels of awareness – especially if you have to drive anywhere! In addition, you want to be able to apply the perceptions and insights gathered during meditation to everyday reality.

The best way to accomplish this is by giving yourself a moment to realize that you have to start breathing normally and turn your thoughts back to everyday matters. Don't open your eyes too quickly, and don't move too fast (or you risk getting a headache). Let thoughts of work, home, kids, hobbies or whatever come back of their own accord. Wiggle your body a little bit, and then try squinting – so your eyes have time to adjust. Put your hands palm-down on the earth to ground yourself. Finally, sit for at least a minute longer, until you feel wholly alert.

Visualization

Witches find visualization very helpful, even though it is not a necessary component of meditation. Visualization helps a Witch review a meditation's goal or focus from a detached perspective.

Think for a moment of the hours you spent as a child imagining things, or daydreaming as an adult. That's what magickal visualization is all about. The only real difference is that now the images you evoke will be will-driven and will have specific functions.

A lot of people underestimate the power of thought and our mind's ability to change reality. That is a terrible shame, and it's a mindset Witches try to avoid. If you cannot see the results from your spells in your mind's eye as an accomplished reality, and trust in them as being the probable outcome, then magick becomes nothing more than rote action and wasted energy.

Visualization unlocks the power of thought. No matter the purpose in meditating or in casting a spell, the Witch can visualize that purpose and use that image to help guide the energy effectively.

For example, if a Witch feels that he needs protection, he might use a combination of meditation and visualization as a way of invoking that sanctuary. Typically, he might envision a blazing blue-white ball of light surrounding either himself or the entire room. When the visualization is firmly in place (that is, the Witch can sense and 'see' the vision, even with open eyes), then everything else that's planned proceeds.

Don't limit your visualization only to mental images – allow yourself to hear, taste, smell and touch. If you have trouble conjuring up images in your mind, try taping visualization guidelines to take you through the visualization, and listen to them while you breathe and relax (also see Chapter 7); sometimes the sound of a voice can transport you where you otherwise could not go.

Designing Personal Meditations and Visualizations

The primary purpose for meditation and visualization in Wicca and Witchcraft is to meet pressing personal needs and to get the practitioner into the best possible frame of mind for magick. There are also seasonally themed, guided meditations.

Seasonal meditations focus the imagery and goals on something appropriate to the time of year. For example, if a coven is celebrating Samhain, which is the Celtic New Year and a festival for the dead, the meditation/visualization may include a time to commune with ancestors and make peace. In contrast, a springtime meditation/visualization might focus on a rising sun to inspire hope for a new project or goal.

A guided meditation is one in which someone (a priest, priestess or leader) talks people through the imagery and the overall process of going in and out of a meditative state of mind.

The final type of meditation/visualization is one that directs energy outwards, to the planet, instead of inwards. Witches and Wiccans both are very aware that our world is in desperate need of healing and support on all levels. Consequently, they may choose to meditate on these needs and direct any resulting insights or energy outwards to figuratively hug the world with magick. For instance, the meditation might be focused on peace, with the visualization providing the image of peace as a blanket of energy settling over the world.

CHAPTER 7

The Sacred Sounds: Prayer and Affirmation

Sound adds a sensual cue to magickal undertakings and transports the practitioner more easily from the mundane into the mystical. Wiccans incorporate prayers and chants into their ceremonies, and Witches often use sound and affirmations as part of their practices.

Prayer

You may have childhood memories of praying by your bedside or at the family dinner table. As the years passed, that practice may have faded away and got lost in the daily shuffle. Nonetheless, prayer offers much to Wiccans (especially prayers directed to a specific god or goddess). Prayer can also become a useful tool for Witches, if it is used as a mechanism for reconnecting with the psychic self and the collective unconscious.

What is prayer?
The answer to this question depends a lot on who you ask. John Bunyan, the 17th-century preacher and writer, thought that prayer is 'sincere, sensible, affectionate pouring out of the soul to God'. In comparison, the American essayist and poet Ralph Waldo Emerson described prayer as the 'study of truth', which implies more of a meditative element.

For the purpose of this chapter, prayer is defined as a means of communicating with Spirit, which in part also means listening. Whether that communication takes the form of a request, thankfulness, worshipfulness or simply opening up to Spirit in truthfulness, if you don't listen as well as talk, a great deal of prayer's effectiveness remains unrealized.

The Role of Prayer in Wicca and Witchcraft

It's taken a while for Witches to integrate prayer into rituals and daily magickal practices. The problem for many has been an overwhelming connection between the idea of prayer and organized religion. Since many Witches come from a past steeped in a faith to which they had no strong personal connection, it's been hard for them to reclaim the power of prayer. Nonetheless, it is happening.

In part, this change has occurred due to the realization that many prayers are really a kind of respectful, deity-directed spell. Think for a moment: when we pray for something, we are indicating our desire for that something to manifest. In spellcraft, the Witch does the same thing, adding will and an awareness of how to build and direct energy into the equation. A Wiccan can also invoke the quarters or Spirit to bless and guide the energy – by all definitions, this invocation qualifies as prayer.

Witches and Wiccans approach prayer as a personal construct. If a practitioner does not follow a deity, then he might not feel a need to pray (and will likely substitute meditation or other thoughtful practices for prayer). If a practitioner honours Spirit in any form, prayer certainly has a place in her magick.

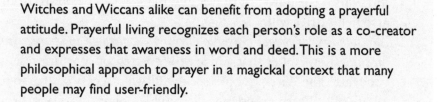

Witches and Wiccans alike can benefit from adopting a prayerful attitude. Prayerful living recognizes each person's role as a co-creator and expresses that awareness in word and deed. This is a more philosophical approach to prayer in a magickal context that many people may find user-friendly.

What to Expect from Prayer

According to Socrates, 'God knows what is good for us'. Prayers are filled with good intentions, yet often good intentions pave the way to trouble. Human beings have limited spiritual vision and frequently don't realize that a 'good' idea may have terrible consequences Thus, the Witch may end a prayer (or spell or ritual) with the phrase 'for the good of all, and it harm none'. This phrase releases the prayer's energy to the Powers so it can be guided for the best possible results, even if those results aren't exactly what is expected.

Seven Steps for Effective Prayer

When a Witch or Wiccan chooses to adopt prayer as a personal method for connecting and communing with the Higher Self and/or Spirit, the next question is: how do I begin? This isn't an easy question to answer when you're dealing with an individualized, vision-driven belief system.

Nonetheless, most Witches do tend to follow some sort of generic guidelines. Here is an outline of seven basic steps for effective prayer:

1. *Meditate on your faith and find ways to sharpen it. Without faith, prayer is pointless.* Ask yourself: what do I believe? How strong is that belief? Belief and willpower work together in magick, and if you lack one or the other, the results will likely fall flat. Faith is very much like a muscle: it requires exercise to get stronger!

2. *Consider the purpose of your prayer in detail.* By clarifying your purpose, you will begin to develop a multidimensional pattern for your wishes into which the power of prayer and magick can be poured. Purpose also helps drive will.

3. *Adjust the words of your prayer to mirror your purpose and have personal meaning.* Remember that you are the co-creator of your present and of your fate. The Witch doesn't see divinity as an easy source to blame for all life's ills. Every mundane effort made opens doorways through which the Universe and the Divine can start answering that prayer.

4. *Make daily, purposeful efforts to help that prayer manifest in your life.* After all, God helps those who help themselves.

5. *Make prayer a part of your daily life, like a spiritual vitamin, repeating any prayers for which you feel the need.* As with any spiritual practice, the more you pray, the better and more effective your prayers become. Repeating a prayer does not equal a lack of faith; it simply reiterates your sincerity and sends out supportive energy for that goal.

6. *Trust yourself and the Divine, and keep your eyes open for possible answers.* This step is probably the hardest, and one with which many people struggle. Trust isn't easy to come by in this world. Trusting yourself, trusting your connection with Spirit, trusting your magick and trusting the Divine to answer is difficult.

7. *When a prayer is answered, rejoice and be thankful! Happiness and gratitude are powerful magick.* If you ask for divine intervention and help on your behalf, it seems only polite to remember to say thank-you. Humankind's manners in this area are woefully lacking. Above and beyond thankfulness being necessary to developing a good

relationship with the Divine, it also creates very positive energy in and around your life.

Chanting

Chants are typically words or syllables (and sometimes the names of gods) that are frequently accompanied by drumming, clapping, rattles and sometimes musical instruments specifically for the purpose of increasing psychic energy. At its height, chanting can create altered states of awareness, including ecstatic trances. It's very hard to distinguish between chanting and mantras, except that chanting does not need to have a religious focus, making it more appropriate for the philosophically inclined or nonreligious Witches.

In a magickal setting, chanting can be done alone or in a group. In a group setting, chanting provides the additional benefit of uniting those in attendance and charging their emotions at a concurrent rate. This process forms the cone of power, which the attendees will send out towards their goal.

How Chanting Works

To understand the chanting process and other uses of sacred sounds a little better, just consider the amount of sound that assails you every day. How does that sound affect you? A honking horn will make you jump or move just by conditioning, for example, while the sounds of gentle bells may bring a smile. This secondary illustration is akin to what sacred sounds strive to produce – rather than continuing to insult our ears with destructive noises, we massage them and our spirits with something uplifting and positive.

Chanting in particular shifts consciousness because the vibration of sound has a measurable effect on the nervous system. Listening to sacred words and syllables brings the mind and spirit together for the practitioner. That unified force then transforms further into the chanting and deepens the meditative state (although this doesn't happen right away or without some practice).

> The deeper levels of chanting in combination with meditation (or ritual) culminate in a coming to terms with self in a very honest and meaningful way. In this setting, surrounded by the sounds of creation, we come to know our spiritual self, which is also the key to unlocking the Divine within.

The initial stages of chanting act like an astral bath of sorts. The main effect is simply that of clearing away useless thoughts and negative energy. Even if a practitioner never gets beyond this point, this result is well worth spending a little time on.

Mantras

According to its generally accepted definition, a mantra is a gathering of sacred sounds used repeatedly for religious purposes. This makes the mantra and chant very closely related (although chants do not necessarily have to have a religious context). The word *mantra* comes from Sanskrit and can be translated as 'delivering the mind'. Among Hindus, it means 'the learning'. Both definitions provide very powerful allusions. This is perhaps why Lama Govinda, a Tibetan Buddhist, taught that mantras are a tool for thinking, but thinking in a distinctively different way, in which truth supersedes prejudice, preconditioning and personal agendas.

The mantra is a mechanism through which you begin to see the spirit housed within your body. This spirit is also consciousness, and the essence that makes each person unique. By recognizing this spirit and returning to connectedness with it, the Witch can focus on the magickal rather than the material world.

In the Upanishads, *Om* in particular is thought to be the basis of all sacred sounds. In this word, we find the alpha and omega of energy – transformation and enlightenment.

A mantra can be a divine name, word or sound that contains power. In the *Om mani padme hum*, the *Om* represents the perfected mind, body and speech that Buddha advocated. *Mani* represents compassion; *padme* represents knowledge; and *hum* is the infinity within the finite. These things mirror the eightfold Path of Buddhism.

Mantras are not limited to just Buddhism and esoteric practices. Islam and Christianity have always regarded the name of God as invocative; repeating it continually is reciting a mantra. In addition, yogis use mantras in performing many amazing physical feats, and of course Western Witches use mantralike words or songs to raise power.

Words have power, and mantras have directed power. Speaking them allows the Witch to reach a heightened state of awareness more easily. It also fills the air within and around the sacred space with supportive energy. This combination creates a very powerful atmosphere of spiritually oriented vibrations, specifically aimed at *delivering the mind* from mundane pursuits (and in turn, liberating the spirit).

The Benefits of Chants and Mantras

Chants and mantras are a discipline of fulfillment and attainment. Reaching a goal or objective, such as successfully walking one's spiritual path, requires discipline. Witches who use chants and mantras do so with a similar purpose, often in combination with meditation.

In addition, doing chants and mantras results in the following:

☾ Self-awareness and confidence
☾ Joy and zeal for life
☾ Freedom of the mind and spirit
☾ Development of personal virtues such as compassion
☾ Harmonious vibrations in and around one's life
☾ A medium through which to experience divinity in sound
☾ Spiritual perceptions of the self
☾ Peace of mind and overall self-control
☾ Exercise of the body (through controlled breath and posture)

Affirmations

Affirmations are a modern interpretation of chanting and mantras. As the word implies, an affirmation is a short phrase meant to support and affirm the individual, which makes affirmations uniquely helpful for self-image issues. The overall idea is to break the chain of negative thinking and replace it with empowering influences.

While life is often focused on getting, affirmations are about manifesting. What's the difference? Ego. Getting is about ego and about somehow justifying the outcome of any situation to suit the ego. And, of course, the real source of that justification is fear, which undermines not only spiritual pursuits but also everyday life.

Psychological studies indicate that affirmations do, indeed, work. Saying yes to yourself and to your potential motivates your behaviour. Repeating the affirmation supports this process by making the thought (and any subsequent action) natural on both a conscious and subconscious level – eventually effecting the specified changes.

Manifesting, in comparison, is about trusting, being and allowing. In consequence, you will never see an affirmation that includes negative words. Rather, affirmations are powerful positive thoughts, stated as an accepted reality. In other words, rather than saying, 'I'll try', the affirmation says, 'I'll achieve. I'll do.' The difference is pretty obvious. In the first statement, there is still a question of accomplishment. The second statement does not revel in uncertainty – it claims the prize. The person who says, 'I can't' gives away power, whereas the person who says 'I am' harnesses that power.

Affirmations embrace what is possible in the human potential despite our circumstances, but they're not boundless. Each of us has limitations. Wisdom comes in knowing what limits we have and the wherewithal to overcome them with time and tenacity.

Your Own Affirmations

Follow this process to formulate successful affirmations:

☾ Know your goal.
☾ Find present-tense statements that reflect that goal as a reality (avoid negative terminology at all costs).
☾ Write the affirmation down and place it where you will often see it.
☾ Include your name (or the words *I* and *me*) in the affirmation. This is not egotistical – affirmations are focused on self-improvement.
☾ Set aside time for affirmations as you would a meditation.
☾ Repeat the affirmation. The more you hear it, the more you'll trust in it as being true.
☾ Give yourself an opportunity to put the affirmation to work through positive actions.

The Power of Positive Thinking

On an elementary level, affirmations illustrate the power of positive thinking by verbally expressing those positive thoughts. People often become what they believe themselves to be. And where do they 'learn' that belief? From other people around them.

Children and adults alike often say cruel and hurtful things. When you hear those negative statements often enough, you begin to believe them. For example, I was often called clumsy and ugly during my teenage years. After a time, I noticed that I no longer fought against the negative comments. I embraced them. They became who I was even in my own mind, and sure enough, I couldn't walk up the stairs without tripping. Realistically, like attracted like – I saw myself in a bad light and became what I had imagined myself to be. Even at the age of 40, this Witch is still using affirmations to break down the walls built by that experience.

Affirmations aren't a quick fix. The longer you've held on to an idea or problem, the longer the affirmation process to release it and replace it with something beneficial. So keep your expectations realistic – otherwise you'll undermine everything you had hoped to achieve.

Magick and Affirmations

In Witchcraft, affirmations can be combined with spells, rituals and meditations. Witches strive to stretch themselves on all levels (body, mind and spirit). Affirmations support that stretching process, especially when a particular goal seems elusive.

Let's put this into an illustration specific to Witches. The Witch or Wiccan who may feel a little unsure about her abilities could choose the phrase: 'I nurture my magickal being and see my power growing daily'. The recognition that we're not fully developed as spiritual people is a balancing point, yet it doesn't hinder the maturation process! In the same way, a Witch suffering from self-image issues could repeat 'I am beautiful within and without; I love myself'. Saying this phrase in front of a mirror several times a day creates a visual connection between self-love and the image seen (the Witch's reflection).

Affirmations are totally portable. You can say them quietly in the office toilets, repeat them in your car, dance to them outside in a rainstorm or whisper them as you go to sleep. And as you do, you will begin to transform your image of self so that it supports your spiritual pursuits.

CHAPTER 8
Magickal Dreaming

I n Wicca and Witchcraft, dreams are not just omens or flights of fancy. They are messengers of things to come and allow communication with the Divine. When you dream, bits of data from the subconscious, superconscious and Spirit can filter through because you've slowed down enough to pay attention.

The History of Dream Interpretation

Dream interpretation has been popular with the public since ancient times, spurred by support from great thinkers and leaders. Julius Caesar, Socrates, Hippocrates and St John were all strong proponents of finding visions of the future, creative inspiration and much more in dreams. The Greeks were great lovers of dreaming, and from the socio-economic hub of Athens, ideas about dreaming travelled around the ancient world. As these ideas spread among kings, merchants and commoners alike, each culture and society added a little more lore to the blend until some symbols emerged as archetypal.

Spiritual dreaming and dream interpretation are certainly not recent traditions. The earliest written dream keys date to 1350 BCE in Egypt, indicating a much earlier oral history. One dream key, *Oneirocritica* (*The Interpretation of Dreams*), written by Artemidorus Daldianus in around 140 CE, became so popular that it was still being printed in the 1700s.

Dream interpretation was not limited to the Western world; the Eastern traditions favoured dream oracles as well. While the oracles at Delphi and Epidaurus were speaking about dreams, Japanese Buddhists were conducting similar rites. In Japanese culture, dreams had a very honourable advocate in the emperor, who was given the duty of sleeping in a special chamber to receive regular missives from Spirit through his dreams.

Since Wicca is considered a religion, it's worth mentioning that the Egyptian, Mesopotamian, Hittite, Hebrew, Druidical and Taoist priests and priestesses (just to name a few) regarded dreaming as a suitable way to connect with the Divine. Even St Augustine and Martin Luther agreed with this concept, as do Native Americans to this day. Wiccans and Witches are far from being alone in honouring dreams as a spiritual tool.

Wiccans and Witches also look to Native American tradition for help in receiving good dreams. That help comes in the form of a dream catcher, which is made like a web to 'catch' nightmares and only allow the right dreams through. Using a dream catcher has become a popular practice.

Contemporary Connections

Although interest in dream interpretation waxed and waned with social contrivance, it received a huge boost at the turn of the 20th century when Carl Jung and Sigmund Freud began writing about dreams. Jung felt that our night visitors illustrated a vast number of universal ideas, sometimes gathered from the collective unconscious. Freud believed that dreams exposed suppressed desires and information hidden in each person's subconscious.

Most Witches and Wiccans would agree with a similar theory. Basically, dreams may recount mundane thoughts and actions, reveal what is overlooked or ignored, look into the future and act as the voice of the Divine. Dreams have the power to teach dreamers about human life and interactions, about the way the world works and about the Divine. They can also remind dreamers of the magick within, universal symbols, spiritual paths and, perhaps most importantly, about themselves.

Types of Dreaming

Everyone dreams, even if they do not remember their dreams in the morning. In fact, dreaming regularly is essential to human psychological stability. Without enough REM sleep (the period of sleep when dreaming occurs), a person can easily begin misinterpreting the real world until daily life becomes the nightmare that they couldn't experience during sleep.

Witches may experience several forms of dreaming. Ritualistic dreaming occurs when the individual purposefully tries to create an atmosphere conducive to receiving spiritually centred dreams. Another form is programmed dreaming, which occurs when the Witch tries to dream up specific imagery by using presleep emblems or symbolism. A Witch who is having trouble with a colleague may visualize that person before going to sleep in the hope of manifesting a dream about him or her. This dream would contain symbols or interactions that would explain the problem and possibly provide a solution.

The third form is lucid dreaming. The dreamer who is aware of being in a dream state has the power to interact with the images, even to change them for a more positive outcome. This awareness is particularly empowering for nightmares, which embody and personify our fears and pains. By engaging the misgivings and fears head-on and changing the outcome of the dream, a Witch realizes that he also has the power to transform waking reality.

The human mind accepts what happens on the dreamscape as a form of truth. For this reason, some psychologists say that experiencing death in a dream may cause enough shock to your body to lead to a physical death.

To illustrate lucid dreaming, an example might be in order. Say a Witch is dreaming about a recent ritual. At the time of the ritual, she felt as though the energy she raised wasn't directed very effectively. In a lucid dream, she has the power to change the ending by mentally raising the cone of power and guiding it directly to its goal. Maybe she can even dream of how the energy will manifest itself in transforming reality according to her magick. Witnessing this in a dream will reinstate the belief that the energy created at the original ritual has also found its home.

Other Forms of Dreaming

Other types of dreams you might receive include telepathic dreams (communication between your mind and that of another without direct personal contact), prophetic dreams (thought to foretell future events) and past life dreams (believed to reveal a previous incarnation of the dreamer's soul). While ritualistic presleep work may help formulate these types of dreams, they also seem to come of their own volition. Why, remains a mystery. Nonetheless, the Witch and Wiccan welcome all three, being thankful for the insights they provide.

Effective Magickal Dreaming

If a Witch or Wiccan wants to manifest a spiritually or magickally oriented dream, how does he or she go about it? As with many of the methods already discussed in this book, the approach is usually highly personal. Nonetheless, there are some similarities in technique throughout the magickal community that anyone can use or adapt. Here are some guidelines:

1. *Prepare.* Before embarking on sacred sleeping, consume only certain foods, fast and/or purify yourself. Foods might be limited to those believed to help in manifesting dreams, such as onions. Fasting is part of purification. You should consume only water to cleanse the body (and therefore the spirit) of any unwanted impurity. Forms of cleansing and purification include smudging your aura or taking a ritual essential oil bath. For example, you could add three drops of chamomile or geranium essential oils (provided you like the aroma) to the bath water – add the oils after you have run the bath, and not to running water as with bubble bath, as this depletes the oil's potency. As for all essential oil use, see the caution on page xii.

Why use onions – of all things – to inspire spiritual dreams? Historically, Egyptians worshipped the onion and invoked it during promissory rituals. Onions were also used in a variety of divinatory efforts in France, Germany and Wales: for instance, the Welsh ate onions on special occasions to inspire dreams about important relationships.

2. *Create a sacred sleep space.* You know the traditional ways of creating sacred space (refer back to Chapter 5 for review) – the only difference here is that you would be setting it up in your bedroom. In addition to

the customary invocations to the quarters, special candles (blue and purple, in particular, are considered excellent 'dreamy' hues) and incense, Witches will invoke a deity to help them in their dreams.

The following incense blend is suitable: 125g (4oz) of sandalwood powder, three drops each of rose and jasmine oil, and a tablespoon each of dried lavender flowers and crushed marigold petals. Consider calling on Isis (who grants healing dreams according to Egyptian lore) or Hypnos (the Greek god of sleep) for blessings.

Other clever ways of accenting the sacred sleep space include scenting nightwear or bedding by tossing them in a tumble dryer with a bundle of dream-accenting herbs; making the bed with soft, comfortable sheets (itchy fabrics don't generally create the deep-sleep state where dreams form); and putting a dream sachet (filled with any of the herbs and flowers that promote dreams) under your pillow.

3. *Employ prayer, chanting and/or meditation.* Prayer, a wish turned godwards, may be used to ask for a dream. Chanting releases vibrations into the room and improves your aura and overall state of awareness. Meditation silences the thousands of thoughts in your mind and turns the focus to one task – dreaming.

4. *Visualize.* Presleep visualization plays an important role in preparing you for a journey through programmed dreaming. Alternatively, you might use symbols and imagery that you feel will inspire a spiritual dream. For example, since the eye is regarded as the window of the soul and represents 'vision' on all levels of being, envisioning an eye may be one option that provides a defined cue to your subconscious and superconscious mind.

5. *Keep a dream diary.* Many Witches record their dreams, either in a journal or with a tape recorder – some creative people even sketch or paint them. Recording a dream serves several functions. First, it often helps clarify the details of the dream. Second, it allows you to review and interpret those details at a convenient time (instead of trying to think out interpretations while rushing out of the door to work).

Third, the meaning of many spiritual dreams may not become clear for days, weeks, months, even years. Therefore, having a record to look back upon and find the 'Aha!' therein is of great help. Such illuminating moments give the Witch faith in her dreams and the power within them to help with daily life, understand the self and connect with the Divine.

Remember that these are guidelines, not edicts. Each Witch will discover what works well and then follow those processes to reach the dream world. Over time, these processes will be shaped into a ritual that honours the self and Spirit.

Sandman Visualization

When you're having trouble relaxing, this visualization often helps. Think of your entire body as being filled with sand. In your mind's eye, reach down and remove corks from your toes. Let the sand slowly flow out, taking with it your tensions and negativity. As each part of your body 'empties', feel how it grows light and unburdened. You may fall asleep during this process; conveniently, this visualization also helps to unblock a lot of barriers for dreams.

How to Interpret Dreams

The Babylonians regarded the whole dream (as opposed to individual parts) as a message. Assyrians held a completely opposite belief: that each element in a dream has specific meaning or ominous portent. The majority of Wiccans and Witches take a stance somewhere in the middle. The entirety of a dream holds import – its continuity, its feeling, the impressions it left upon waking. But the details are also important. Sometimes the human mind leaves clues in small, seemingly insignificant items.

The length and amount of detail in a dream isn't really an issue. For one thing, time is elusive in the dream world – what appears to be a moment can translate into hours of real time, and vice versa. Similarly, short dreams with only one or two images can be just as insightful, if not more so, than lengthy ones that require a lot of sorting.

> 'We have in dreams no true perception of time – a strange property of mind!...The relations of space as well as of time are... annihilated, so that while almost an eternity is compressed into a moment, infinite space is traversed more swiftly than by real thought.'
>
> Hubbard Windslow, 19th-century clergyman

With this foundation in mind, let's look at the methods Witches, Wiccans and many other people employ to effectively interpret their dreams:

1. *Note the first gut feeling about the dream.* Don't just brush off first impressions – they're important. Very often the initial feeling or ideas that come to mind upon waking are spot-on. And if the meaning of the dream seems obvious, it probably is exactly as it seems.

2. *Try to interpret any references to obvious internal or external influences –* such as something seen on TV or in the newspapers, or obvious personal fantasies and memories. Internal or external influences hold import to a dream. It's possible you could simply be dreaming about those memories or feelings, but it's also likely that those influences are important to the situation or question at hand.

3. *Look at the dream as a whole.* Is there a theme to it? What's the overall setting and feeling? Try to see the big picture.

4. *Look at the details.* Does there seem to be a repeated message? It may come through words, objects, colours, aromas or symbols that are duplicated or have the same connotation. Alternatively, write down each component and the meaning it has for you, then compare them to the impressions from the whole dream.

5. *Consider the dream's patterns, progressions or cycles.* For example, a dream that begins in spring and ends in winter might be connected to the flow of time, the change of seasons and so on. Patterns often prove important to the overall interpretation.

6. *Meditate on the dream.* When time allows, think about the dream and all the impressions you've gathered. If you think of new parts of the dream previously forgotten, add those into the process. Make note of any notions that come to you during this re-examination.

7. *Finally, look to dream keys for help.* Remember that many dream interpretation books don't include modern symbolism and rely on information gathered at the end of the 19th century, when this art was in its heyday. Some good modern books that have a spiritual focus include *The Language of Dreams* by Patricia Telesco and *Dream Dictionary: An A to Z Guide to Understanding Your Conscious Mind* by Tony Crisp.

Remember that not all dreams have deep spiritual meaning; in fact, they are in the minority. Most dreams have to do with odd things your mind retained during the day or week, or other things you've been mulling over. So don't be disappointed if sacred sleep doesn't always produce the desired results.

Recognizing a Spiritually Generated Dream

How can you know for certain if you have had a dream of import – a dream in which Spirit or the higher self has visited you? There are several signs to watch for:

☾ The dream produces a dramatic emotional response (fear, joy, sadness, release and so on).

☾ The dream exhibits uncanny realism that leaves the dreamer somewhat confused upon waking.

☾ The dream is repeated for several nights in a row (three being a common number).

☾ The dream includes information or learning to which the dreamer has no conscious access.

☾ Images from the dream disrupt waking reality by returning to the forefront of the dreamer's thoughts regularly throughout the next few days.

(The dream includes a blazing light or sense of a higher power, which is often overwhelming to the dreamer.

(The dream is unusually multisensual. For example, if you do not usually have a sense of smell in your dreams, this additional dimension points to a uniquely multifaceted experience.

Some spiritual dreams (especially prophetic dreams) may not become apparent until quite a while after the experience. So even if you're not certain the dream had magickal overtones, record the content anyway.

Common Dream Symbols

As you review the following list of magickal dream interpretations, please remember that dream interpretation is a highly subjective art based on your own perceptions and experiences. A wise Witch knows that answers cannot always be found in one book, let alone dozens. The first book to read in any partial system is the book of *you*.

ABYSS: In the Tarot, this is the place where faith is tested, the place from which the Fool leaps to discover his or her magick. Alternatively, it may represent fertility (the womb), and new beginnings.

ALTAR: An in-between place or bridge between the mundane and the eternal, an altar may quite possibly represent the need to give or receive by way of an offering.

ARROW: The Warrior's rune, the arrow is a call to action and discovery of personal power.

ATHAME: The ritual knife of Wiccans, the athame represents the reality that magick is a two-edged tool that can be wielded to help or harm.

BELLS: A message of protection or warning, bells may also be an advisory that you need to centre and focus.

CAKES: Typically eaten during or at the end of ritual, cakes represent wishes, an initiation or other sacred rites.

CANDLE: Enlightenment, the light that shines within each soul. The behaviour of the candle can be interpreted in this context.

CAULDRON: Because a cauldron has three legs, Witches associate it with the threefold Goddess and her influence. With this in mind, it also represents traditional feminine qualities: wisdom, nurturing, creativity and insight.

CIRCLE: Sacred space, completion, wholeness, equity and cycles.

DANCING: Integration or participation in something greater than yourself. Pay attention to where and with whom you are dancing in the dream to gain more insight into its meaning.

DIVINATION TOOLS: These tools represent the need to examine something closely or gather more information.

FIRE: A call to gather with community, fire may alternatively represent the power of light over darkness or a heated situation.

GOBLET: Another strong feminine symbol of the womb and the Goddess. Drinking from one cup is a Wiccan and Pagan symbol of unity.

GYPSY: Unexpressed psychic potential.

INCENSE: Prayers or requests being directed to Spirit, incense alternatively represents cleansing and life as a ritual.

INVOCATION: The call of your soul to the Divine for assistance or presence.

KNOT: Binding negative or unwanted energy (or holding energy in place until it's needed).

MAGIC: Personal power that requires responsibility and control.

MIRROR: Reflecting energy in one direction or another, the mirror may also represent the need to reconsider your self-image.

MOON: Believed once to be the source of a Witch's power, the phase of the moon changes the meaning. A full moon, for example, would indicate coming into the full awareness of magickal potential, whereas a waning moon might indicate that inner resources are wanting.

PATH: The course of your spiritual progress. Make note of the path's condition. Is it well-tended? Filled with rocks or holes? This condition should be highly indicative of how smoothly your path is progressing.

PRIEST OR PRIESTESS: A representative of your inner voice that acts as a spiritual guide, or perhaps a call to consider embarking on suitable spiritual studies to reach this level in the community.

SALT: The need to purify, banish or preserve something.

STARS: Wishes, dreams and hopes. Alternatively, stars represent outside influences impressing themselves on a situation (similar to astrology).

STONES OR CRYSTALS: Each type of stone or crystal has unique symbolism based on the folklore and superstitions behind it. An eye agate (which has round, eye-like markings), traditionally used for protection from the evil eye, represents the need for safety. A magnetite (also known as lodestone), on the other hand, represents something that will approach you because it is known for its magnetic (attractive) qualities.

SWORD: An alternative to an athame, the sword wields greater power and therefore bears greater responsibility.

UFO: A large number of witches and Neo-Pagans trust in the possibility of life in other worlds: to quote Carl Sagan, 'Anything else would be a terrible waste of space.' The UFO reminds dreamers of their place as citizens of a very large universe.

WATCH: Many Wiccans remove their watches in the sacred space because magick works outside normal time–space constraints. In consequence, this dream may be asking to what you are directing your attention: the temporal or the eternal?

WEB: The intertwining of all things; life's network, where everything from the smallest neutron to the largest galaxy is connected, including your life.

Because this is an abbreviated list at best, it's good to seek out another dream guide or, better still, the advice of a Witch or Wiccan gifted in the art of dreaming and dream interpretation. Like the oracles of old, he or she may often be able to provide perspectives that others would miss when locked into the 'box' of rational, deductive thought. Although logic has a place in dream interpretation, the psychic, intuitive voice is even more important, because it is from this voice that spiritual missives often originate.

CHAPTER 9

Hexcraft:
Spell Methods
and Components

What would a book about Witches be without a healthy portion of spellcraft fundamentals? In the long legacy of Witchcraft, spells have always been the primary method in the Witch's kit, perhaps because they are an easily accessible form of magick. Some spells need nothing more than the Witch's presence to manifest power.

Spellcraft in Perspective

This chapter will introduce you to some of the most popular forms of spellcraft as exhibited in today's community – and throughout the ages. Although the chief ingredients or words used in spells may have changed, depending on the culture and social climate, the basic processes have not. This is wonderful for the Witch who looks to tradition or who simply wants to honour history in her practices.

In the Book of Exodus, Moses wielded a staff to bring water from a rock. Modern Witches might equate this to a water-witching tool or a magickal wand that directs the energy of a spell.

Mind you, respecting tradition does not limit the modern Witch. A lot of people who are new to magick often ask if it's OK for them to create their own spells. The answer is a resounding yes. Think of it this way: someone, somewhere had to come up with the idea for the first spell – and the hundreds of thousands of spells after that. Personally created spells are a birthright and are often considered a very important step in the Witch's training and adeptness.

Why did so many ancient spells include animal parts while modern ones do not?
The ancients honoured the power in nature by using it literally rather than symbolically. Since then, Witches have come to realize that this approach is neither ethical nor earth-friendly. Spellcraft and witchery have adapted to new times and societal situations, their powers growing with added symbolism.

A comprehensive overview of spells and their origins is not possible in a book of this size. What is possible is to share snippets of history and sample spells used hundreds of years ago, which are still used today.

Sympathy and the Law of Similars

To understand how spells work, it is necessary to understand sympathy and the Law of Similars. Sympathy basically means that a symbolic item, when properly used, has the power to act on something or someone by virtue of its sympathetic relation. For example, to heal a cut made by a dagger, put salve on the dagger – it will help heal the wound caused by it, due to the relationship between the wound, the dagger and your action. Furthermore, this action would help keep similar wounds from happening again because you're effectively 'forgiving' the dagger for cutting you.

f@ct

One example of a sympathetic spell comes from ancient Rome. A magistrate would strike a pick while summoning Jupiter so that the god would bear witness to a promise being made and likewise strike down any person who dared to break the oath.

The Law of Similars is a little different. According to this law, there is a divine fingerprint in nature, one that gives clues to an item's spiritual function. For example, red plants might be used in magickal cures for blood problems, and a heart-shaped leaf might be part of a love spell. Poppets (described in Chapter 4) were designed with the concept of sympathy and the Law of Similars in mind. The Egyptians were the first to utilize them in spellcraft, making the dolls very carefully, dressing them and adding incantations that designated the poppet's desired effect on the person it represented.

Little did our ancestors know that scientists who study subliminal perception would confirm their practices. Today, figurative representations play a part in everything from advertising to religion, affecting the subconscious in specific ways. Witches certainly aren't left out of this picture. You can still find many spells that employ an item's shape as part of the overall meaning, such as using a phallus-shaped stone in a spell for male virility. In this manner, Witches believe they are giving greater dimension to the energy a spell creates, and therefore it will manifest more specifically.

A Blessing Look, a Healing Touch

Although this theory has no proof, some believe that physically oriented spells were probably among the first to develop. People always had eyes, hands and feet – so why wouldn't they have used them? And since there was so much symbolic value ascribed to these parts of the human body, the mental connection needed to make the magick work was already there.

Eyes are the windows of the soul. Feet hold up the body and transport it, offer great stability, but also have the power to kick and crush things. Our hands serve, heal, build, welcome, support and offer aid, and have a million other responsibilities. You might have noticed that priests and priestesses around the world maintain eye contact with the people they serve and often use their hands in blessing; this approach creates a very real bond and helps energy flow more freely from one person to another. The Witch's methods are really no different.

The following list contains some examples of physically oriented spells:

BANISHING: To rid herself of an enemy, the Witch may stamp out that person's path through the woods, symbolically taking power over the person's very footsteps.

ENCHANTMENT: Trying to charm another person or object might include a long come-hither look as part of the process or the whole of the spell in order to weave the person desired into the magick.

HEALING: Nearly all healing spells employ hand motion and touching the patient. In modern times, people have learned much about the importance of touch, which gives this approach even more merit.

Never at a Loss for Words

Charm (verbal spell) was probably another common form of ancient spellcraft. This probably has a lot to do with linguistics. A variety of magickal processes, which seem to appear later in history than charms (such as the making of talismans and fetishes), use words that link them back to charms. This approach makes sense if you consider that a wise Witch realizes that he can always rely on his voice, his gift of speech.

Certainly, this particular form of spellcraft is pretty convenient – it goes with you everywhere.

The word *charm* comes from a Latin word *carmen*, which means 'incantation'. Many charms rhyme or have a distinct rhythm in their delivery, making it easier for the Witch to commit them to memory – no need to carry a huge grimoire around, no scrolls to get damaged in the rain en route to market.

In addition to rhyme and meter, charms utilize a variety of other magickal ideas in their mechanisms. For example, a Witch might wait until the first night of a full moon to recite the charm, then recite it thrice each night thereafter. The full moon represents 'fullness' or coming to manifestation, and the intuitive mind. The number three represents the body-mind-spirit connection or the triune nature of many of the world's divine figures. In this manner, the Witch combines lyrical verse with other symbolic systems to improve the results of the charm.

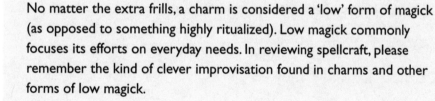

f@ct   No matter the extra frills, a charm is considered a 'low' form of magick (as opposed to something highly ritualized). Low magick commonly focuses its efforts on everyday needs. In reviewing spellcraft, please remember the kind of clever improvisation found in charms and other forms of low magick.

Written Spells

Many wise people were more literate than the rest of the populace; written spellcraft followed on the heels of verbal charms. Words have power, and the written word in many cultures was revered as a gift of the gods, especially among the Egyptians and Greeks. With this in mind, it's not surprising to discover that written spellcraft came to be considered more potent than verbal forms.

Written spells relied on the methods used for making charms. They might be timed by auspicious astrological conjunction or be written a set number of times. With written magick, specifically, the word's meaning, the colour of the ink, the shape of the paper and even aromatics added to the ink or paper contribute to the overall effect of the spell. Why go through all this fuss? Because Witches believe that the more dimensions magick has (with sensual dimensions being especially significant), the better the results will be.

One of the oldest, and most well-known written spells is the Gnostic spell that uses *Abracadabra* (no, we're not pulling a rabbit out of a hat). In the original Chaldean texts, *Abracadabra* translates as 'to perish like the word', and it was customarily used to banish sickness. The process was pretty simple. *Abracadabra* was written in the form of a descending triangle on parchment, which was then laid on the inflicted body part. Then the paper was stuck in the cleft of a tree and left there so that as time and the elements destroyed the paper, the magick would begin its work.

This whole process is a great example of magical symbolism, sympathy and similars — the word disappears into nothingness; the paper disappears into nothingness; and, therefore, the disease or illness takes the hint and follows suit.

Knot and Candle Spells

Knot and candle spells can also take their place in history among the more common spells. Making a knot has never been a complicated matter. A knot can be made of just about anything, and the symbolic value of binding or releasing certainly wasn't lost on our ancestors. Candles were similarly handy and linked with much symbolic value.

Knots for Good Luck

Knot magick most likely originated with the arts of weaving, sewing and fishing, all three of which use knotting in one form or another. A woman weaving her husband a scarf would bind a little magick into every strand to protect his health. A fisherman would tie knots in his fishing net to attract a better catch. (A seafaring fisherman might also knot a rope and hang it from his sail. When winds weren't favourable, releasing one knot would also release a light wind to take the boat where it needed to go.)

Although knot magick developed independently in different cultures throughout history, it generally has two elements in common. First is the use of numeric symbolism in the knot spell, such as tying a money knot four times (four is an 'earth' number associated with prosperity). Second is the binding of specific energy into each knot with incantations or symbolic objects: for example, if a fisherman wanted to attract fish, he or she might bind a small piece of bait into the net and release the knot as the net was lowered.

Modern Wiccans and Witches still use knot symbolism in the following types of spells:

☾ Bindings and banishings (especially of illness and negative energy).
☾ Channelling energy into a specific location (the energy can be captured in the knot and then released when most needed).
☾ Fixing relationships.
☾ Tying up the loose ends of a situation.

Candle Magick

Candles may be used in magickal spells as either the focus of the spell or as a component that sets the spell's overall mood and tone. As a focus point, the practitioner can manipulate the candle. Lighting the candle represents igniting the energy; carving the candle indicates the intention of the user; and pinning the candle marks the melting spot at which the magick will be released (like an **X** marking the spot on a treasure map).

The symbolic value of the candle goes further. The flame represents the element of fire, which in turn signifies inspiration, passion, energy and cleansing. Spells that require a fire source as a focus or component can easily be cast with a candle instead of a full-blown bonfire.

Witches also anoint candles with various oils and consider each candle's colour, which should correspond to the goals of specific spells. For example, a pink candle might be chosen for a friendship spell because pink is a gentler form of red, which usually represents passion. As for aromatic oils, the ancients associated sweet pea scent with friendly energy, and the scent of pineapples with hospitality.

Traditionally, anointing a candle is called 'dressing'. Begin at the bottom of the candle and rub the oil upwards when building energy, or from the top down when banishing. Work from the middle when you want to achieve a balance.

Component-Oriented Spells

It is reasonably safe to say that there is not a stone, plant, animal or other natural item that hasn't been used at one time or another for magickal purposes, especially spellcraft. If you think of a spell as a magickal recipe, you will begin to understand why the components (that is, the ingredients) are so important. If the components are not measured correctly, if they are not added to the mix at the right time, if you don't give them enough time to 'bake' properly, the magick goes awry. The magickal ingredients give flavour to the magick, and this has been the case throughout history.

So what constitutes a good spell component? Anything that's essential to the recipe – anything that builds the energy until it's just right. It's important for all the ingredients to mesh on a metaphysical level. Their energy needs both continuity and congruity. Of course, the Witch herself can be the key component of any spell, with but a word, a touch or a wish.

To illustrate this point, here is a list of possible components for a prosperity spell:

ANIMAL SYMBOLISM: Fish or rabbits (both prolific)
AROMATIC CORRESPONDENCES: Orange oil
COLOUR SYMBOLISM: Gold or silver (for the colour of coins)
HERBS: Saffron, the herb of kings
NUMERIC SYMBOLISM: Four for earth or eight for completion
TIMING: Waxing to full moon for 'fullness'

Putting such a list together provides numerous options for any Witch. He could make orange saffron incense to burn or possibly eat blessed fish dinners for eight days. Or he might begin the spell on the waxing moon and carry a gold coin in his pocket.

Of course, some spells come in prefabricated form (ready to use by simply following the instructions). However, if those instructions or ingredients don't make sense to you or break personal ethics, the spell will not work. A good working knowledge of components is essential to effective spellcraft.

Creating and Adapting Spells

With the previous example in mind, it's easy to see that there will be many times when a Witch or Wiccan will want to adapt a spell or make one of her own. The next obvious question is: just where do you begin?

Adapting a spell is far easier than creating one. When a Witch examines a spell, she looks for continuity and comprehensiveness.

☾ Does the spell really target the goal at hand through its words, actions and components?
☾ Does it do so on a multisensual level (hearing, sight, touch, taste and smell)?
☾ Does every part of the spell make sense and excite the Witch's higher sentiments?

If the answer to any of these questions is no, the Witch tries to find a substitute spell.

For example, many old love spells call for blood as a component. But modern awareness of disease makes using blood inappropriate. Alternatives would be to utilize a red juice or crushed berries that also have loving magickal qualities: strawberry or passion fruit juice would work well. In this manner, the Witch can still use the basic spell process while relying on components that are safe and support his ethics.

Magick doesn't have to be complicated to work. Complexity doesn't imply power, nor does simplicity mean weak magickal results. If anything, the simpler the better – it gives you more time to focus your mind and spirit on the task at hand.

Creating from Scratch

What's the difference between adapting a spell and designing one from scratch? Quite a bit. Now you no longer have a template to work from, you must devise all the actions, symbols, timing, wording and other components of the spell. Following these steps will help you create spells that can be just as effective as ones you learn from this book and other sources of Witchcraft and Wicca.

1. Boil down the purpose of the spell to a word or short phrase.
2. Find the ingredients suited to that goal (by using correspondence lists and resource books).
3. Consider the best possible timing for the spell.
4. Decide if you want a verbal component (incantation). If so, write it so that it includes your components and your goal.
5. Bless all the items you will be using as part of the spell (this rids them of any unwanted energies).
6. Consider any actions that might help support the magick and where best to place them in the spell process (for example, lighting a candle at the outset to illustrate your intention).
7. Focus your will and begin the spell, building energy.
8. Guide the energy as far as you can mentally, then release it and trust in the outcome.
9. Keep a journal of your successes and failures for future reference.

Of course, it's not necessary to always use every step of this process. There will be moments when you can't conduct a spell at 'just the right time', or when you don't have perfectly suitable components. The key here is to have things as close as possible to that ideal state so that the resulting energy is also that accurate.

Sample Spells

Having been a Witch for over 16 years, I have some favourite spells that I use regularly and find successful. Using the information given here for adapting spells, you can enjoy them too. For simplicity, I've set them up according to the spell's goal.

Turning Negative Energy

Take any reflective surface (pieces of aluminium foil or small mirrors, for example), and put them under the light of a midday sun (symbolically this turns away all darkness), saying:

> Negativity away,
> Darkness away,
> Banished by the light of day!

Put these items in every window of your home, and make sure that each one is facing outwards.

Attracting Luck

Find a coin minted in the year of your birth (if you can get one that has a high silver or gold content, all the better). Wrap the coin in a cabbage leaf (a good-luck food) and tie the bundle with a ribbon or string to bind the energy (choose the colour of the string to correspond with your 'lucky' or power colour). Leave the cabbage leaf where it will naturally dry without going mouldy (preferably during a waxing moon cycle so that luck 'grows'). When it is completely dry, wrap it in a natural-fibre cloth and carry it with you regularly.

An alternative to a cabbage leaf (and something quicker) is to wrap the coin in green paper (or choose another colour you consider lucky).

Finding Love

Gather a good-size handful of rose petals (preferably given to you by a friend or loved one so they're already filled with good energy). Take them outside your house or building and scatter them on the path or drive leading to your home, saying:

> Love find your way,
> Love come to stay!

Continue repeating the incantation until you reach your door. Retain one rose petal to carry with you as a love charm so love will follow you home.

Improving Prosperity

Based on the threefold law, take a £5 note and wrap it in yellow art or writing paper, saying:

> Return to me
> By the law of three.

Send this anonymously to someone you know who is in need of a little extra cash. This spell usually yields a £15 return within three weeks.

Maintaining Health and Vitality

Take an old knitted glove that you've worn and stuff it with health-giving dry herbs (symbolically, you are stuffing yourself with all that positive energy) – some good options include caraway, coriander, fern, geranium petals, juniper, marjoram, nutmeg, tansy and thyme. When you've done this, sew up the opening (so the health remains where you put it), tie a strand of your hair around the index-finger of the glove (to remind you of good health and its blessings), and keep this with your clothing.

Ethical Spellcraft

As with all forms of magick, Witches have some general guidelines that constitute morally and karmically responsible spells. These guidelines include:

☾ Never designing a spell that impedes another person's free will.
☾ Never working with languages or symbolic items that have little meaning (or are not fully understood).
☾ Never using a spell that includes components or methods that violate personal taboos or ethics.
☾ Avoiding spellcraft if you are ill, angry or otherwise off-centre, as this can affect the outcome dramatically.

Believe it or not, sticking to these guidelines still leaves a lot of leeway for personal vision. And what kind of results can you expect from spells? Well, this depends on your focus, your willpower and how detailed you became with the spell. Bear in mind that, just like a computer, spells do what we tell them to do: so if you perform a spell to find a perfect companion and get a wonderful dog, your magick certainly has manifested! It just did so within a broader scope than you really wanted because you left out some details. Spells, being designed with energy, will always take the easiest and most direct route to manifestation, so the outcomes can be interesting – to say the least.

CHAPTER 10
Handy
Spellcraft Magick

Charms, amulets, fetishes, talismans and other types of portable magick comprise a huge portion of the Witch's kit. In times when people travel both short and long distances without a second thought, these types of accessible items are becoming even more important. Taking spellcraft on the road has never been easier.

Defining Terms

Charms, amulets, fetishes and other forms of handy magick are rather like empty, uncharged batteries. The words and pieces used to make each object get filled with the Witch's will and magickal energy, and the result is something that slowly releases its power into the Witch's life as he or she carries it.

In modern vernacular, the words *charm*, *amulet* and *talisman* are often used interchangeably. From a historical perspective, however, they were not the same. To respect tradition and begin understanding what makes each process unique, it's important to define the terms.

Charms were probably the original form of portable magick (see Chapter 9 for more on charms in spellcraft). As we have seen, the word 'charm' comes from the Latin *carmen*, which means 'incantation' or possibly 'song'. This would imply that, at least at the outset, charms were nothing more than sacred words uttered with intention. Later on, the term was also applied to small symbolic items that were carried to encourage good fortune or avert evil. In either case, charms remain active once they have been created (unless the Witch intended otherwise), and typically, their energy lasts less than a year.

Charms play an important role in various magickal traditions. In many tribal cultures, a person could not claim the title of Shaman until he or she knew how to contrive dozens of traditional charms.

Amulets, by comparison, are passive until something external creates a need for their energy; therefore, their energy tends to last longer. An amulet's main purpose is protection; specifically, it wards off unwanted magick or other baneful influences such as lightning and theft. In some cases, amulets were contrived for purposes similar to charms, such as improving strength, increasing personal wealth and augmenting magickal power. The word 'amulet' comes from Latin *amuletum*, which means (you guessed it) 'charm'; it's no wonder people still confuse one with the other.

The Greeks called amulets *amylon*, meaning 'food'. This definition implies that people used food offerings to ask gods and goddesses for protection (and may have even eaten or carried a small bit of that food as an amuletic token).

Talismans are also used as active participants in magick. The Witch's wand is a good example of how a talisman operates because it transports energy and helps in casting spells. A Wand is a talisman of power (akin to the Rod of Moses). Many old stories tell us that talismans had indwelling spirits that were commanded by the magick user to do specific tasks. Instances of this nature are rare today, and the word *talisman* is now used to refer to any token that has been created during auspicious astrological times with the right materials.

f@ct

Aladdin's lamp was a kind of talisman. The lamp held a jinni, which is a very powerful spirit constrained to obey its owner. Other examples of items with talismanic virtues include the self-setting table, the cornucopia, the purse of Fortunatus and the refilling food bag of Arabic, Greek, European and some African folktales.

Finally, there are fetishes. The word probably comes from Latin *facticius* ('artificial'), by way of the Portuguese *feitico* and the French *fétiche*. Basically, a fetish can be any object. The important point is that the person who carries it must either have a strong emotional connection to the object or regard it as representing a higher authority (such as a nature spirit or the Divine).

For a good example of a modern-day use of a fetish, a labyrs (the double-headed axe) could be worn as a fetish, as it is a symbol of femininity and the goddess.

The Advantages of Using Handy Magickal Objects

Charms, amulets, talismans and fetishes are remarkably flexible and provide a great deal of creative leeway. In particular, they allow you to do the following:

☾ Choose personally meaningful base components that support your magickal goals.
☾ Design particular items for long-term, short-term or one-off use.
☾ Pattern the magick so it can be activated or turned off as needed.
☾ Create portable items that have all the same energy signatures for which spells and rituals are devised; you don't have to carry spell components or all your ritual tools when leaving home.
☾ Fashion effective magickal tools in a reasonably short period of time.

Charms

The three types of charms are spoken, written and physical. Verbal charms are easiest, since they require nothing more than some clever phrasing and your vocal cords – very convenient! A charm is like a poem: many charms, both ancient and modern, rhyme or have a poetic rhythm about them. The following example is a simple verbal charm from Europe:

> Leaf of ash,
> I do thee pluck
> To bring to me
> A day of luck.

This little ditty isn't a literary masterpiece, and your charms don't have to be either. What's important is that the charm expresses your wish or goal, and that it's easy to remember. Keeping it simple and memorable, you can repeat it whenever it comes to mind, giving the original charm more energy to work towards manifestation.

It's quite common for charms to be repeated a specific number of times. This repetition gives the charm a musical attribute and wraps it in the Witch's will. The other reason for repetition is the mystical value of numbers (also see Chapter 19). Using the aforementioned example, to add this dimension to the charm, a practitioner might repeat the phrase several times, the number of which could be her 'lucky' number, eight times (the manifestation number) or perhaps 12 times (the number that represents cycles coming to fruition).

Verbal charms can also include music. The Greek mathematician Pythagoras (circa 500 BCE) used music as part of his spells for foresight and healing.

Physical Charms

The little ditty used to illustrate a spoken charm can be followed easily by a physical charm. As the Witch speaks the word 'pluck', she takes the leaf from the ash tree, and carries it all day to inspire good fortune. Many physical charms are derived from nature; a four-leaf clover is a famous and typical example that already bears symbolic value and inherent power and simply needs to be activated by the carrier (often by using a verbal charm to empower it).

During the 19th century, man-made charms became very popular, specifically in the form of charm bracelets, often given as presents. Each charm had meaning and its own special blessings for the recipient: an anchor represented strong foundations; a heart was the gift of love; and a flower charm conferred health.

A good example of a physical charm is a lucky coin charm. To make your own, you'll need to find a coin minted in the year of your birth (or in a year that has special significance for you, such as the year you discovered Wicca). If this can be a coin with a high silver content, all the better – silver is a metal aligned with the moon and the energy of good fortune. Empower the coin for luck by repeating the following incantation:

> By word, will and this silver coin,
> Magick and fortune herein join!

Carry the coin with you or place it where you need the most luck.

Written Charms

Because magi and wise people were often literate, it's not surprising that they eventually came to express their magick on paper, as this medium provided the practitioner with even more options for symbolic value. Now the colour of the ink, the colour of the paper, the pattern created by the paper or words, and even an aromatic placed on the paper can be used to support the spell.

The words in written charms must reflect the goal of the magick by their meaning and by either the way they are written or what happens to them afterwards. For instance, if you're trying to get rid of a habit, you might write the name of that habit backwards on paper or write it on the paper and then burn it so that it disappears. Another good example of a written charm was the ancient healing charm *Abracadabra*, which worked to make sickness disappear by writing *Abracadabra* on a piece of paper and placing it on the inflicted body part (see Chapter 9 for more on this charm).

A Love Charm

This charm requires all three elements of traditional charms: verbal, written and physical. To work the charm, you will need red or purple art or writing paper (red and purple are the colours of passion and romance), rose oil, a picture of you and your mate, scissors and a red pen. Dab the paper with the rose oil, saying:

> Rose of love, this charm's begun,
> That I and _____ [name of your partner]
> will always be one!

Cut the paper into the shape of a heart. In the middle of the paper put a picture of yourself and your beloved, writing your names underneath, and keep it in a safe place to safeguard that relationship and keep love alive.

Amulets

Amulets are usually fashioned out of carved stone, metal, animal parts or bunched plant matter. With stone and metal, the more precious the base material, the better the amulet is thought to work; with plants, nearly every plant has been used at one time or another.

As far as animal parts go, the animal was chosen for its qualities so it could transfer those qualities to the bearer of the properly prepared amulet: for example, wearing an amulet formed out of lion skin would offset fear when the bearer was in battle or on the hunt.

> In old times, Greeks drank peony tea or carried a leaf with Athena's name written on it to safeguard themselves from hexes; Japanese carried double walnuts to fend off the evil eye; Romans attached garlic to doorways to keep away Witches, even as modern Witches hang it in their kitchens.

Amulets were also commonly chosen for their shape or where they were found. For example, Europeans often carried a holey stone (any stone with a hole going through it) to ward off malicious fairies (which would be trapped in the hole). A crystal found adjacent to a sacred well known for its healthful qualities would be carried as an amulet to protect the bearer's well-being. In this regard, amulets and charms have a lot in common.

The major difference between making charms and amulets is the fact that the ancient magi were very precise in their instructions on how to make amulets: the base components had to be organized and measured precisely, and any carvings had to be done in an exact order. Say, for example, a Witch wanted to create a health amulet for a sickly person. Copper would be a good base material. An emblem for recovery would be applied to the copper base first, since that was the primary necessity. Afterwards, a symbol for ongoing protection from sickness would be added. This seems like a natural progression – and it was! It was (and still is) customary for the practitioner to recite charms over the amulet as it was created.

Amulets Around the World

A good example of a readily recognized amulet in Western tradition is the horseshoe placed over a doorway. To work properly, the horseshoe must be found, rather than taken from an animal. Some people mount it upwards to catch any negativity, while others mount it downwards so it can rain blessings on everyone who enters.

Amulets in other cultures include:

BRASS RING (LAPLAND): Worn on the right arm to keep ghosts away.

GOD FIGURINES (ASSYRIA): Buried near the home to protect all within.

LAPIS LAZULI EYES (EGYPT): Placed in tombs to safeguard the soul's journey.

METAL RATTLES (ANCIENT ROME): Tied to children's clothing for overall protection.

MINIATURE CARVED CANOE (IROQUOIS): Protection from drowning.

MONKEY TEETH (BORNEO): For strength and skill.

PEACH STONE (CHINA): General ward against evil.

SPRUCE NEEDLES (SHOSHONE): To keep sickness at bay.

Strength and Safety Amulet

The idea for this amulet comes from India. To make the amulet, go out at dawn and look for a small piece of bark from the east side of a tree (where it gets the morning light). Bind this with a piece of yellow or gold-toned yarn, saying:

> Gathered from where the sun awoke,
> The power of protection and strength I invoke!

Wrap the bark in a natural white cloth (so it won't get damaged) and carry it with you often.

Amulets don't always have to be carried. They can be worn, placed with valued items, put on pet collars, hung in windows, planted in gardens or put anywhere else their protective and safeguarding energy is desired.

Talismans

Talismans have a lot in common with amulets in that their materials must be appropriate for the talisman's function. For example, when making a talisman to prevent drunkenness, amethyst is an ideal base component because it helps with self-control (see Chapter 16). To this base all manner of other methods and materials may be added. It is especially important to create the item at a specific time and recite incantations over it.

A rather interesting difference between talismans and other magickal items is that the talisman can influence its owner from a distance – it doesn't need to be in the right place at the right time. For example, when a husband gives his wife something personal before going into battle and asks her to keep it safe (which, in turn, extends protection to him), that object assumes the powers of a talisman. Although talismans are more potent than either charms or amulets – at least in terms of how far their energy extends – their power gets used up rather rapidly as a consequence. As you remember, Aladdin only got three wishes.

While some Witches might disagree, others consider poppets to be talismans as well. They are fashioned to represent a specific individual or thing, and are then bound to that person or thing by a personal item (a piece of clothing or hair, for example). Because the maker has a strong emotional bond to the poppet and uses that bond to affect a person over a long distance, the poppet qualifies as a talisman.

A Talisman for Finding Lost Objects

For this talisman, find a branch that's shaped like a Y, which is the traditional shape for the water-witching wand used in dowsing for wells. Do not go out and break off a branch from a living tree, but find a fallen branch that seems to appeal to you. For best results, you should gather the branch when the moon is in Libra.

After finding the branch, wrap it top to bottom with gold-toned, white and purple yarn braided together. Each time the braid wraps around the branch, repeat an incantation along the lines of:

> Within this braid my wishes bind,
> Whatever I look for I'll surely find!

The next time you lose something, take the talisman out and hold it in your hand while you're looking for the lost object. Repeat the incantation to activate the talisman's energy further. Alternatively, you can hold the two-pronged end of the Y with your hands as is done in dowsing and walk in the area where you think the item was lost. If the long part dips down, that's where you should look.

Fetishes

Fetishes are a little hard to describe outside the context of charms and amulets because they're very similar, except for their representative power and emotional connection (discussed in Chapter 9). For example, if you are working with a love charm, you would use a picture of yourself and your loved one. Because the photograph has the power to evoke an emotional response, the charm could be considered a fetish.

In modern magickal practice, fetishes are most often used for one-off spells. In such a case, the Witch makes up a bunch of fetishes at the same time, all of which have the same purpose. If a Witch uses a bay leaf (to represent Apollo) bound into a natural yellow cloth (for creativity) and empowers those bundles with an incantation, then he can use one of the bundles any time he feels the need.

Activate the energy of single-use fetishes by carrying them, burning them, burying them or floating them on moving water. Burning releases your wishes to the heavens in the smoke and disperses the energy. Burying helps the energy grow. Floating in water helps transport the energy where it's desired.

A Bad Luck Fetish

We've all run into streaks of bad luck. Make a couple of these fetishes to neatly disperse that negative energy. You'll need three pennies, three pieces of loosely woven cloth (in your lucky colour), and three pieces of white string. Use the string to tie each of the pennies into the cloth while reciting an incantation:

> In luck I trust, in luck I believe,
> Within this bundle, protection weave!

When you want to activate the fetish, take it to a remote location and put it into the earth, saying:

> Bad fortune's come, but not to stay.
> I command it now to turn away.

Turn away from the bundle and don't look back, leaving all that negative energy behind you.

Magick on the Road

People have always been very creative in making their charms, amulets talismans and fetishes. If one component wasn't available, they found something else that suited the task. As long as the symbolism held meaning and worked, they didn't make a fuss over having to make the substitution. This adaptability provides the modern Witch and Wiccan with a great prototype for using anything and everything in handy magick.

Quick Solutions

What do you do when you're on an aeroplane, for example? Well, the napkin can be used to make a written charm for pleasant travel, and the in-flight snack items may contain garlic as flavouring (protection) so they can be eaten as amulets. The only limit here is your imagination!

CHAPTER 11

Ritual: Methods, Constructs and Means

Ritual is one of the key ingredients in a magickal lifestyle, whether it is to honour a time of year, a god or goddess, or a personal transformation. To be a Witch or Wiccan, you need to know how a ritual is put together, how to build energy through that ritual and how to release it towards your goal.

Introduction to Rituals

Rituals play important roles in a great number of cultures and religions, as well as in personal lives. The way you prepare for your day is a ritual. The particular pattern of road navigation you use to get to work is a ritual. Human beings are creatures of habit. Rituals make us comfortable and provide a kind of continuity in life – something regular and dependable. They help control life's hectic pace and provide a way for us to recognize our place in the Circle of all things. Just watch nearly any family at Christmas – what you're seeing is a ritual and each person's place within the ritual, the family and the greater society. Perhaps most importantly, rituals contain a great deal of information about historical and cultural customs and traditions, as well as beliefs of social groups and individuals.

Ritual is like a spiritual instruction book to the universe, complete with blueprints. Ritual participants express a desire or goal to the universe, and the energy in and around their lives is patterned to mirror that desire or goal. In effect, each person becomes the magick!

What Does Ritual Celebrate?

Any number of things. Some rituals work to empower a divine figure (usually on his or her sacred day). Other rituals mark the Wheel of Time, the annual progression of the moon cycles, seasons, equinoxes and solstices. Yet others celebrate or honour the events that make us human: birth, marriage, death and all the minor events in between. Finally, a ritual can have a specific purpose for any one, or all, of the people assembled to perform it, such as a rite of healing or a ritual focused on helping crops to grow. In this manner, the energy raised during a ritual holds the potential of touching the needs and thoughts that lie at the heart of each individual and the world as a whole.

The Wiccan Ritual

Looking at Wicca and Witchcraft from the outside raises a lot of questions. Why do Witches design rituals in a particular way? How do you create or adapt rituals effectively? For a Wiccan, ritual is ultimately about fulfilment – fulfilment of everything it is to be a Witch or a Wiccan, or a human, for that matter. During ritual, the eternal and the temporal dance on the same stage. Human spirits can become one with the Divine, their energies merged with each other and the energy of the world in ways that even passion cannot replicate. Ritual brings the unseen, timeless realm to our doorstep and allows us to freely explore it. It also provides a construct through which we can build more energy than spells provide and direct it outwards to a need or goal.

Ritual is both personal and communal. It can evoke deep individual experiences and perceptions, or initiate incredible meaning for a whole. In this setting, each Witch or Wiccan needs to learn to be comfortable with the idea of eventually becoming a priest or priestess. In a group setting, someone trained for the job usually fills those shoes, or each member takes a turn. Solitary practitioners find themselves fulfilling the role rather quickly, however, simply because there is no one else to carry out the function. Although that might sound a little daunting to some readers, remember that you have already become a minister in your life each time you make a moral choice alone and each time you make a decision about your spiritual path.

Not all Witches or Wiccans work ritual frequently, and many do not follow the exact processes provided in this chapter. Each ritual, and each group enacting a ritual, is likely to have its own flavour and form, as unique as the people at that gathering. That is how it should be, for among Witches human diversity is a strength, not a weakness.

How to Construct a Ritual

Wiccan rituals fit a variety of tried-and-true magickal methods together into a congruous whole, rather like a spiritual jigsaw puzzle. Dancing around a ritual fire, singing, chanting, meditating, casting a spell, crafting amulets, making wishes, pouring libations, asperging the participants or the sacred space or praying – every part of a ritual has purpose and meaning in relation to the whole. Great care is taken that there are no wasted or meaningless words and actions, which would only undermine the productivity of the event. A ritual without meaning becomes a liturgy to which the participants have no connection and therefore cannot effect magick.

Key Elements in a Ritual

Although not every ritual you create or attend will have all these elements, any of these applied in meaningful combinations will help generate similarly meaningful results:

AMBIANCE. The right environment for your ritual is essential. Just as with spellcraft, your working space is very important. You don't want anything to distract, interrupt or otherwise take you away from the ritual at an important juncture. Set the right mood by using appropriate decoration, aromatics, altar configuration and so on. All these components should reflect the ritual's purpose.

In addition to the basics, don't overlook little meaningful touches. A bundle of newly opened blossoms at a spring ritual, or a candle for your ancestral altar at Halloween are two good examples. Well-chosen thematic music, incense and decorative items can make a big difference in the way a ritual progresses. These touches have the power to affect your senses, which in turn affect both the conscious and subconscious mind where the will resides.

PERSONAL PREPARATION. Everyone in attendance should be in the right frame of mind. Each person participating in a ritual is important. Witches gather in circles to demonstrate visually and spatially each participant's equal responsibility and relevance. Everyone who chooses to participate should feel wholly comfortable with the ritual and its components, should understand the ritual and its goals, should be well rested and should be ready to put aside daily stress and mundane thoughts to focus on the goal. All the preparation methods mentioned in Chapter 5 can certainly be applied in this context.

For the good of all, anyone who cannot fulfill all three parts of the preparation process is better off not participating. One person's lower energies or distractions become a weak link in the total circle of the power of creation and the direction of magickal energy.

TOOL AND COMPONENT PREPARATION. Do you need a complete altar set-up? Do you need special costumes? What about a special altar cloth, candles and crystals? A ritual might require any of the following tools:

- ☾ Asperger
- ☾ Athame
- ☾ Cauldron
- ☾ Circumference-marking material (like chalk)
- ☾ Cup
- ☾ Drum
- ☾ Feather or fan
- ☾ Foods or beverages
- ☾ Incense or oils
- ☾ Incense burner
- ☾ Objects representing the four elements
- ☾ Offerings
- ☾ Masks (or other props)
- ☾ Salt
- ☾ Smudge stick
- ☾ Statues
- ☾ Sword
- ☾ Wand

Everything that the ritual requires should be cleansed, otherwise an item's lingering energy could alter the course of the magick. Furthermore, each ritual object should be charged for its task in the ritual. Refer to the cleansing and charging methods described for tools used in spellcraft in Chapter 4.

LOCATION, LOCATION, LOCATION. If you're a solitary Witch, you have a lot more options than 30 people might. And if you live in a heavily populated city, it is likely that few inexpensive halls or parks allow public gatherings. Accept your limitations, and plan with the goals of the ritual in mind. Where a ritual takes place has a tremendous effect on the participants and the resulting magick: for example, it's far more difficult to hold an earth-healing ritual indoors, away from nature.

Make sure that your space can safely hold all the people participating in the ritual. Don't forget to include the space needed for conducting the ritual – if you're going to do a spiral dance, you need a *lot* of room. Sitting and meditating, by comparison, requires far less space.

Whenever possible (and safe), working outdoors in a private location seems to improve a ritual. Being away from concrete, telephones and TVs helps set a better tone for spiritual undertakings.

PROGRESSION. Rituals need to follow a logical progression, like a play. Each should have a defined beginning (such as creating sacred space), with something specific taking place afterwards on which all participants focus their attention. The ritual's progression creates the ritual's pattern – the actions and words that become tradition.

The beginning of any ritual sets the tone for everything to follow. In particular, it transports the participants to that place between the worlds and unifies their hearts and spirits, directing them to the ritual's goal. A typical beginning in a group setting may include breathing in unison, holding hands and calling the Watchtowers (the elemental guardians of the four quarters of the sacred space that 'watch' over the sacred space when invoked and honoured). Practitioners of solitary rituals may take a moment for prayer or meditation, followed by invoking the Circle.

After this, what happens varies dramatically, depending on the ritual and its goals. As mentioned previously, there may be the weaving of spells, dancing, singing, drumming, meditations, visualization, divination and so on. Whatever takes place after a Circle is cast needs to be congruent with the beginning of the ritual.

SENSUOUS CUES. As with spellcraft (Chapter 9), the more sensuous input during a ritual, the more energy it's likely to raise. As participants work their way through the ritual, everything perceived through their senses helps them to maintain focus and direct energy: when the Circle is trying to raise energy, drumming might get faster or chanting might get louder, for example. Each cue communicates the goals of the ritual to the superconscious and the Divine, and therefore nourishes the magick.

ENDING. Human beings like closure; solid endings also bring participants' attention back to mundane matters. A ritual without a defined ending is like forgetting to print the last chapter in a book; it leaves both the participants and the energy hanging. Since the ritual takes place in sacred space, it's rude to leave the Watchtowers just sitting there waiting to be released and thanked. Furthermore, participants really need this time to wind down a bit (or ground out, as Witches say). End the ritual by deconstructing the Circle, saying a closing prayer or stating a parting wish; then follow with hugging, talking and eating some crunchy food to get everyone's feet back on *terra firma*.

Seasonal Rituals

The Wheel of the Year is the Wiccan model of the annual calendar, which Wiccans view as a circle. There are eight major observances that are important to Wiccans and that many Witches also observe. Furthermore, every season has specific meaning and symbolic value, and within each season there are other celebrations that mark the Wheel of Time's ever-forward motion.

The following calendar marks the eight most important occasions in a Wiccan year:

THE EIGHT POINTS OF THE WICCAN WHEEL OF THE YEAR	
Candlemas	2 February
Spring Equinox	Late March (around 21)
Beltane	1 May
Summer Solstice	Late June (around 21)
Lammas	1 August
Autumn Equinox	Late September (around 22)
Samhain (All Hallows' eve or Halloween)	31 October
Yule	Late December (around 22)

Candlemas comes in February, at the outset of the year. Also known as the Feast of Brigid, this day is a time to work magick for the land, the welfare of young animals, the return of the sun to the world, health, transformation and divine providence. It is also a time for meditations designed to help the seed of our spirit grow to maturity.

Next comes the spring equinox in March. Spring is an upbeat, hopeful season when the earth returns to beauty. In keeping with this energy, the spring rites focus on fertility and abundance. It's also a great time to cast spells focused on new projects so they get off on the right foot.

The third notch on the wheel is Beltane, one of the most festive of all rituals, complete with a plethora of flowers, dancing and pure fun. Beltane is a fire festival in which wishes are often tossed into the balefire, or people jump the fires to ensure conception. The Maypole is the centrepiece of all this frolicking, the pole itself representing the masculine aspect, the ribbons representing the feminine and the weaving of fate's threads for the coming year. If you're a lover of fairy lore, this is one of their favourite holidays. Leave them a little offering of sweet bread and cream to make them happy.

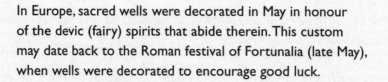

In Europe, sacred wells were decorated in May in honour of the devic (fairy) spirits that abide therein. This custom may date back to the Roman festival of Fortunalia (late May), when wells were decorated to encourage good luck.

The summer solstice in June is the halfway point in the Wiccan year. Although the earth is filled with bounty, winter is just around the corner, so prudence is wise. This is traditionally the time of year when Witches harvest magickal herbs for greatest potency. The ritual's focus includes inventiveness, luck, health and power.

August brings Lammas, which means 'loaf mass'. As one might expect, bread features in this celebration, specifically the baking of loaves from the first harvest of wheat. Lammas celebrates the grain spirit, a great provider. Lammas originated from the ancient festival for the god Lugh, said to preside over craftspeople. With this in mind, the Lammas may have one of two main points of celebration: it is the time to celebrate your craft and inspire your art further, and it is also the time to symbolically harvest the magick that you've nurtured up to this point in the year.

Autumn equinox rolls the wheel one more step forward in September. Days begin to grow shorter, and the harvest is gathered in abundance. However, the gathered food must last a long time, so at least one of the themes for this celebration is frugality. The autumn equinox is also a good time to give thanks to the earth and Spirit for all their blessings.

Samhain, or Halloween, is the holiday that children of all ages really revel in. Halloween originated from the Celtic New Year. According to Celtic lore, this is the time when the veil between worlds grows thin and both spirits and fairies are able to visit the earth more freely. It's no surprise, then, that Witches pick this time of the year to honour their ancestors and work magick for protection and improved psychic insights. Divination attempts are said to be most successful during Halloween.

f@ct

Costumes and carved pumpkins or turnips at Halloween used to have a different purpose: to fool or frighten mischievous or baleful spirits.

The last spoke on the annual wheel is Yule (or what most people call Christmas). This is the end of the solar year, when the sun reaches its lowest point in the sky, only to begin again to gain strength. The symbolism of a reborn sun wasn't lost on early theologians, so they adopted this holiday as Christ's birthday. For the Witch, Yule is a time to honour nature spirits, celebrate the sun's return, and commemorate ties to family and tribe. As is the case around the world, we too exchange gifts and gather with those we love.

Lunar Observances

Legends and witching lore say that Witches gain power from the moon. Where did this adage originate? Perhaps it came from ancient Greece, where Hecate (goddess of the moon) also taught and protected Witches.

And at least part of the tale may have come from the Witches themselves, who did, in fact, gather beneath the moon to work their magick and conduct rituals.

The tradition of using the moon's monthly cycle and its symbolism to empower spells, charms and rituals has not disappeared in modern times. Many Wiccans and Witches still celebrate Esbats (full or new moon rituals) or plan their magick according to the phases of the moon.

The first crescent moon represents the youthful Goddess. This is a traditional time to weave magick directed towards steady improvements, improving insight and creating opportunities. Repeating spells throughout this phase (or any phase) increases the power behind them.

The full moon represents the Mother aspect of the Goddess. The Mother offers us wisdom, maturity, nourishment, creativity and fertility. The three days of a full moon are among the best times to weave any type of positive magick, because this time marks a powerful fullness of metaphysical power.

After the full moon passes, its light and visible surface slowly shrink. The waning moon represents the Goddess in her Crone stage. The Crone knows life's mysteries and has grown content in who and what she is. This time of the lunar cycle supports any magick aimed towards lessening and decreasing (or banishing), and it's a great time to focus on ridding yourself of negative thoughts, forms and habits that you've outgrown.

Finally, the dark moon is like a three-day death (followed by rebirth with the next crescent). Witches use this time for introspection and for leaving behind anything from the past that holds them captive.

Names for the Full Moon

In Shamanic traditions (many of which bear strong similarities to Wicca, and many of whose customs Wiccans have adopted), every full moon throughout the year has at least one descriptive name. Following are the names of each moon cycle, as adopted from the Shamanic customs by some Wiccans. This list only shows *one* name per month, even though there are several other alternative names (depending on the particular culture or tradition).

JANUARY: Frost moon

FEBRUARY: Starving moon

MARCH: Storm moon

APRIL: Water moon

MAY: Corn-planting moon

JUNE: Honey moon

JULY: Raspberry moon

AUGUST: Gathering moon

SEPTEMBER: Spider-web moon

OCTOBER: Leaf-falling moon

NOVEMBER: New snow moon

DECEMBER: Long night moon

Rites of Passage

Rites of passage are rituals that mark important moments in the wheel that is our life. The birth of a child, coming of age, marriage, eldership and death are five rites of passage that immediately come to mind. At the birth of a child, we welcome his or her spirit into the world. This process often includes an introduction to all the elements and a blessing.

When that spirit comes of age, he or she has the right to become a fully recognized adult member of the community and begin participating fully in ritual (if he or she so wishes). The coming-of-age ceremonies vary enormously from culture to culture, but they generally include elements of learning, initiation and social affirmation. This is also a time when magickal tools are often presented as gifts, for which the spirit is now expected to become responsible.

The marriage ceremony allows the community to witness and support the adult's choice of life partner, and links two spirits into a harmonious one (in which neither individual is lost). A magickal marriage often includes the jumping of a broomstick or sword at the end of the ritual. This rite marks passage into a new life together and also fosters fertility.

Eldership honours a person's wisdom and contributions to the community. Some things do get better with age, and magick is certainly one of them. The Neo-Pagan community does not view old age as a detriment; it is celebrated, and the insights old Witches offer are gratefully accepted.

At the end of a Witch's life, her spirit is ushered on to its next form of existence. This ritual is typically called a Summerland rite. At this gathering, people open the Circle for the spirit of that individual to join them in one last dance and song, and to say their farewells. In this way, the Circle provides peace and closure, trusting that everyone will meet again in another life.

'We must get back into relation, vivid and nourishing relation to the cosmos and the universe. The way is through daily ritual, and is an affair of the individual and the household, a ritual of dawn and noon and sunset, the ritual of the kindling fire and pouring water, the ritual of the first breath, and the last.'

D.H. Lawrence (1885–1930)

Other Personalized Rituals

The Wheel of Time has many more special moments than are outlined in the eight-spoke festival calendar. In the centre of this wheel resides the individual Witch, who experiences so many things in a day, let alone a year. In consequence, Witches and Wiccans alike may call together their covens or friends for any number of personally meaningful rituals, or they may enact them alone. Among these we find rites of initiation, rituals of healing, new job celebrations, birthday festivities, forgiveness rituals, earth-healing gatherings and so on.

Realistically, you can create and enact a ritual for anything that has deep meaning to you. These additional rituals bring the magick home to your heart. In each of these rituals, you are no longer celebrating a cycle of the earth or a phase of the moon – you are celebrating your humanity and important events in your daily life. All too often we don't pause at these junctures and give them their due attention, but we should, and that's exactly what Witches try to do!

CHAPTER 12

Divination Tools and Methods

Diligent research reveals at least 300 methods of divination around the world. While a book of this nature obviously can't explore them all, it can provide good information on how divination works, how and why Witches use divination, and how to find a method that will work best for you.

The Origins of Fortunetelling and Divination

It might seem odd to see the interest in fortunetelling on the rise in these technically advanced times. Astrological predictions appear in many newspapers. People consult phone-in psychic hotlines; some even buy a pack of Tarot cards in an effort to understand the here-and-now better and take a peek into the all-elusive future. Why is this happening?

It's not just Wiccans and Witches generating the market for such things – human curiosity about the future and about things considered 'unknowable' by normal means is nothing new, and is certainly not limited to magickally oriented people. From the first moment humans realized there would be a tomorrow, it was natural to wonder about what it would bring. With such inquisitiveness, the next natural step was to create 'tools'. At first, these tools were nothing more than observation: our ancestors watched the movement of the wind, the changing shape of the moon, the way plants grew and how animals travelled, in an attempt to discern when to grow crops, travel, have babies, heal and handle other common needs.

True to human creativity, it didn't take long to develop other forms of divination. Astrology, for example, dates back to about 2,000 BCE, with roots in oral tradition that stretch back even farther. Before television, radio and the Internet, novel ideas had to spread slowly from person to person via caravans, traders, priests and neighbours.

Today, thanks to the advent of the media and advertising, an awareness that psychic tools exist has spread rapidly around the world, spurring a tremendous growth of interest in, and use of, divinatory methods. It's only natural that Witches and Wiccans would be part of this movement, since they already focus on spiritual pursuits.

Now, as then, each divination system has some connotation of culture and societal setting in its formation. Some systems are complex, some as simple as tossing a coin, but all strive to unlock an inner door into the future. Similarly, each person using these systems does so in the hope that the system being used is the key to the psychic self. Diviners seek information about any number of pressing issues, from matters of the heart to job-hunting, on which they lack perspective. In this manner, they are participating in an age-old tradition but in a whole new way.

Divination or Mediumship?

How does the work of divination differ from what a medium does? Mediums, prophets and channellers relinquish themselves in whole or in part to spiritual powers such as a ghost, angel or the Divine. A fortune-teller using a tool never undergoes such possession; instead, his or her tools become the focus for both the diviner and the questioner. Rather than hearing a far-off voice that seems to be coming from a familiar face, the divining tool becomes the 'voice' and provides the symbolic value that the reader must then interpret with all the wisdom he or she can muster. Both approaches to 'seeing' have merits and disadvantages – the real key is determining the one with which you're most comfortable.

Most people aren't ready to just step aside and let an unknown entity use their body for a few minutes. Nor is everyone wholly at ease with that same entity directing the course of decisions. On the other hand, many people find indirect divination systems highly approachable and well within their comfort zone, even if they only try it for entertainment.

Buyer Beware

Speaking of entertainment, be careful to avoid charlatans who use people's thirst for spiritual experiences and information to get rich while giving little in the way of sound readings in return. It's important that you always keep this in mind when you seek out a reader. Not everyone who divines is good at it, so go with word-of-mouth recommendations rather than a fancy advertisement. In addition, be aware that divination systems have their limits and not all of them are well conceived. Use your consumer sense to guide you (it's a good idea to bring a healthy dose of logic into this picture).

All caution aside, both mediumship and divination offer a window between the worlds, reaching beyond concrete reality. When you feel you need a witchy outlook and can't quite get a handle on things through normal means, turn to this chapter as a guide. Here you'll find instructions for several simple divinatory techniques and commonsense guidelines on how to read the signs you receive from them. Whether it's casting dice, laying out cards, gazing in crystal balls or scrying a fire, you can learn the ways that help Wiccans and Witches 'see' the world just a little bit differently – with the eyes of the Spirit.

Divination Tools

The number and variety of the divination forms certainly call for a pause to applaud the creative and inquisitive nature of our ancestors. Their divination tools included the following interesting items:

- ☾ Butterlamps (Tibet)
- ☾ Calfskins (several Shamanic traditions)
- ☾ Chanting (Celtic Europe)
- ☾ Dolls (Eurasia)
- ☾ Drums (Lapland)
- ☾ Handwriting (ancient Rome)
- ☾ Horses (Germany)
- ☾ Ink (Persia)
- ☾ Lightning (ancient Greece)
- ☾ Masks (Mayan)
- ☾ Popcorn (Navajo)
- ☾ Rods (Saxon)
- ☾ Tablets (Egypt)
- ☾ Wind (New Zealand)

Thankfully, historians kept note of these types of methods, and many of the old ways have been reborn into the New Age, alongside the growth of the interest in the occult in general. Witches and Wiccans incorporate many divination tools into their efforts to reveal the future, tools that people relied on hundreds and thousands of years ago. The following sections include some of the most popular methods of divination.

The Tarot Deck

Tarot is a divinatory tool whose symbols are used for myriad additional tasks, from meditation and visualization to spellcraft and ritual. The

Tarot consists of 22 major arcana cards; each one tied to a letter of the Hebrew alphabet and a position on the Tree of Life. There are also 56 minor arcana cards separated into four suits, each one representing an element: swords are air, coins are earth, wands are fire and cups are water.

Each of these four suits deals with specific life matters. Cups cover matters of relationships and the heart. Coins are concerned with mundane issues such as fame and fortune. Wands speak of changes, movement and communication. Swords deal with challenges and opposition. Together, the 72 represent the whole of humankind's spiritual and material experiences.

tips

The earliest Tarot cards are thought to date back to 15th-century Italy, probably commissioned by the Duke of Milan and painted by court artist Bonifacio Bembo. The cards may have been named after the River Taro in northern Italy.

Runes

Runes have roots in Scandinavian, Italian and German traditions. To make runes, slices of wood, pieces of clay or tumbled stones are etched with up to 30 emblems and drawn or cast upon a surface. The order of the runes or where they land determines the interpretation.

In addition to being a favourite divination tool, runes can also be used as a magickal language or for spellcraft. Some witches like to write in runes in their Books of Shadows for privacy purposes. While another Witch will recognize some symbols, most other people won't be able to decipher the meaning. In spellcraft, runes can be etched, drawn or painted onto another object (such as paper, cloth, stone or wood) to evoke specific energies.

Rune illustrations and explanations appear on the following page. For ease of reference they are presented in A to Z format, although in divination runes are traditionally grouped in three sets of eight, with each group known as an *aett*.

Algiz: Balance between heart and head, safety, personal restraint.

 Fehu: Frugality.

 **Ansuz:** Listening and speaking effectively; wisdom, advice, reading signals properly.

 **Gebo:** A gift (given or received), working in cooperation.

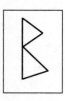 **Berkana:** Growth.

 **Hagalaz:** Psychism, a new sense of freedom.

 Dagaz: Attainment, wealth.

 Inguz: Freedom and liberation, abundance, insight.

 Ehwaz: Developing personal attributes (often as a result of changes).

 Isa: A time of being alone to release the past.

 Eihwaz: Preparation, fortitude, overcoming, foresight.

 Jera: Cycles.

Kano: Keen insight, openings.

 **Raido:** Balance, travel, communication.

 **Laguz:** Matters of the heart, going with the flow.

 **Sowelu:** Conscious mindfulness, life's energy, the sun's blessings.

 Mannaz: A new start, improved sense of purpose, personal maturity, transformation.

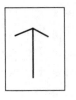 **Teiwaz:** Self-control, forbearance, warrior energy.

 Nauthiz: Knowing your limits, dealing effectively with personal shortcomings.

 Thurisaz: Thoughtfulness and meditation, new duties.

 Othila: Weeding out old ways of thinking and being.

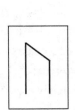 **Uruz:** Slow progress, thinking things through completely, inner strength.

 Perth: Spiritual beginnings, something unseen or unknown.

 Wunjo: Abundance, happiness, health, blessing.

Other Methods of Divination

Here are some additional methods of divination. Although the list is by no means complete, these are some common tools Witches use to look into the future.

ASTROLOGY. By 1600 BCE, there were already 7,000 astrological omens listed on tablets in Babylon, but it was not until around the 1900s that natal charts became a popular form of this art. China also has a form of astrology in which each year is named after one of 12 animals, each of which has characteristics that shape the year and the traits of persons born during that year.

BONE, SHELL AND STONE CASTINGS. The use of bones, shells and stones for divination shows up in settings as diverse as China, Japan, Rome and South Africa. In each setting, the manner in which the bones and shells land on a surface (the pattern they create) determines the interpretation. Other commonly 'cast' items include nuts, rods, seeds and runes.

DICE. Divination by dice became popular around 1200 BCE, thanks to the need to entertain people during long voyages. The number of dice used varies from tradition to tradition, three being employed in Tibet while some American systems use only one.

I CHING. The *I Ching* is approximately 3,000 years old and originates in China. It includes a system of hexagrams, each of which has a meaning. The hexes are derived by tossing the coins and making note of which side comes up on all three. Originally, the *I Ching* employed yarrow sticks to form the hexes instead of the coins utilized today.

OMENS AND SIGNS. Augury is the art of foretelling the future by reading omens and signs. In early civilizations, this skill was left in the hands of a holy person (a shaman or priest), and exactly what omens and signs were read varied from culture to culture: in Rome, for example, bird observation was popular, while in Egypt thunder was an important portent.

PENDULUMS. Pendulums seem to appear first in ancient Rome as a tool for determining the outcomes of forthcoming wars. This particular method is actually a form of dowsing, similar to that done with a Y-shaped branch to discover the resting place of water.

This is, of necessity, a very abbreviated review of what can be very complex systems. For research purposes, read *The World Atlas of Divination*, edited by John Matthews.

Proper Care of Divination Tools

Witches should take very good care of their divination tools. First of all, these items are sacred and should be honoured according to their importance and function within a spiritual context by the manner in which they are treated. A second, more pragmatic reason for taking good care of divination tools is so that unwanted hands don't damage them and render them useless.

Remember that anyone or anything handling a tool can unintentionally put energy into it. Having a special place for these items makes perfect sense; anything from natural fabric pouches to stained glass boxes will keep them physically and psychically safe.

Care of divination tools doesn't end there. The tools should be cleansed and recharged regularly, depending on the medium you have chosen. Crystals are often soaked in salt water to dissipate any lingering unwanted energy, while Tarot cards might be smudged with sage by wafting the smoke from a smouldering sage smudge stick over them. A Witch might place her hands palm down over her tools and direct white-light purifying energy into them.

As for recharging, Witches believe there is power in the elements, in the sun, in the moon, in sacred spaces and so on. Acceptable means of recharging include putting a tool in the light of the sun or moon, near a source of the wind or on the altar. Think of this process as the spiritual equivalent of jump-starting a battery and then refilling it.

The charging method chosen sometimes has to do with the nature of upcoming questions. For example, if a Witch planned to pose a lot of questions that required more intuitive insight (as opposed to conscious thought and planning), he would likely charge the system by the moon, which represents the psychic self. Conversely, for questions pertaining to very concrete matters, sunlight makes more sense because it represents the rational self.

All this fuss may seem a little confusing and difficult, but it's important to Witches and Wiccans. When you respect a tool, it's far less likely to be misused; when you treasure a tool, it tends to last longer; when you use a tool consistently, it becomes more effective in your hands. The way Witches tend their tools is an outward expression of inward philosophies and ideals. This conduct also illustrates an important concept to Wiccans and Witches, namely that all the different parts of their craft and magick are tied together, work together and help and enrich each other.

Picking a Divination System

The first question any magickally inclined person asks about a given divination system is: will it work for me? While that may seem like a very obvious consideration, the answer isn't quite so clear. Each divination system has unique symbols, depending on the creator's vision and the methods used. So how do you choose? Try using the following list to help you decide.

1. Which of your five senses elicits the strongest response? Does any particular divination system appeal to that sense? Tarot cards are highly visual, whereas stone sets or wooden runes appeal to touch-oriented individuals. While sensuous cues aren't indispensable in divination, they certainly provide another dimension: humans perceive the world in specific ways, and primarily through their sensuous experiences, as well as through how the mind interprets the sensory input.

2. Does the divination system exhibit any cultural influences that elicit a response or that interest you? For example, the *I Ching* originates in China. If you are interested in ancient China, have Chinese ancestry or integrate Chinese folklore or symbols into your magick, you might find the cultural appeal of the *I Ching* helpful.

3. What symbols do you like? What symbols make you uncomfortable? If more than a quarter of any particular method's symbolic values

makes no sense to you, and if you are unable to connect to them mentally or spiritually, it's highly likely that this system will not work effectively for you.

4. Does the given medium have enough symbolic value to answer the kinds of questions you have in mind? This question is particularly important. The Tarot can be quite specific, since it offers 72 different symbols. Runes generally only offer 21 symbols; casting stone sets have anywhere from seven to 13; and flipping a coin offers only two possible results! Most Witches and Wiccans recommend the middle ground – a somewhat diversified system with at least 13 emblems (for the 13 phases of the moon throughout the year).

A divination system such as using coins is called binary because of the two-result answer. It will provide yes/no, move/stay, up/down answers, but no details. This kind of system has its merits under specific circumstances, but won't provide a lot of room for psychic growth.

5. If the system has a few problems but you really like the whole, is there room for personal adaptation? In looking at a tarot deck, it's quite normal to dislike some of the art or symbols. In this case, you can look at others of of the hundreds of sets available, or get some blank cards and create substitutes with emblems that you can relate to or like better. In the same way, if you don't like all the crystals in a stone set, go out and buy some to substitute into the mix.

There is nothing wrong with this adaptive approach, as long as you maintain some kind of continuity within the system. I would not, for example, recommend putting non-Japanese images and symbols into the Japanese Tarot, because that breaks the feel and focus of the set. The overall accord makes a big difference in how effectively and accurately the system works together.

6. How durable and portable is the system? In a highly mobile society, where pets, children and coffee wreak havoc on everything from a Witch's ritual robes to altar cloths, these considerations are very

important. If you happen to travel frequently by broom or plane, you'll want a small system that's easily packed.

One nice solution to the durable/portable problem is having one special tool that you keep in a safe place, and another more portable system to use on the road. Runes, stones and dice work particularly well for those on the road.

7. Price versus quality? The price of a divinatory system does not necessarily indicate its quality. For example, a stone set with seven tiny crystals and a pouch priced at £12 might be made at home for about £7 (small tumbled stones may sell for £1 or so each, depending on the type and quality of the stone, and you can make the pouch yourself). On the other hand, the price of tarot decks is pretty reasonable (provided you like the art).

This list of questions is only a guideline, not an edict, but it's a good place to start. Ultimately, the most important point about any divination tool is that you have a strong affinity with it and understand the symbols it employs. Without this, it simply won't work effectively.

Using the Divination Tools

After going through the trouble of finding the right divination tool, it doesn't make sense to just leave it lying on a shelf somewhere. So the next obvious question is: how do Wiccans and Witches go about the divination process? The answer here isn't cut-and-dried. Bearing in mind that magick is a vision-driven methodology, it stands to reason that each person's approach to divination is pretty well unique. Luckily, there are some generally accepted processes on which most beginners can depend.

To begin with, a wise Witch always makes sure she is healthy, well rested and focused before any reading. A tired body, mind or spirit will affect the interpretation (usually in a negative way). Similarly, anger, frustration, depression and other negative emotions often lead to dark, dismal interpretations. Next, the witch finds a quiet, comfortable place to work the divination. Interruptions can really put a reading off track because they break the concentration and ambiance.

Some Witches spice up the surroundings to look and feel more magickal. This is accomplished by lighting a candle, burning some incense, putting on New Age music or doing whatever else it might take to turn thoughts from the mundane towards more spiritual pursuits.

Try using a yellow candle when you do a reading. Yellow is the colour of inspiration. Alternatively, you could try purple, the colour of spiritual and religious endeavour.

As far as setting the stage for the rest of the reading, Witches often recommend making sure that there's a suitable surface on which to use the tool and a comfortable place to sit. Candle scrying, for example, is best done at a table where the flame of the candle is about eye-height when the questioner or reader sit in an adjacent chair. Similarly, a detailed Tarot reading requires a large, flat, clutter-free surface on which to spread the cards. Some Witches also like to put a special covering cloth on this surface, one that is only used for readings. Traditionally, such a cloth is made of all-natural fabric and might have painted or embroidered symbols (such as runes) or personally significant images.

Finally, it's not uncommon for Witches to add other ritualistic overtones to the whole process. Here, 'ritualistic' refers to actions or processes that are repeated ritually each time a reading is undertaken. Examples include washing hands to remove any unwanted energies that could skew the reading, and smudging the area in which the reading takes place with sage smoke to clear the 'vibes'. Doing these things or enacting similar ones each time helps to create a different mindset, which gets you ready to receive information from the Spirit.

Reading for Yourself

Witches know that divination is meant to be a helper, not a crutch, and that it shouldn't be abused. Nonetheless, there are moments when they want more information before making a fair choice or deciding on a course of action in a specific situation. These are the moments when a reading could prove very helpful.

If you are emotionally charged about making a decision, you will have difficulty reading for yourself. Only you know whether you're in the wrong state of mind. If you hesitate to read for yourself, find a reading companion – another trusted Witch with developed psychic skills – for an unbiased spiritual perspective.

Reading for Others

If you thought a Witch's decision about reading for herself was difficult, reading for others isn't any simpler. Above and beyond deciding whether they're in the right frame of mind and making proper preparations, a Witch must also consider whether he can put aside personal opinions about the person or the question at hand. This concern is very important, as otherwise, the reading will reflect the reader's opinions rather than whatever message Spirit is trying to communicate. The phrases 'sharing truth in love' and 'constructive criticism' come to mind here – the goal of a reading is to help, not harm, and delivery matters.

Generally a Witch will decline to divine for someone towards whom they have ill will, or for those individuals about whose questions they know too much information. Both circumstances tarnish the quality and accuracy of any reading, because the human mind tends to bring personal feelings and knowledge into play.

One way to resolve the knowledge issue is to ask the questioner to keep his or her question unvoiced. Unless a Witch needs to know the question for clarification purposes, he may simply have the questioner focus on the question throughout the reading. At the end of the session, the questioner will be asked whether the question was answered. If not, the reader can ask about the question and review the reading again for specifics. However, not all Witches work this way – the choice is individual and may even change from situation to situation.

Reading Fees

In addition to the way in which each person directs the reading session, another element in divining for others is whether the Witch should charge for her services. Some feel that spiritual gifts should be free and available to all, while others believe that energy should be compensated in some manner, either by barter, trade or cash. Both schools of thought have merits, and both have adherents.

Perhaps it is true that people value what they pay for more than 'freebies' – even if a Witch only trades reading for reading, both individuals receive and both give. That kind of balance and symmetry is something for which Witches and Wiccans often strive.

What to Expect from the Readings

Each divination session is unique and tends to yield unique results. Some seem to provide no information whatsoever, others seem to answer questions that were never posed, and still others seem to contain terribly vague answers. Each of these three situations usually has specific causes and at least a few potential solutions.

When readings offer vague answers or provide no information whatsoever, the theory is that the lines of fate and the future are simply too tangled at the moment for a clear, concise response. Think of time as a tapestry, with the past and present being fully formed into a mosaic, and the future all bundled into a large, multicoloured ball of thread. Since we are beings of free will, even the most detailed predictions can be wrong.

Another explanation is that sometimes the person asking the question really needs to act on his own. Rather than depending on a divination system to guide his action, he needs to turn to his own inner voice and trust it. Some people become dependent on psychics, and Witches don't consider that a healthy way of living. Eventually, each individual needs to become his own guru and psychic.

How Accurate Is Divination?

Accuracy often depends on how adept the Witch is with his tools, as well as on the person asking the question and how open and honest she is with her inquiry. And, of course, accuracy also depends on the future's fluid, uncertain nature.

Divination isn't a perfect art with carved-in-stone answers. Instead, the hope is that a reading provides an alternative viewpoint and options that the questioner may not have considered.

You may receive amazingly accurate readings from total strangers, and terrible ones from friends. Some readings hit the nail on the head immediately, and some carry a message you may not understand for six months or more.

CHAPTER 13

Elemental Magick: Earth, Air, Fire and Water

You have already learned that the four quarters (east, south, west and north) have elemental associations – earth, air, fire and water – that are relied on to gather the Sacred Circle and are used in spellcraft and rituals. This chapter takes these associations further and discusses elemental magick in more detail.

Defining the Elements

The elements are the four primary substances encompassing creation (all physical matter). But this definition alone doesn't touch on the spiritual part of the equation. Following the Wiccan saying 'As above, so below', Witches believe that each earthly thing also has a presence and form of expression in the astral world. In consequence, each element (earth, air, fire and water) has been given astrological, mineral, plant, mystical and lunar correspondences and specific magickal attributes, including personalities.

Earth: The Solid Element

In the eyes of a Witch, earth is the home of humans and all other beings, as well as a storehouse for all kinds of spiritual lessons. The earth element resides in the northern quarter of creation (the top of the sacred wheel) along with the gnomes, whose name means 'earth dwellers'. Gnomes are said to have a great sense of humour and clever minds. They enjoy humans who are kind and honest, and will often help such individuals. Other earth spirits include the dwarves of European fairy tales, the *bergbui* (Teutonic mountain giants), *kubera* (Hindu guardians of the north) and *simargl* (Slavic guardians of all plants).

The magickal energies embodied by the earth element include patience, foundation and harmony. Earth is the element in which the soul puts down roots so it can reach safely towards the heavens. Other traditional applications for the earth element include magick aimed at slow and steady progress, fertility, financial security and overall abundance.

Global Myths and Superstitions

A good deal of earth's magickal symbolism is illustrated in global myths and superstitions. Nearly every tribal culture regarded earth in a maternal aspect. For example, there are Native American stories that tell us about how the soul waits for rebirth in the earth's womb (under the soil). Similarly, there are dozens of myths, including those of ancient Sumer and Guatemala, that describe humankind as being shaped from soil. According to the ancient Greeks, the heavens were born into existence from the womb of Gaia, the mother who oversees the abundance of all the earth.

Russians had a unique way of using soil for divination. They would think about a question, dig a small hole in the soil and lean down to listen to the earth's mouth. The belief existed that if one knew how to listen with spiritual ears, the earth would speak. This 'speech' might not come directly from the soil, however – the trees might rustle, an animal might run across the path or a bird might fly overhead. If such a thing happened, it was considered a natural omen and interpreted according to custom.

And what of superstition? Well, many farming traditions include giving offerings of bread or mead to the soil to ensure a good crop. It is from this custom and various Roman planting rituals that Witches come by land and seed blessings today. In fact, soil was used as a component in many old spells. People buried symbolic items to banish something or encourage growth: for example, to remove sickness, one healing spell instructs a sick person to spit in the soil and then cover that spot and walk away without looking back. To speed recovery from illness, patients were encouraged to grow health-promoting plants in the soil from their footprint. And if you wished to ensure a lover's fidelity, you would be advised to gather a little soil from beneath your foot and place it in a white cloth bag (for protection). It was said that your lover would never stray after that.

In the Slavic tradition, the soil was so sacred that it was sworn on when making a promise. The person making the promise placed one hand on the ground, taking the earth as his or her witness of the pledge, which was considered irrevocable.

Air: The Elusive Element

Air resides at the eastern quarter of creation. Here the sylphs, lovely winged beings, fly into the human imagination. The ancients believed that it is to these creatures that people owe their thanks for many oracular messages from the gods. Sylphs are also said to interact well with the other elementals, combining their efforts with those of the undines to make snowflakes, for example. Other air spirits from around the world include *ga-oh* (the Seneca spirit of the four winds), *boreas* (the Greek personification of the north wind) and *austri* (a Norse dwarf who traditionally rules the air).

Spiritually and mundanely, air is the most elusive of the elements because it is invisible, intangible and very moody. It can be gentle or fierce, damp or dry, and each of these moods has slightly different magickal connotations. For example, a damp wind combines the power of water and air to raise energy that motivates and nourishes. The air element is applicable to traditional spells and rituals such as transformation, magickal dreaming, contemplation, renewal, working with spirits (ghosts), communication and movement.

Air in Mythology and Spellcraft

A good deal of air's evasive ability is found in legends. For example, one of the most widely known folklore motifs is that of a man being sent to catch the wind, which has become a metaphor for an impossible task. Another motif is the sacredness of speech, the ability that depends on air. In the biblical version of creation, God's breath created life, and it was the Word that was fertile.

Many myths named the directions of the wind and provided them with dramatically different personalities. The ancients believed that the wind is influenced and changed by the corner of creation in which it originates. This idea translated into magickal methods nicely. If a wind is blowing from the south, it can represent fire and is said to generate passion, warmth or energy for spellcraft; similarly, a wind moving from the west brings water energies; from the north, it brings earth energies; and from the east, it doubles the strength of the air element.

We see a fair amount of directional wind work in spellcraft. For example, always scatter components in a wind moving away from you to carry a message or to take away a problem. Magick for new projects is best worked with the 'wind at your back', for good fortune. When trying to quell anger, opening a window to 'air out' the negative energy has great symbolic value; and, of course, when a Witch needs a wind, he or she has but to whistle! This is an ability said to have been passed down through families of Witches for generations.

Fire: The Element of Clarity

Fire takes up the southern quarter of creation. Here the salamanders, the tiny lizardlike tongues of flame, dance joyfully. Their life is tied to the fire, and when it is gone, so are they. Other manifestations of the fire spirit include the will-o'-the-wisp of European and American stories, the hobgoblin (a European fire-tending fairy), Logi (the Teutonic giant who governs wild fire) and Shawnodese (the spirit of the south in some Native American traditions).

Magically speaking, the fire element empowers spells and rituals focused on banishing negativity or fear, dramatic purification, purity, enlightenment, power and keen vision (the ability to see in the darkness). Because of its warmth, fire represents our passions, emotions, kinship and an in-gathering of people. It was around the fire that our earliest tribes gathered to cook, tell stories and celebrate life.

fact

The great predictor Nostradamus turned to the fire element regularly for his visions. In one of his writings we read: 'Secrets are revealed by the subtle spirit of fire.' Pyromancy (divining by fire) continues to be a favourite means of divination among Witches and Wiccans (see also Chapter 12).

Fiery Myths and Superstitions

Throughout Europe, superstitions about fire were strongly connected to the home. A person would never play with another person's hearth fire without permission because it angered the hearth spirit. This, in turn, could be disastrous for a family, because the hearth fire represented the home's heart and family unity. It is from this idea that we come by the tradition of bringing small gifts when we visit someone's home – originally those gifts were an offering for the hearth spirit.

The myths of fire often recount how, originally, fire was so powerful that only the gods had this element. In Greek mythology, Prometheus stole fire from the gods to give it to humankind. According to the people of the Congo, fire came to earth from a angry god who tossed down a burning log, and in Finland the first earthly fire was started by the god Ukko's sword.

> When fire came to humans from the Divine, it had retained its magickal powers. To this very day, shamans and elemental Witches alike will tell you that fire is the most difficult element to control due to its volatile nature. Handle it incorrectly, and you will be burned!

In spellcraft and ritual, fire is generally used in one of the following ways. As the best source of light, fire is set up in a special way (usually without chemical additives) so its energy supports the gathering. Moreover, items are released to the fire either to destroy a type of energy or to release energy into the smoke (which in turn carries the desire to the winds).

Water: The Element of Movement

Magickally, water resides in the western part of creation. Here the undines, better known as mermaids, live and frolic in the waves. Other water spirits from around the world include Aganippe (a Greek water nymph who lives in the stream that provides poetic inspiration to the Muses), *apo* (Persian water spirits), *gahongan* (Iroquois water spirits) and Nakki (a Finnish water genie whom you can bribe with coins).

The magickal energies embodied by water include wellness, gentle transformations, movement, tenacity, abundance and nurturing. In addition, because the moon affects the tides, water has a lot of the same correspondences as the lunar sphere in its full phase for spell and ritual work.

A variety of items can be used to symbolize the element of water in spells and rituals, or at the western quarter of the Circle. These items include a ball, a cauldron, a goblet, driftwood, a holey stone, kelp, a mermaid statue, rainwater, a painting of the ocean, seashells or anything that contains liquid.

Water Mythology and Superstition

To understand the symbolic value of water a little better, consider the world's myths and legends, which are filled with sea gods and goddesses who protect sailors and provide for whole communities. Many creation myths begin in the water or contain water as a key element to that first, vibrant burst of energy that started all things; thus water also often represents creativity on a very physical level.

Water legends carried over into superstitions. Reverence for water has taken on many forms and customs, from dropping coins into sacred wells (to ask the water spirits to grant wishes), to pouring mead into the sea (as an offering) before going on a voyage. And as with the superstitions tied in with the other elements, a lot of these beliefs translate nicely into a magickal setting.

For example, a Witch would dip her broom in water and shake it out to bring rain. This is a perfectly good example of sympathetic magick. The joke about rain coming after you wash your windows or car works on the same principle – there's really little difference! A modern Witch wishing to invoke rain might follow a similar process.

A very popular application for water in spells and rituals is for healing and protection from sickness. According to European custom, dew gathered at dawn banishes illness, making it a good base for curative potions. Similarly, bathing in the water from a sacred well, dipping your hands into the ocean's water three times (then pouring it behind you so the sickness is 'behind' you) or releasing a token that represents your sickness to the waves are old spells that easily work in today's setting.

Scottish lore advises a person searching for physical beauty to bathe in heather water beneath a full moon. This folk spell relies on the connection between the moon and water. In modern times, heather sprigs are still sometimes used to asperge the sacred space in order to purify it for those walking the Path of Beauty.

Spirit: The Fifth Element?

Spirit (also known as aether or ether) isn't an element as such, but it is often included in a list of magickal elements as the fifth point of the pentagram. It's even harder to define than air. Spirit is the binding link between the four quarters of creation, and is thus the source of magick. Spirit resides within and without, around, above and below all things. While we can experience earth, air, fire and water directly with our temporal senses, Spirit is elusive and depends on both the Witch's faith and spiritual senses to be experienced.

This underlying, life-sustaining energy we call Spirit has been known by many other names. Among the Native Americans, we hear the name Grandfather, or Arch of Heaven. In Hindu writing, *atman* is the spiritual essence of creation. The Polynesians and the Jains have a similar idea but call it *mana*, or *jiva*, respectively – that which animates all life, or the life principle.

In spells and rituals, Spirit usually comes into play if the Witch or Wiccan chooses to call upon a divine figure to bless and energize her magick. Alternatively, it can come into the equation if several devic (fairy) entities are being invoked and need to be able to work together. Spirit provides the medium in which any and all elements exist equally well.

The Elemental Beings

If you look at the world's folklore, you'll discover a nearly universal belief that each element has a specific set of beings who reside within or have power over it. Most Witches agree, if only by acknowledging that there is far more to life and our world than readily meets the eye. Each of these elemental creatures has a function and is intimately connected to the element in which it resides. The personalities of these creatures are often reflected in that element. For example, the traditional sylph is an air deva and tends to have a very whimsical, lighthearted nature; similarly, elves are earth beings who keep to the trees, striving to protect nature's sacredness.

What are some names of elemental beings?
In Benin (a former kingdom of western Africa, now part of Nigeria), one elemental is called *aziza* (little people). The *aziza* live in forests, working magick much like the elves of European lore. Tibetans have the *sa-bdag*, who bear remarkable similarities to the fairy folk of Western stories, and the *chinoi* of Malaysia are beings who live in flowers.

While logically minded people might shake their head at such notions, that doesn't seem to keep dreamers, artists, psychics, children and pets from seeing these marvellous entities. Each person perceives them a little differently (because they live on a different vibrational level). Nevertheless, it seems that elementals continue to interact with humankind in intimate and interesting ways.

Magickally speaking, the elemental beings are considered more powerful than humans when in their element, and if they so choose they can be very helpful to Witches. Mind you, devic beings have agendas and projects of their own, so they're not to be commanded like children or invoked without thought. Witches believe that all elemental beings warrant their respect, especially if the Witches presume to honour nature in their workings.

The processes to invoke an elemental being and work with it are too lengthy to describe in this book, and they're also considered more 'adept'. If you'd like a book that looks more closely at this subject, try *Dancing with Devas* by Patricia Telesco.

Elements Expressed in Personality

Each Witch has one element to which she most strongly responds; this is called her power element. In addition, each Witch has a personality element. Knowing both these aspects of personality helps a Witch greatly.

Your Power Element

First, let's look at the element to which a Witch or Wiccan responds – the power element. By working with that element, the Witch has the power to energize both herself and her magickal processes. Basically, the element becomes a battery. The Witch can tap into the powerful subconscious effect of the element to improve the results of her working and to shape her personal meditations and visualizations.

How do you determine your power element? By paying attention. Go to places where you can experience each element intimately. Stand in a strong wind, sit by an ocean or waterfall, watch a blazing fire or walk into a cave, which is the earth's womb. Which location (closest to which element) makes you feel the most alive? Where are your senses tingling to the point where they feel more accurate than before?

Once you determine which element energizes you, then you can find ways to expose yourself to that element more regularly in order to refill your inner well. This exposure is especially helpful when you're feeling spiritually limp. Here are some ideas to get you started:

EARTH: Work in the garden; sit (as close to the ground as possible) with brown or black crystals in the palm of your hand; take a long walk in the woods; keep a potted plant where you work.

AIR: Put an electric fan near your desk; open windows; practise breathing exercises; go to a windy location and let the breeze embrace you.

FIRE: Dance the ritual fire; light a candle; put fire-aligned oils on a lamp to turn up the energy; sit next to a heater; sit in a sunny location.

WATER: Take a long bath or shower; play in the rain; drink a glass of spring water; go swimming; run through a lawn sprinkler.

But what about meditation and visualization? What's great about that setting is that you do not need to have actual contact with an element to receive its positive effects. For example, a water Witch might listen to a nature CD with the sounds of water and envision himself at the beach, being caressed by ocean waves. When a water Witch needs healing, he might envision the waves gathering all his negativity and sickness and washing it out to sea. This kind of creative visualization, because of its symbolic value, can prove just as potent and transformational as direct exposure to your power element. Just give it a try!

Personality Elements

To discern your personality element, ask yourself the following questions:

☽ What are your likes and dislikes?
☽ How do people describe you?
☽ What hobbies (or art forms) attract your attention?
☽ What's your temperament?

Do any themes appear in your answers? Next, look over the following descriptions of elemental personalities for more insight:

EARTH PEOPLE: Very grounded, they like stability, plan out everything and have little patience for procrastination or flights of fancy. Their favourite colour may be black, brown or forest green, and their hobbies often include gardening.

AIR PEOPLE: The world's gypsy spirits, they enjoy adventure, long conversations and risks, and hate to be restricted. Their favourite colours may be yellow or white, and their hobbies can include hang-gliding or flying kites.

FIRE PEOPLE: Passionate and energetic (sometimes to the point of burning out), they dislike wishy-washy sorts who, they feel, have no spine. Their favourite colours are solar red and orange with periodic intense blues, and their hobbies might include salsa dancing.

WATER PEOPLE: They like to go with the proverbial flow. They are healers, motherly types and nurturers who unnerve you with their psychic insights. They may find it hard to understand those who cannot control their anger. Their favourite colours are purple or blue, and their hobbies might include fishing or swimming.

Once a Witch establishes her elemental personality, how does she use this information? Usually, it will help improve her interpersonal communication and help her understand better the way her magick works. For example, fire people are naturally uncomfortable with water people. Their relationships might be steamy, but eventually that's all that's left – hot air! Similarly, the relationships between earth people and water people get muddy. In terms of magick, fire people have to maintain a more rigid control on their energy because of the propensity for explosive energy.

Sometimes an individual's personality element can be the same as his or her power element, but often they are two different elements or a combination of more than two, one of which is predominant. By way of illustration, let's say that a Witch's power element is water and his personality element is air with an earthy subtext. This Witch is an avid communicator and networker who is also strongly focused on stability. Water as a power element actually helps balance his air and earth elements and provides more symmetry. This Witch is slowly learning to work with the fire element, with a similar goal of personal coherence in mind. From this example, you can see how working with power and personality elements can be of tremendous value to the Witch in magick and in his daily life as well.

CHAPTER 14

Kitchen Witchery: Eat, Drink and Make Magick

Kitchen magick (also known as hearth magick) is among the simplest schools of witchery and is easily applied to many spiritual paths. Kitchen Witches are similar to hedge Witches in their methods and outlooks. Although the kitchen Witch may work alone or in an eclectic group, the keywords for this person's approach to magick are finesse, frugality, functionality and fun!

The Kitchen Witch's Philosophy

A kitchen Witch definitely adheres to the keep-it-simple outlook. Looking to her ancestors, she has a long history of practicality on which to base this tradition. This approach is simple, and makes perfect sense: if something is available and contains the right symbolism, it should be used in kitchen magick. Just a few decades ago, there were no superstores and no Internet, and people had little time for lengthy spells and rituals, so they turned to nature's powerhouse and the home for fast and functional magick. The modern kitchen Witch continues to practise this approach today.

Functionality, Finesse and Frugality

With finesse, the kitchen Witch brings personal flair and vision into every spell or ritual she performs. With frugality, the kitchen Witch keeps magick affordable, enjoying a positive spiritual path without breaking the family budget. Looking to functionality, the kitchen Witch considers every item in and around the house as having potential for magick. Functionality, finesse and frugality work hand-in-hand. If something is not functional, why expend time, money and effort on it? For that matter, it just wouldn't appeal to the kitchen Witch's higher senses.

Kitchen Witches are fun. Their quirky approach to Witchcraft is quite liberating and playful. They believe that life itself is an act of worship, and anything else you can bring to that altar just makes the proverbial cake all the sweeter!

Equation for Successful Kitchen Magick

The basic equation for successful kitchen magick is:

Simplicity + Creativity + Personalization = Power

Simplicity allows the kitchen Witch to focus completely on the goal rather than on the process of getting there. *Creativity* allows the Witch to see the spiritual potential in even the most mundane items. *Personalization* makes the practice meaningful, and it is the meaning that provides the most support for manifestation of the magick.

With this formula in mind, today's kitchen Witches do not ascribe to the media's message that fancier is better. On the contrary, instinctive, intuitive things should come naturally, without a lot of fanfare. Kitchen Witches make every effort to keep Witchcraft part of their everyday life, serving spiritual energies and mundane efforts on one plate. Furthermore, kitchen magick should always reflect the individual Witch's principles; if you don't abide by these principles, you are not really practising kitchen magick.

The Home and the Hearth

The kitchen Witch's philosophy and focus begin and end at home. Wherever you live can function as your sacred space; what makes it 'sacred' is how you treat it. Every item and action in the kitchen Witch's life, from brewing coffee to brushing teeth, can be spiritual if she chooses it to be so. How? By being a little inventive.

The coffee pot 'perks' up energy along with the flavoured coffee chosen for its magickal association; and brushing your teeth with mint toothpaste improves communication. Just because something is technological doesn't mean it's antimagick. If Granny had any of the kitchen toys of today, she would have used them in magick with all due pragmatism, and the modern Witch should certainly follow suit.

The Folklore of Hearth Magick

Many kitchen Witches look to folklore, superstitions and old wives' tales for magickal ideas. A whole lot of magick resides in these old stories, and they are very easy to follow. For example, how often have you seen people toss spilled salt over their shoulder without a second thought? That practice comes from a superstition that tossing spilled salt over your shoulder keeps evil away, and it gives the kitchen Witch food for thought: why not use salt as part of her magick for protection?

Another bit of hearth lore is that the oven or the fireplace (wherever you cook) is the heart of the home. That's why people often built this part first. Each house has a hearth spirit that keeps warmth and love within the home. With this old belief in mind, many kitchen Witches have small altars near their cooking space. In addition, a wise kitchen Witch always brings a small gift for the hearth spirit when visiting magickal friends so as not to anger that important protector of family unity.

There are many other ways that superstition influences the kitchen Witch. For example, he probably doesn't cut lettuce, as to do so cuts away luck and prosperity. Also, once served to the table, foods should be passed clockwise to inspire blessings. These folkways have obvious charm and potential power, and they allow the kitchen Witch to reclaim a heritage without wandering far from the hearth fires of home or having to give up modern conveniences.

Gods and Goddesses of the Kitchen and the Hearth

Every culture tells of divine beings that govern either the entire home, the pantry or the hearth. These entities include:

- ☾ **Bannik (Slavonic):** God of all household matters, who also oversees prophetic attempts.
- ☾ **Dugnai (Slavonic):** Goddess of bread and the home.
- ☾ **Fornax (Roman):** Goddess of the oven.
- ☾ **Gucumatz (Mayan):** God of domestic life.
- ☾ **Hastsehogan (Navajo):** God of home (a house is often called a *hogan* in Navajo).
- ☾ **Hehsui-no-kami (Japanese):** Goddess of the kitchen.
- ☾ **Mama Occlo (Incan):** Goddess of domestic arts.
- ☾ **Okitsu-hiko (Japanese):** God of the kitchen.
- ☾ **Pukkeenegak (Eskimo):** Goddess of providence (especially food).
- ☾ **Tsao-wang (Chinese):** God of the hearth.
- ☾ **Vesta (Roman):** Goddess of the hearth fire.

Kitchen Magick in the Kitchen

Of course, the ultimate expression of kitchen magick begins in the kitchen. Here the Witch makes foods, beverages, potions and notions that fill and fulfill body, mind and spirit. To accomplish this, the Witch first does a little practical decorating: she hunts up some aromatic pots or amphoras, Witchcraft-themed trivets and refrigerator magnets, a candle or two and maybe god and goddess salt and pepper shakers.

Once the kitchen has a more magickal feel, the next step is to choose the tools for the job at hand. I like using a wooden spoon as my wand and a butter knife for an athame. These items are in my kitchen all the time, absorbing my personal energy, and they maintain a congruity of symbolic value in the sacred space. What other utensils could you use? Nearly anything that's handy and that has the right symbolism: use straining spoons to strain out negativity, a blender to whip up energy, a microwave to speed manifestation, and soap for cleansing or asperging.

Don't overlook the names of products in and around your kitchen, as these can often provide a clue as to how you might apply them. If you buy washing powder, use Tide to reflect on the pulse of life and Surf for energy or to improve your outlook.

Steps for Making Magick in the Kitchen

1. Set up the space so it reflects your magickal needs and goals.
2. Choose kitchen tools appropriate to the working.
3. Choose your ingredients to support the process; in other words, match the magickal meaning of the foods, spices and beverages with your goals and intentions. Don't forget to consider colour and numeric symbolism as well. (This is also a good time to invoke the magick Circle, if you were planning to set it up for this particular spell.)
4. Chant, incant, visualize, sing. Empower whatever you're creating while you're making it. Make sure you do this at the most propitious time. For example, chant over bread while it's rising so the energy may likewise rise.
5. Serve the food in a manner that represents the desired manifestation. For example, if you're working for joy, pattern the blessed food on the plate so it looks like a smile.
6. Say a prayer before using or consuming the results.
7. Trust in the magick.

It doesn't matter whether you're creating edibles or beverages, or just mixing up spell components that come out of the sacred space of home. What matters is that the meaning is there, and that the symbolism works in your mind and heart.

Food for the Spirit

People making spiritually enriched foods all around the world. For example, the Japanese eat a special glutinous-rice dish on their birthdays for luck, much as Westerners eat cake. As recently as a century ago, people still baked and brewed by the phases of the moon to improve the outcome of the recipe. Kitchen Witches revel in and embrace this kind of approach to food magick.

To take this concept into a specific scenario, say you're preparing food for Samhain (Halloween), a festival for the dead. You might begin with potato soup (potatoes have eyes with which to recognize the spiritual world, and they help keep us rooted in this realm).

Next, try a bean side dish for protection and insight. Cooked haricot or kidney beans would work especially well here, and for more symbolic protection, remember to season the beans with onion and garlic. And for dessert, why not make an apple pie to reflect the harvest? If you decide on this, make sure that you rub the apples first to rub away any 'evil'.

Relationship Rescue Pie

Imagine you have a bunch of apples, want to make a pie, and wonder about what kind of magick to whip into it. Well, apples represent health, cinnamon is a good love herb, ginger improves overall energy and vanilla inspires love. Combine these ingredients, and it sounds like the ideal dessert when your relationship with your partner needs a pick-me-up. Cut the pie crust so the top has the outline of a heart that warms up as the pie bakes.

Here is the complete recipe:

Ingredients

8 medium apples, peeled and sliced thin

$1/2$ teaspoon ginger

$1/2$ teaspoon cinnamon

$1/2$ teaspoon nutmeg (or to taste)

$1/2$ teaspoon vanilla

30g (1oz) flour

2 shortcrust sticks, prepared and rolled out according to directions on the packet for a 23cm (9in) pie

2 tablespoons butter

Directions

1. Preheat the oven to 220°C, 425°F, gas mark 7. Put one of the rolled shortcrust pieces into the pie pan. Toss the apple slices with the spices, vanilla and flour; then put them into the pie crust. Dot the top of the apples evenly with bits of the butter. Put the other half of the pastry over the top of the pie, securing it at the edges while saying:

   Secured within, so my magick begins.
   Transform anger with love, and bless from above!

2. Gently draw a heart in the top of the pie using a fork so that energy bakes into the crust. Bake the pie in the preheated oven for about 45 minutes, or until the crust is brown and apple juice is bubbling through the heart pattern.

Strength and Safety Soup

Here's a recipe that can be a main dish, side dish or starter during those times when you feel you need more protection. Garlic and onions are the key ingredients.

Romans used garlic for strength, and many other people have considered it a protective herb. Egyptians used onions to keep away baleful spirits, and fed them to their slaves to ensure vitality. This recipe also relies on the number four for its earthy energy, which provides the magick with foundations to take root in our hearts and lives.

Ingredients

1 large Spanish onion
1 large red onion
1 bunch spring onions
1 white onion
4 sticks celery, diced (optional)
1 tablespoon butter
4 small cloves garlic, peeled and crushed
500ml (16fl oz) beef stock
500ml (16fl oz) chicken stock
500ml (16fl oz) water
4 dashes (1 tablespoon) Worcestershire sauce (or to taste)
Garlic powder and onion power (optional)
Croutons and grated cheese (for garnish, optional)

Directions

1. Slice the onions and place them in a frying pan with the butter and garlic.
2. For a hearty broth, add 4 sticks of diced celery (to be fried with the onions). Magickally, this ingredient will provide you with psychic insight and a sense of inner peace.
3. Gently sauté the onions and celery, if desired, until golden brown.
4. Stir the vegetables anticlockwise as they cook, to banish negative energies, saying:

   Onions for health, and to keep ghosts at bay,
   Garlic for safety all through the day!

   Keep repeating the incantation slowly until the onions are done.
5. Transfer the onions into a large soup pan, adding the stock, water and Worcestershire sauce (you might also add a bit of garlic powder and onion powder, but that's optional). Cook this mixture over a medium-low flame until it is reduced by about a third.
   Serve the soup with croutons and grated fresh cheese, if desired.
   Visualize your body being filled with white light as you eat it.

Magickal Properties of Common Culinary Items

After reading recipes such as these, you're probably wondering what magickal associations apply to the various edibles and spices in your home. Here is a brief alphabetized listing of some of the items in your kitchen and their correspondences:

CULINARY ITEM	MAGICKAL ASSOCIATION
alfalfa sprouts	frugality, providence
anise	love, enthusiasm
bacon	financial prosperity
banana	male fertility
bay leaves	energy, health
beef	grounding, abundance
bread	kinship, sustenance
carrot	vision, the god aspect
celery	foundations, peace
chicken	health, new beginnings
coffee	conscious mind, alertness
eggs	fertility, hope
honey	creativity, joy, well-being
lemon	cleansing, longevity, devotion
mint	rejuvenation, money
olive	peace, spirituality
pineapple	hospitality, protection
potato	healing, foundations, earth energy
rice	blessings, fertility, weather magick (rain)
thyme	fairy folk, health, romance
vinegar	purification
wine	celebration, happiness

For more detailed information, I recommend Scott Cunningham's *The Magic in Food*, Paul Beyerl's *A Compendium of Herbal Magick* and Patricia J. Telesco's *Kitchen Witch's Cookbook*.

Sacred Space of the Home

Although you might begin to think that kitchen magick has no place outside the kitchen, just the opposite is true. Most kitchen Witches strive to carry special energy into every nook and cranny of their home. How do they accomplish this? In the same way they prepare their kitchen (refer to the list of steps for successful kitchen magick on p 167).

The Witch sets up every room so that it somehow augments magick. One simple way is to have elemental decorating schemes: for example, place a shell in the west part of the room, a candle in the south part of the room, a fan in the east part of the room and a potted plant in the north. Make sure that each item set up as an elemental point is blessed and energized before it goes in place. Regularly cleanse and re-energize these items so they radiate only positive energy.

An alternative way of stressing the spiritual nature of the home is to work magick in various rooms as appropriate to that room. The living room or family room is ideal for magick focused on kinship and unit; the bedroom is suited to sleep, passion and dream-working; the cellar or basement might be a good place to work earth-oriented magick because of its close proximity to the ground. Consider how you (or the majority of the residents of your house) use each space, and then apply that theme on a spiritual level.

House Candles

House candles are an important part of the kitchen Witch's household repertoire. They honour the whole living space and represent the spirit of the entire house, including all the influences that previous owners or tenants have had on the overall energies of the home. Making your own candles is a special, magickal task.

The easiest approach is to make container candles, which can be left burning safely for several hours at a time. Look for glass containers, such as those used for seven-day devotional candles, or something else that can be regarded as fire-safe.

You will also need some wax and a wick. Wax can be collected from other candles you've used in magick (to recycle), because they're already saturated with energy. A note of caution here: make sure that the spell for which the candle was used somehow supports the goal of household harmony and peace.

Melt the wax over a low flame; if you wish, you can add aromatic oils or very finely powdered herbs at this time. Again, the aromatics and herbs you use should mirror your goals – include apple for joy, lilac for harmony, myrrh for health, jasmine or roses for love, cinnamon for luck, bayberry or mint for prosperity, magnolia for peace and violet for protection. This is also a good time to incant, chant or pray, indicating your intentions in verbal form.

Put the wick into the glass container, keeping it in place by tying it to a pencil that is placed horizontally over the top of the container and adding a small weight (such as a crystal) to make sure that the wick hangs straight down at the bottom. Let the wax cool slightly, then pour it slowly into the container. Cool and use as desired.

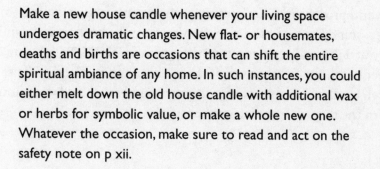

Make a new house candle whenever your living space undergoes dramatic changes. New flat- or housemates, deaths and births are occasions that can shift the entire spiritual ambiance of any home. In such instances, you could either melt down the old house candle with additional wax or herbs for symbolic value, or make a whole new one. Whatever the occasion, make sure to read and act on the safety note on p xii.

Once you have a house candle, all the residents of the house should be present the first time you light it. You want the contribution of each person's energy so the candle itself becomes a representative of unity, trust and love. Hold hands, say a prayer or do whatever else feels appropriate, and let the candle burn for a while. Afterwards, light it at any time when household stress, sadness or other negative feelings seem to accumulate.

For a detailed look at candlemaking, as well as safety tips and other useful information, look at *Exploring Candle Magick* by Patricia Telesco.

Charming Chores

Another way of working magick into your home is by incorporating metaphysically enhanced methods into your routine chores. Look around your home, and a few magickal ideas will be sure to come to mind. Here are some examples: add some lemon or lime juice to the water for washing the floors, dishes or clothing – the resulting aroma will support the goal of getting rid of negativity wherever it lies; or dust with a feather duster to lift heaviness and tickle your aura at the same time.

Another idea is to sprinkle carpet freshener mixed with charged powdered herbs over the rugs. The herbs will soak up the negative vibes and will be neatly sucked up by the vacuum. Finally, try stuffing a variety of herbs in an old, clean stocking and tossing the bundle in the shower or tumble dryer. In the shower, the bundle will help shift your aura to something more positive; in the dryer, it will heat up and energize your entire wardrobe. The options are endless!

You can anoint doorways and windows for luck, health, protection, peace and prosperity. These are the in-between places in your home where magick stands between the worlds. Alternatively, burn incense and place pot-pourri in various rooms according to your needs. Try placing a bunch of lavender in the family room if there's been tension in the house. Be it a hovel, hotel or houseboat, this is your sacred space and you should reclaim the magick from its every corner!

CHAPTER 15

Colour, Texture, Shape and Scent in Magick

Every sense you can add to a spell, ritual or other metaphysical process improves the potential for manifestation and integration, and provides a new dimension to the conscious and subconscious mind, as well as to the universal powers. To bring all the senses together, you must understand the role of each sense and how to combine sensual cues effectively.

Senses in the Sacred Space

You already know that the four elements reflected in each quarter of the sacred space play an important role in conducting magickal works (see Chapter 13 for a brief review). Similarly, the senses are present there as well. Beginning in the east, we have the sense of smell, which depends on air – the atmosphere – to bring us various aromas. This sense also has strong connections with our vital breath.

Witches associate the southern quarter of the Circle with vision because we need the fire to illuminate the night and our Path. In the west resides taste (which has a correlation with saliva – water), and in the north we have touch, which may be why we use touchstones to this day (to stay connected to earth and concrete reality). And what about hearing? Most Witches associate that ability with Spirit, because learning to listen to that voice within us (and all around us) is one of the most important abilities anyone can develop.

The human ear contains some 20,000 tiny sensory hair cells that work as sound receptors. The movement of these hairs produces electrical impulses that the brain uses to interpret sound waves. That earwax you find so annoying is produced by the ear to help conduct sound.

Witching Colours

Psychologists have already demonstrated that colour has an amazing capacity to act on the human subconscious. Shared communal experiences among early people created an instinctive reaction that we still experience today. Consider that many children are afraid of the dark, and when left in a dark-coloured room, they tend to become subdued. In the same way, bright blue rooms encourage hopefulness and happiness. This deep-seated, natural reaction is what gives colour so much potential in Witchcraft.

Applications for Colour in Magick

Always consider the colour of the tools you use in your spells and rituals. The colour of each of the following objects plays an especially significant role in the magickal mood you need to create for the manifestation of your goals and purposes.

☽ Altar cloths
☽ Candles
☽ Decorative items in and around the Circle
☽ Libations and post-ritual foods
☽ Light bulbs for the sacred space (such as elementally coloured ones at the four quarters)
☽ Paint for the walls of your magickal workrooms
☽ Robes or daily clothing (often seasonally dependent)
☽ Spell components (including plant parts)
☽ Visualizations (especially those integrating light imagery)

ASTROLOGICAL COLOUR CORRESPONDENCES	
Aries	Red
Taurus	Yellow
Gemini	Red or purple
Cancer	Green
Leo	Yellow, gold, orange
Virgo	Sky blue, violet
Libra	Violet
Scorpio	Reddish brown
Sagittarius	Orange or purple
Capricorn	Brown or blue
Aquarius	Sea blue or green
Pisces	White, purple or aqua

The key to successfully using colours in a magickal way is to balance their traditional correspondences with your own feelings and preferences. Overall, your gut reaction to a hue is more important than its customary meaning. You are the one wielding the magick; therefore, the colours you use have to make sense in your mind if the symbolism is to work. Let's take a look at the basic colours and their magickal associations:

BLACK is the colour of night, historically a time for Witches to gather for ritual. Black has been associated with forbearance, rest, constancy, the planet Saturn (and by extension, Saturday) and the number eight. It is also the colour of mourning and sometimes of evil intentions or negative emotions. Witches tend to use black in magic aimed towards banishing or as a way of representing a mock death so something new and positive can be born.

It's important to remember that the intensity of a colour also implies its intensity in the sacred space. Bright yellow, for example, has strong associations with the sun and fire, whereas pastel yellow is more closely aligned with the air element and has a far gentler message.

BLUE is very different from black, being the colour of a clear sky. Traditionally, blue is linked with Venus, Fridays, the number six and the astrological sign of Capricorn. Among Druids, blue was a sacred colour that denoted someone who'd achieved the rank of bard (a formally trained storyteller often entrusted with the oral history of a group), while Christians associated it with the Virgin Mary. Magickally speaking, blue is used to encourage wisdom, insight, happiness, truthfulness, patience and peace.

GOLD is a form of yellow, but metallic. To most Witches, it represents solar energy and the god aspect. Gold was part of many magical healing rites in Europe for a very long time, giving it associations with health and recovery. In addition, we can use this colour to connect with the masculine energies of the universe and with attributes such as leadership skills, logical thinking, conscious awareness and problem-solving.

GREEN has many aspects, being the predominant colour of vibrant, growing things. It's associated with Mercury, Wednesdays, the number five and the astrological sign of Cancer. In the sacred space, various hues of green are applied to support maturation, steady progress, healing, hopefulness and transformation.

DAILY COLOUR CORRESPONDENCES

Sunday (the sun's day)	Orange or yellow
Monday (the moon's day)	White
Tuesday	Red
Wednesday	Green
Thursday	Purple
Friday	Blue
Saturday	Dark blue

ORANGE resides somewhere between red and yellow in its energy. It's associated with the astrological sign of Leo and Sunday, and it releases a friendly warmth. Typically, orange candles or other items are used in spells and rituals directed towards understanding theories, directing your will effectively, kinship, kindness and harvesting the fruit of your labour. It may also be applied for mental alertness that isn't quite as intense as that provided by gold. To understand this difference, just consider how your eyes feel when blinded by the sunlight at noon, as opposed to the gentler orange light of the sunset.

PURPLE is a spiritual hue. It corresponds with Jupiter, Thursday, the number three and the astrological signs of Sagittarius, Gemini and Virgo. Meditating on purple inspires an awareness of Spirit and ancient knowledge. Magickally, it supports any spiritual undertaking, centring, psychic awareness and wisdom.

RED is for passion and fire. Its correspondences include Mars, Tuesday, the number nine and the astrological signs of Aries and Scorpio. Lore tells us that certain fairies and ghosts are afraid of red because it symbolizes life's blood. With this in mind, Witches continue to use red for protection as well as for energy, health, dramatic purification, love, stamina, motivation and desire.

WHITE is an all-purpose hue. It is magickally neutral, because it can represent any type of energy due to its purity. Its correspondences include the number seven and the Goddess. For thematic magick, white is best suited to oaths, safety, sincerity, the divine self and enlightenment.

YELLOW represents kindness, belief and friendship. It's associated with the astrological signs of Libra and Taurus, the season of late spring and early summer, and uplifting occasions. Magickally, many Witches rely on yellow when they want to improve communication or inventiveness, make themselves charming, strengthen productivity or attract general blessings.

Try wearing the colour that's associated with your birth sign to understand how that sign affects you. Or wear other birth sign colours to develop specific attributes associated with that sign. Wear white or silver during lunar rituals to honour the moon, and yellow or gold during solar celebrations to honour the sun.

Chromatomancy

Witches don't only use colours as components in magick – they also use them to see the future; divining by colour is known as chromatomancy. For example, if a dream has a predominant colour, there is symbolic value in that dominance.

In general, dark hues tend to reveal sombre moods or something that you're trying to hide from yourself, while bright colours are liberating and happy. Bright red presents the message of 'stop' (just as a bright red light does for traffic); blue implies faithful communication; and green can represent jealousy from the dreamer or someone else in his or her life.

Colourful Candle Magick

The significance of coloured candles varies considerably from the general colour symbolism described above. Although the reason for this variation is unknown, it might have something to do with the special powers of candles and candle magick. Since coloured candles are very easy to come by and candle magick is one of the simplest forms of the Craft, you will certainly find this information useful in your magickal experiences.

☾   Black candles are used in spells for determining the truth (getting to the bottom of things) and in earth-oriented rituals (where they represent the rich soil).

☽ Brown candles ground energy and also support spells to augment the conscious mind (that is, they provide foundations in the here-and-now).

☽ Burn dark blue candles to augment instincts and spiritual dreams. Sky blue encourages safe travel and overall awareness.

☽ In comparison, gold is on the other end of the scale. Gold candles improve the conscious mind (remember, gold is the colour associated with the sun) and are burned to bolster personal skills and overall luck.

☽ When you're ready to work on money matters, don't forget to light green candles.

☽ Pink candles are good for friendship.

☽ When you need to compose yourself and show real authority, try burning purple candles.

☽ Red and white seem to maintain their significance in candle magick (refer back to the description of each colour and its significance in the previous section).

☽ Silver candles emphasize occult learning.

☽ Violet candles should be lighted in spells and rituals for personal progress, inventiveness and the awareness of universal law.

☽ Burn light yellow candles when you feel your self-assurance waning, or to help with divinatory efforts.

For additional candle magick, carve a symbol on the candle that represents your goal. Dab the candle with a corresponding aromatic oil while reciting a chant or a prayer that details those wishes to the Universe. Put the candle on your altar, surrounded by crystals. And don't forget timing – light the candle during a waxing moon for positive energy, or during the waning moon for banishing unwanted things from your life.

Textural and Tactile Cues

Do you consider yourself a 'touchy-feely' person? Good – you can use tactile sensations as a cue to improve the outcome of your magick. One of the ways this sense manifests is through the clothes you wear. If you were to put on a smart shirt and a pair of fluffy slippers, this wouldn't feel right, would it? The feel of specific fabrics sends specific signals to the brain, and the formal feel of a smart shirt would not be congruent with the sensation of your feet clad in comfy slippers.

The following list describes the basic fabrics and the sensory cues they provide. Note that each person's reaction will be slightly different; see what works for you, and modify this list accordingly.

CHIFFON: Represents the air element, freedom and revealing secrets.

COTTON: Represents casual fun, being comfortable in your skin and practicality.

DENIM: Stands for hard work, durability and strength.

FLANNEL: Represents security, rest and platonic emotional closeness.

ITCHY FABRIC: Allows you to stay alert or locate the source of trouble.

SATIN: Sexy and sensual, with a natural coolness; helps keep your wits about you.

SILK: Sets the mood of expertise without ego; presence and composure.

WOOL: Gives a sense of authority and professionalism, but is still warm and approachable.

Witches don't only look for textural cues in clothing; they also get tactile or textural input directly from other individuals, through both physical and aural expressions. Sensing auras may also prove very helpful to you in your personal interactions.

Sensing the Auras of Those Around You

Smooth auras imply peace and balance; itchy ones indicate insincerity or incompatibility; bumpy ones denote illness or difficult situations; auras with static reveal miscommunication; and sticky auras may indicate a tendency for a 'clinging' personality. And that's just for starters!

A hot aura reveals areas the body is directing energy towards (and therefore might indicate an injury). Emotionally and spiritually, the hot aura speaks of a high-energy person (sometimes with a heated temper). A cold aura signals poor circulation and implies aloofness.

Learning to sense these energies isn't as difficult as you might think; a lot of people have a natural aptitude for it. Just consider how being in a tightly packed lift makes you feel on one day as opposed to another –

just because of the people who are around you. This is a natural reaction to close aural proximity and one you can hone over time.

The Magick Touch

Touching is essential to human well-being, and there are a lot of different kinds of touches that take place: there is the comforting hug, the supportive hand on the shoulder and the welcoming handshake. Witches can translate these touch-based gestures into functional magickal symbolism – for example, a spell focused on self-love might include hugging oneself, and a spell between two individuals aimed at commitment to a specific goal could be sealed with a handshake.

Consider the texture of the items you use in the sacred space. A magickal procedure focused on smoothing the way in a relationship or a job could use a smooth crystal as a component.

Shape It Up!

Magick is made up of patterns, as are all forms of energy. Each pattern is like a fingerprint, indicating where the magick came from and where its intended designation lies. Witches often say, 'As within, so without; as above, so below.' This adage may help you understand that all things on the spiritual plane have some kind of representation in the here-and-now. Shape is the manner in which metaphysical patterns manifest themselves in the mundane world.

According to green Witches, the shape of any natural item is like a blueprint for how it should be used in the sacred space; so if you find a heart-shaped stone or leaf, it's best to apply it to matters of the heart. We see a heart, we think love – and that thought produces positive energy in support of the overall goal.

For techno-Witches, man-made objects with specific shapes also hold potential for that kind of symbolic value. For example, use old CDs to represent cycles. To break a cycle, break the CD and dispose of it. CDs are circular, so they have the right shape to help you manifest that goal.

By far the best shapes to use are simple geometric forms. For one thing, you can take other small items and design them easily into circles or squares – beans, rice, mashed potatoes, coloured paper and so on (edible items can be shaped and then eaten to internalize the power of that pattern). For another, these shapes are very easy to visualize if you want to add them to meditation.

Shape Correspondences

The following is a very generalized list of the basic shapes and their symbolical meanings:

ARROW: Warrior energy, directional guidance, hitting the mark
CIRCLE: Cycles, chakras, sacred space, the moon
CIRCLE WITH A SLASH: Refusal or banishing
CROSS: The four corners of creation, the quarters, change
DIAMOND: Prosperity and abundance (often financial)
SQUARE: Earth energy, foundations, truth and fairness
STAR: Wishes and dreams, protection
TRIANGLE (POINT DOWN): Decreasing energy, banishing
TRIANGLE (POINT UP): Increasing power, the Goddess, fire
X: Goals and ambition

As you can see, the meaning behind each shape makes perfect sense on both the conscious and subconscious levels, which is why it's potent spiritually. Logistically, any shape can have meaning (just look at ink blots), but simple shapes free the mind to focus on the magick rather than on the complex pattern. That doesn't mean that Witches never employ elaborate motifs – in fact, two of the most popular emerging patterns in many spiritual traditions are the mandala and the labyrinth, both of which can get very intricate. Witches typically meditate on these patterns and draw on them as a focus or walk them as a kind of physical prayer.

The oldest remaining labyrinthine image (2500 BCE) is a stone-carved relief found in Sardinia. The famous myth about Daedalus and the labyrinth appeared in Greek mythology in the 5th century BCE. Labyrinths are sometimes called 'mandalas of the Western world' because of the many similarities in function and symbolism between the two patterns.

Magick on the Winds

How often have you heard someone say 'something smells fishy' or 'stop nosing about'? Language provides a lot of clues about how important various senses are to the human interpretation of the world. These types of phrases indicate that the sense of scent is used psychically as well as physically.

The Witch trusts her instincts regarding the symbolic value of any given scent. For example, a certain perfume may make you think of your mother, and therefore you could use that as an aromatic in spells or rituals to inspire your own maternal nature. Another person might associate that very same perfume with an old rival and never wish to use it in magick at all, because of the negative energy lingering in her memories.

Other examples of spiritual applications for aromatics include:

☾ Spraying oil mixed with water on ritual tools or on your chakras. (You can use essential oils by misting – add a few drops of your chosen oil to water in a mister bottle, and spray the mixture.)

☾ Placing elementally aligned scents in their proper quarters of the sacred space.

☾ Burning incense.

☾ Using bundles of scented flowers on the altar or at the four quarters. (These bundles will also work as visual aids if they're chosen for their colour as well as their smell.)

☾ Choosing spell, ritual and meditative components by the symbolism of the scent.

One of the most wonderful things about smell-oriented symbolism is that it's very subtle. No one thinks anything of air fresheners, incense or pot-pourri sitting around the house these days, even if the clever Witch has chosen all those things for their magickal potential! For example, if a Witch's home needs a good vibrational cleaning, he might burn a sage smudge stick (to get the negativity out of the air), leave out some lemon pot-pourri (to sustain the cleansing process), and burn spicy incense (to rejuvenate the energy).

Some Common Magickal Correspondences for Scents

APPLE: Happiness

BASIL: Serenity, love

BAY: Strength (honours Apollo)

BAYBERRY: Abundance

CEDAR: Bravery

GARDENIA: Spiritual harmony, well-being

GINGER: Calm spirit, overall perkiness

GRAPEFRUIT: Banish the blues

HONEYSUCKLE: Conscious mind (focus)

HYACINTH: Self-control and peace

LAVENDER: Antistress, personal regulation

LILAC: Improve psychic awareness

LOTUS: Focus on spiritual life

MYRRH: Meditation

NARCISSUS: Self-image

PEACH: Manifest goals and wishes

ROSEMARY: Memory retention, banishing

SANDALWOOD: Spirituality

THYME: Work with fairy folk

VANILLA: Increase magickal power

VIOLET: Attraction

So how do you tie this all together? Well, Witches might scent their clothing with a specific aromatic so it saturates their aura. For example, if you're having trouble at work, try a blend of rosemary, ginger and honeysuckle. The rosemary helps with staying on task; ginger improves energy yet helps maintain composure; and the honeysuckle keeps the conscious mind keen. Be aware, however, that essential oils should not be dabbed onto the skin or clothes that are in contact with the skin – they may also stain fabrics – so use perfumes or less powerful aromas.

Other alternatives include making bundles of aromatic sachets and placing them where they're most needed, anointing commonly used objects with perfumes, bathing or washing your hair in aromatic soaps, and so forth. Just consider your surroundings, the circumstances and the main goal of the magick. Outside the sacred space you have to be a little more creative and discreet – can you see yourself moving anticlockwise through the office with sage? Nevertheless, there are plenty of options open to you, so don't be afraid to be a bit creative – after all, that's what Witches do best!

CHAPTER 16

The Mineral Kingdom

Since Witchcraft often turns to nature's storehouse for ingredients, let's look at the minerals, stones, metals and shells Witches use in their magick. The human fascination with and appreciation of these objects, which seem to have their own personalities, only add to their power in the hands of a clever Witch.

Stones, Shells, Metals and Minerals in Witchcraft

To review what you have already learned so far, you will need stones, shells, metals and minerals for the following forms of magick:

☾ Pendulums and other divinatory methods
☾ Healing methods
☾ As portable charms, amulets, talismans and fetishes
☾ As components in spells and rituals
☾ As images in visualizations
☾ To improve the growth of plants and the magickal energies they bear
☾ To mark the sacred space and honour its energies

In a world of ongoing change, these objects remain constant and firm. Expressions that respect and refer to this kind of metaphoric value for rocks in the English language include *gems of truth, rock solid, clear as crystal* and *strong as steel*.

Gemstones

Gemstones are truly nature's treasures. The warm glow of a ruby, the transforming face of a well-cut moonstone and the incredible strength of the diamond did not go unnoticed among the ancients. Gems appeared on sacred altars across the world as suitable offerings to the divinities, and they cropped up in global superstitions with a multitude of virtuous powers – gems could heal, protect, inspire fertility, indicate the outcome of battles and improve crop growth! Some historians and folklorists have even raised the possibility that the original intent for wearing jewellery was more based on the talismanic quality of its gems than mere decoration.

Some people believe that the power of gemstones is related to their rareness and expense. This principle may go back to the concept of making offerings to gods: anything that was scarce and valuable was more acceptable to the Divine.

The following is a list of the gemstones used most commonly in Witchcraft, as well as their corresponding symbolism and powers.

AQUAMARINE: A gift of the sea goddess, this stone bears the power of the full moon and helps manifest harmony, bravery, intuitive awareness and a stronger connection with our superconscious.

DIAMOND: Bravery, strength, invulnerability, clarity and devotion. Among Hindus, Arabs and Persians, the diamond represented overall success. Lore recounts how diamonds were formed by a thunderbolt.

EMERALD: Metaphysically, the emerald supports magick for faith, foreknowledge, strengthening the conscious mind and resourcefulness.

Hebrew legends tell us that the emerald was one of the four stones presented to Solomon (along with lapis, topaz and carbuncle); these stones represented his authority and wisdom. In Egyptian and Greek mythology (as recounted by Albertus Magnus), emeralds were originally discovered in a griffin's nest.

GARNET: This gem was used in the Middle Ages to protect the bearer from nightmares. Witches use garnet for devotion, good health and kindness. Non-gemstone-quality garnet is also available.

JADE: Jade has long been used as an amulet to inspire harmony, love, longevity and the proverbial 'green thumb' for those with poor luck in gardening. Low-quality jade is widely available.

OPAL: For those born in October, opal is a luck stone that improves memory.

PEARL: Pearls are sacred to Isis in Egypt and Freya among the Saxons, and are also an overall good symbol of the Goddess, the moon and the water element. Magically, pearls are suited to spells focused on love, happiness and prosperity.

PERIDOT (CHRYSOLITE): When set in gold, this gem turns away evil, nightmares and malevolent magick.

RUBY: Rubies are considered the most excellent amulet for health, mental clarity and harmony.

SAPPHIRE: This gemstone brings divine blessings, the ability to understand omens and signs, luck, success, improved meditative states and devotion.

Crystals

In the distant past, crystals were just as valuable as gems, simply because of their gemlike qualities and their scarcity. Today, crystals are far less costly and much more available than gems. The following is a list of some crystals you might wish to consider using:

AGATE: Those that look like eyes were used to protect from the evil eye curse (and can still be used for protective magick).

AMBER: Lore tells us that amber came from the tears of a setting sun, and as such it's still used as a solar/fire stone. Witches also use it in healing magick (to capture disease much as it did insects).

AMETHYST: Amethyst is a peaceful crystal that helps with self-control, business cunning, courage and safety in battle.

APACHE TEARS: This is a type of obsidian that many Witches carry for luck.

AZURITE: The blue colour of this crystal makes it ideal for dream magick and overall harmony.

BERYL: A transparent to translucent glassy mineral, beryl is used to promote harmony in relationships, success with legal issues and motivation. Transparent varieties of beryl in white, green, pink, blue and yellow are valued as gems.

BLOODSTONE: Used for wish fulfillment, success, understanding weather omens and safeguarding health, the bloodstone is an especially lucky stone for those born under the astrological sign of Pisces.

CALCITE: Calcite comes in a lot of colours, giving it a variety of potential magickal applications. Generally speaking, however, the energy of this stone is suited to encouraging spiritual growth, inner healing and improved focus.

CARBUNCLE: The blood-red colour of this stone might be the source of the legend that carbuncles are created from the eyes of dragons. The magickal correspondences include insight, health and intuitiveness.

CHALCEDONY: This offers good fortune, protection from evil and improved communication and attitudes. According to legend, Mohammed wore a ring with this stone set in it. Carnelian, a pale-to-deep or brownish red variety of chalcedony, provides extra protection.

CAT'S-EYE: The visual impact of this stone alone gives it strong associations with vision, especially our inner sight. Beyond this, superstition tells us that cat's eye is a stone that manifests beauty, luck and prosperity.

CHRYSOCOLLA: Use this opaque charcoal-coloured stone to banish fear and re-establish logical perspectives.

CITRINE: A pale yellow variety of crystalline quartz, citrine is a great stone for banishing nightmares and improving psychic abilities.

A lot of crystals were used on sailing vessels for protection. In Greek tradition, we find carbuncle, chalcedony and beryl. The first two kept sailors from drowning at sea, while beryl safeguarded them from fear during storms.

FLOURITE: This crystalline stone seems to strengthen the conscious mind and thinking skills.

LAPIS: Use lapis to improve magickal insights, psychic abilities, happiness and overall meditative focus.

MALACHITE: A light to dark greenish stone, malachite can improve sleep or be carried for protection, specifically to remain aware of any forthcoming dangers or problems.

MOONSTONE: Under the rule of the moon, this stone bears very similar energy to the lunar sphere. Use magickally to motivate foresight, psychism, inventiveness and nurturing abilities.

OBSIDIAN: One of the favourite stones for scrying mirrors, this is sacred to the patroness of witches, Hecate.

ONYX: Wear onyx when facing adversaries in figurative or literal battle.

QUARTZ: An all-purpose magickal stone, quartz represents infinite potential. The colour of the quartz often varies its applications (for instance, use rose quartz for friendship and love magick).

TIGER'S-EYE: In Rome, soldiers carried this into battle for safety. In modern times, this yellowish-brown stone appears in spells and rituals aimed at improved stamina, good fortune and prosperity.

TOURMALINE: While this stone has little in the way of known ancient usage, it comes in a variety of colours, offering Witches flexibility in its applications. Overall, tourmaline seems to balance energy.

TURQUOISE: Safety in travel, rain magick, visual acuity, strength in friendship and improved awareness.

Metals and Minerals

A goodly portion of the correspondences for metals and minerals comes to us through alchemists, the medieval chemists who searched for gold and instead discovered many other substances and their properties. Alchemists believed that everything on this planet could be broken down into key elemental correspondences; they often worked during the waxing moon to improve the results of their studies. Take a look at the following list of metals and minerals to familiarize yourself with their magickal correspondences and traits.

BOJI STONE: A projective stone Witches use to inspire symmetry, peacefulness and a sense of foundation.

BRASS: Brass is a fire-oriented metal that exhibits energy similar to gold but on a gentler scale. It's popular in healing and prosperity magick.

COPPER: The preferred metal for making witching wands, copper conducts energy and inspires health, balance and good foundations.

FELDSPAR: This substance is made of aluminium silicate and other minerals. Egyptians used feldspar as a tonic for headaches and other minor ailments. Magickally, it's associated with love, fertility and working with the fey.

FLINT: Durability; protection from mischievous fairies.

GOLD: The metal of the sun and the god aspect, gold confers strength, leadership, power, authority and victory to the bearer.

HEMATITE: Pliny recommended this iron ore to attract positive energy and exude charm. The ancient writers put hematite under the rule of Mars, which would also give it the powers of protection and strength.

IRON: Strength, safety, protection from spirits. Some consider iron an antimagick metal, which is why Witches prefer not to cut magickal herbs with an iron knife.

LEAD: Greeks inscribed pieces of lead with incantations and then used them as amulets to ward against negative charms and spells. Lead's weight provides it with symbolism for reconnecting to the earth (keeping one foot on the ground), having a firm anchor and overall practicality.

MAGNETITE (LODESTONE): The magnetic quality of this stone makes it ideal for attracting overall good vibrations into the Witch's life. In particular, it's good for relationship magick.

fact

First discovered in 400 BCE in Lydia (present-day Turkey), magnetite appeared around the world in a variety of lore. In the East Indies, people put it into the monarch's crown to improve his charm. Alexander the Great gave pieces of magnetite to his armies to protect them from evil influences (particularly genies).

METEORITES: Because they come from celestial realms, meteorites are good for meditation and for directing your attention to your place in the greater scheme of things. The other mystical qualities include promoting astral projection and improving understanding of universal patterns.

PYRITE: Carry this to protect yourself from being fooled.

SALT: At one time this substance was so valued as to be used as currency in Rome. Today Witches use salt or salt water for consecrating items or the sacred space, for banishing and for overall protective energies.

SERPENTINE: A greenish, brownish or spotted mineral used as a protective stone, mostly health-oriented.

SILVER: The metal of the moon and the Goddess, silver inspires insight, dreams, psychic awareness and creativity.

STEEL: Steel is typically used to protect the bearer from fairies, or to afford general protection (especially when made into a ring).

TIN: A lucky metal, especially if you put it in your shoe.

Plain Stones, Shells and Fossils

In addition to gems, crystals and minerals, there are other stones and stonelike objects that people have used in magick, and that modern

Witches and Wiccans continue to use. Each item, both simple and sublime, speaks with nature's symbols and the voice of Spirit. Each carries a specific energy imprint that the Witch activates and directs for specific goals.

CORAL: Red and pink coral are the preferred types for protecting children. Carry coral for wisdom and insight, and to connect with the water element or lunar energies.

In the Pacific, people place coral in graves to safeguard the spirits of the dead. Hindus carried coral to protect the bearer from malevolent influences.

CROSS STONE: Sometimes called a fairy cross, this is a gifting stone that (because of its shape) honours the four quarters and their corresponding elements.

GEODE: The geode has the power to create a natural womb for energy, and is an ideal Goddess emblem.

HAG STONE: Also known as a holey stone, it's a plain rock found near the water that has a hole going all the way through it. This stone stimulates health, luck and blessings, and is considered the gift of the sea goddess.

JET: This ancient fossilized bit of wood provides strength and courage, particularly in difficult situations.

LAVA: Being born of fire, lava burns away sickness and negativity.

PETRIFIED WOOD: If you can determine the tree from which a piece comes, this fossil's energies will be connected to that type of tree. More generically, petrified wood helps you honour cycles in your life and improves the longevity of beloved projects.

PUMICE: This is a very light stone. Carry a piece of pumice when you wish to ease your burdens and make the road ahead a little less difficult.

ROUND STONE: To discover a perfectly round stone is considered good fortune, so if you find one, keep it. It also represents the Sacred Circle.

SAND DOLLAR: A fossilized sea urchin, the sand dollar provides protective energy, especially for your personal resources and energies (note the natural pentagram design).

SHELLS: Another gift from the sea, shells help us reconnect with the ancient ocean mother. They're good charms for improving divinatory ability, for learning to go with the flow, and for acquiring the ability to listen to the voice of Spirit.

STALAGMITES AND STALACTITES: Once carried for protection and male fertility, stalagmites produce upward-moving energy, while stalactites move downwards. Stalagmites and stalactites may be used as magickal symbols of increasing or banishing power, respectively.

WHITE STONE: Among the Celts, a white stone found adjacent to a holy well could help the bearer see fairies.

Watching Stones Grow – Divination Methods

There is an old saying that to learn patience, you should watch the rocks grow. Although Witches don't go to this extreme, they do watch and use rocks in a variety of divination methods. Perhaps the best known of these techniques is crystallomancy, or crystal scrying. In this approach, the Witch gazes into a crystal, sometimes while it sits on a special material, and watches for images to appear on the surface.

According to St Augustine, Persians were the first to incorporate crystal scrying into their divination practices. Other historians credit the Romans, at least for eventually introducing the art to the rest of Europe. No matter its origins, however, scrying was mentioned in 5th-century texts that include recommendations for using a variety of stones, such as quartz, obsidian and aquamarine.

Old magickal texts always recommend proper preparation of the crystal before using it for divination. Preparation methods varied significantly, depending on the culture and the author. Some called for washing the crystal in special waters, reciting prayers or incantations over it, and waiting for a specific moon phase before making an attempt to solicit the stone's indwelling spirit for help. In some cases, dependence on that spirit was so strong that shamans actually fed the stones blood or wine, or slept with them, to appease the spirit and improve rapport.

In our day, Witches have kept to the majority of this traditional groundwork; about the only real change from olden times is that now they understand that a definite psychological element is involved in scrying. As a Witch stares at the surface of the stone, she is in deep concentration and breathing regularly, and enters a trancelike state. While in this heightened level of awareness, messages can seep through from the subconscious, the higher self and/or Spirit. These messages appear to the Witch as images in the stone.

Stone Scrying for Beginners

Find a good-size crystal that has a nice surface on which to focus your attention. (Remember, discovering what works best for you will come as a result of trial and error.) Put this crystal on a dark cloth and either place it on a table in front of you or in the palm of your hand.

Next, think of a question. Don't look at the surface of the stone; look at a point within it. Let your vision blur, breathe deeply and keep looking. Be patient with yourself. It takes time to get this approach to work effectively. If clouds, colours or shapes begin to appear, you're doing it properly. Make a mental note of what you see. Continue looking until the images stop, then interpret them according to the list provided in this section, or according to your own instincts.

The beauty of this divination method is that it's highly portable. Nonetheless, it has its limits – most people do not get incredibly detailed responses from scrying, making it more suited to simple inquiries than ones requiring a lot of information.

For example, clouds are moving up and to the right are interpreted as *yes* or *go ahead*. If they are moving down and to the left, it means *no* or *stop*. And if the clouds are swirling, there is no definite answer at the moment. Here is a brief list of some of the interpretive values in the colours of the clouds that may appear:

BLACK CLOUDS: A negative omen
BLUE CLOUDS: Joy
GREEN CLOUDS: Another good omen (the proverbial green light)
PURPLE CLOUDS: Spiritual matters

WHITE CLOUDS: A good sign

YELLOW CLOUDS: Unpleasant news

Stone Casting

Stone casting is another divination method that uses shells, stones and minerals. To divine through stone casting, the Witch takes a collection of stones and tosses them on a surface. The way each stone lands, the overall pattern and the symbolic value of the stone are all points that he interprets. Casting systems seem to provide a little more input and randomness than crystal scrying. A person could try to contrive what they 'see' in a crystal to mirror their hopes and wishes, whereas in the stone-casting method, stones land on a solid surface. Since their location is not open to conjecture, this decreases the chance that the Witch might inadvertently influence the reading's actual meaning. (For more information, see Chapter 12.)

Sleeping with Rocks (Dream Interpretation)

The symbolic value of the mineral kingdom also comes into play when Witches interpret their dreams. While dream imagery is subjective, a few archetypes do exist: a clear crystal, for example, represents clarity, either in the dreamer's thoughts or psychically. If the stone stands alone, it often represents the self.

If a specific type of crystal appears in a dream and the Witch recognizes it, she can look to a variety of lists to see how that stone has been used historically in magick, or what its basic symbolism is.

Besides acting as harbingers of things to come, the way crystals or gems look and what happens to them in the Witch's dream is important. In the dream of the lone crystal, should that stone shatter, some very difficult emotional or physical situation for the dreamer – one that's quite literally shattering to his confidence or sense of self – may be on the horizon.

According to traditional dream keys, onyx portends arguments, malachite a peaceful resolution, lapis suggests that magickal awareness is growing, and jet warns of sadness ahead. Carnelian brings luck; moonstone speaks of improved foresight; and beryl predicts a happy relationship on the horizon for the dreamer.

Diamond Dreams

What if you dream of diamonds? A lot depends on the context and the other symbols present in the dream (not to mention the dreamer's impressions of those symbols and the diamond within that construct). Here are some interpretations:

☾ Devotion or faithfulness (Europe and the USA)
☾ Forbearance and strength, often physical (Europe)
☾ Good luck (Middle East, Egypt)
☾ Victory, success and zeal (India)

Make sure to consider all other aspects of the dream before jumping to any one conclusion; see Chapter 8. For more information on the lore and history of stones, take a look at *The Curious Lore of Precious Stones* by George Frederick Kunz.

CHAPTER 17

The Plant Kingdom

The folklore and mythology of Witchcraft is very closely intertwined with that of the green world. For example, a Greek myth explains that Hecate's daughters taught Witches how to use herbs for both healing and magick. Since Hecate is regarded as one of the patronesses of Witchcraft, it's not surprising to see the magickal arts intertwined with plants, both then and now.

An Introduction to Green Witchcraft

Throughout history, various herbal remedies thought to have magickal properties eventually became what is known today as green Witchcraft, a popular form of magick. Although it is connected with wild magick (see Chapter 18, which discusses the magickal properties of the animal kingdom), this particular version of the Craft is particularly focused on plants, flowers, trees and herbs as a mainstay for components, symbols and energy.

The tenets of green Witchcraft are as numerous as the plants found on this planet. Some plants are recommended as helpmates to magick, while other plants seem to deter witchery. In the latter category, rowan bound with red thread is one of the most popular antimagick charms; to be able to recognize a Witch, elderberry juice would be dabbed on the eyelids; and to find immunity from the Witch's spells, marjoram flowers would be carried. Plants that help Witches include anise, which helps them avoid the ire of an invoked spirit; eyebright or mugwort, which improves psychic awareness; or periwinkle, which increases the power of a Witch's magick.

A medieval book on herbal arts explains that if a woman grows hemlock in her garden (for use in spellcraft) *and* owns a broom with an ash handle (to keep from drowning), she must be a Witch. And if her garden receives no sunlight and a hawthorn hedge grows around it, that's to keep her magick within and curiosity seekers out!

Philosophy, Ethics and Practices

Green Witches have a little bit of Buddhism in them. Buddha said that to know the Divine, feel the wind on your face and the sun on your hands. In effect, that is the heart and soul of green magick – that intimate connection to, and appreciation of, nature. The wonders of creation have become part of the green Witch's very spirit. Green Witches consider every flower, leaf, blade of grass – yes, even weeds – alive and sacred, filled with magickal potential.

And in fact, all these growing things are. Take the gardener's foe, the dandelion. Since the time of ancient Greece, dandelions have been used in medicine, rubbed on insect bites to ease the itching and to help contain fevers. Magickally speaking, Witches use dandelions in solar-related rites or to improve psychic awareness, or in matters of hospitality.

As in wild magick, green Witches recognize that humankind does not have dominion over the earth. They know they walk on sacred ground, so they make a point of respecting the natural world.

Putting Belief into Practice

The first step in practising green magick is to reconnect with nature. You can't honour something you have no intimate connection with, and you certainly can't call on the energies of plant spirits without spending some serious time around plants. For Witches in the concrete jungle, this specific step presents some challenges: you might have to go to a park, a botanical garden or a greenhouse to get a healthy dose of natural energy.

The green Witch strives to work in partnership with her plants. To that end, the green Witch's garden is organic and her household is one of diligent recycling. Living this way expresses the green Witch's reverence for nature's gifts and ethical considerations in a practical way that brings the green witchery into daily life.

How else might a green Witch bring her philosophies and ideals into daily life and spiritual pursuits? There are lots of ways, including:

☾ Watching plant behaviour for omens and signs.
☾ Gathering loosened leaves and petals for magickal components (or to use in pot-pourri), rather than harvesting them.
☾ Using plant matter as charms, amulets and talismans.
☾ Adding plant matter to incense.
☾ Combining plants with other traditional magickal methods (such as floating petals with wishes or burning a herb and observing its behaviour in divination).

☾ Collecting and waxing plants for decorative touches in her Book of Shadows.

☾ Creating specially themed gardens for her plants.

Green Witches do not assume that traditional correspondences for flora are necessarily correct. Instead, they trust in their personal awareness of the natural world to determine applications. The amount of sunlight and water, as well as soil conditions, affect the way a plant grows, how strongly its flowers will smell and its brightness of colour – that is, how the plant will turn out will also affect the magickal energy within it.

Putting this concept into practice isn't difficult if a green Witch has a garden. He could keep a journal regarding growing conditions for each plant he intends to use magickally. This tome becomes a gardening grimoire of sorts, to which he turns when considering the manner in which the plant should be used spiritually. By way of illustration, garlic grown in a particularly wet season may show an energy signature that isn't as fiery as typical garlic. In fact, it may offer a balance of fire and water energy, which is ideal for healing.

All of this may sound rather complex, but after a time it becomes – well – natural! That is how it should be. When human beings began to separate themselves from nature and her cycles, they also lost touch with its magick. Green Witches reclaim that birthright.

Now, if a green Witch cannot grow plants (something that drives an avid green Witch to distraction, because she loves to keep her fingers in the earth), how can she determine these types of energies? Typically, through meditation. In this situation, the Witch holds the plant matter in the palm of her hand, closes her eyes and extends her psychic perception to try to get an indication of the best use for that item. The images or sensations this process produces cue the Witch: for example, if the plant feels warm, it could be used to 'warm' a cold heart.

Divine Flowers and Plants

For Witches who honour a specific god or goddess in their sacred space, plants provide another means to please and appease these beings. The mythologies of hundreds of deities worldwide mention plants as suitable offerings, as protected items or as something into which that divinity transforms.

The reason a particular plant was sacred to a deity changed depending on that god's or goddess's temperament. Frequently some poor mortal was transformed into a flower, tree or herb because of divine jealousy or wrath. When she found Pluto flirting with a maiden named Minthe, Persephone's jealousy turned to wrath – and Minthe was turned into mint. Similarly, violets are the innocent victims of Venus and Cupid.

In Rome, another name for Venus was Myrtilla because of the predominance of myrtle flowers on her altars. Roses are also sacred to this goddess, purportedly growing from her bath water!

Cultures all around the world have gods and goddesses who, by their name or job description, are intimately connected to plants. For example: Kama, the Hindu god of love, bears flower-tipped arrows; the Persian plant god Haoma's plants offer healing; and the Aztec Xochipilli is known as the flower prince.

There's also Zemyna, from the Baltic region, who gave birth to all plants; Vidyadhara, from Tibet, who teaches how to use the magickal property of plants; and Han Ziang-zi, a Chinese immortal who made flowers blossom as he desired. All of this information is quite useful to eclectic Witches who may choose to respectfully blend cultural traditions. By being aware of which plants are sacred to which deities, the Witch can bring those special energies into his sacred space by putting the plant on his altar, making it into incense or oils, or perhaps creating foods and beverages, if they are edible ones.

A SAMPLING OF SACRED PLANTS AND THEIR PATRONS

PLANT	DIVINE PATRON
Apple	Aphrodite, Hera, Odin, Zeus
Basil	Vishnu
Bay	Apollo, Eros
Catnip	Bast
Corn	Demeter, Mithra
Daisy	Freya, Thor
Dandelion	Hecate
Fennel	Prometheus
Garlic	Hecate
Hawthorn	Flora
Heather	Isis
Iris	Iris, Hera
Lavender	Hecate, Saturn
Lily	Kwan Yin, Juno
Marjoram	Aphrodite, Venus
Mint	Pluto
Mustard	Mars
Parsley	Persephone
Pine	Cybele, Pan, Poseidon
Primrose	Freya
Rose	Bacchus, Eros, Isis
Sage	Zeus
Sunflower	Apollo, Demeter
Violet	Io, Zeus
Willow	Ceres, Hera

Petal Portents

Speaking of divine things, how about the role of plants in the Witch's divination kit? Divination by flowers and plants are known as floromancy and botanomancy respectively. There are several different ways in which these methods work.

First, observe plants in their natural state. A myrtle plant blossoming unexpectedly near your home portends joy and a full year of peace. Stumbling over the first blossoming daffodil of spring foretells financial improvements, and if this happens on a Friday, the prosperity doubles.

Luck comes to those who find a four-leaf clover or a five-petal lilac. A healthy growing wisteria speaks of sound friendships. And if you wonder when those friends will arrive for a visit, a geranium planted near your door will tell you. Watch it, and when the head turns a different direction, expect guests soon!

A more active approach to divination involves purposefully manipulating the plants. To divine the name of the person you'll marry, cut a fern stalk and observe its lines. If you can float a candle on a freshly harvested holly leaf, prosperity is forthcoming. If a harvested ivy leaf stays green all night on New Year's Eve, the coming year will be healthy. Tossing flower petals on water and watching their movement is an effective kind of scrying. Burning plant parts and observing the behaviour of the fire is a form of pyromancy (divination by fire).

Yet another way to apply plants to divination is by making carefully preserved leaves and flowers into a set of runes or perhaps a green Witch's Tarot. To accomplish this, you need a good base medium (stones, wood or sturdy art paper) and appropriate decoupage covering. In this case, the meaning of each rune or Tarot card is determined by the symbolic value of the plant depicted. The beauty here is that this approach really allows the green Witch to create a divination system that speaks with nature's language and includes personal vision in its making.

Blossoming Divination Pendulums

You can also make homemade pendulums out of plants. If you want to do this, choose a plant that represents your question in some way and secure it to a thread or yarn in a way that creates a kind of pointer – for example, an unopened rose has a natural tip that can be observed. Tie the rosebud so it hangs with the tip down.

After securing the herb or flower, put one elbow on a secure surface, steady the pendulum and concentrate on the question. The movements of the pendulum provide the answer. Generally speaking, movement from left to right means the answer is negative, and movement up and down means that the answer is affirmative. Circular movement means that no answer is presently available. Bobbing movement instructs that hesitation may be in order. Diagonal movement represents conflict or barriers to overcome. Square movement represents the need to establish some foundations before proceeding further.

Plants and Dream Divination

Plants appearing in dreams have special significance for green Witches. Blossoming flowers imply fulfillment and the opening of new skills (either magickal or mundane), and symbolize hope and potential. Gardening portends a coming surprise. Buttercups represent business success; carnations speak of love; irises predict forthcoming communications from friends or loved ones; and primroses herald new friendships.

What if a Witch has trouble remembering dreams?
In this case, green Witches recommend placing a mistletoe leaf under the pillow to inspire prophetic or spiritually oriented dreams.

Phyllorhodomancy: Divining by Roses

In the Greek tradition, the rose was sacred to Aphrodite, the goddess of love. A person with a question (particularly about a relationship) would put a rose petal in his left hand and clap it with his right. The louder the clap, the more positive the omen.

Another system of rose divination instructs the questioner to watch three freshly cut roses that haven't begun to open yet. Each one represents a specific answer: yes, no or maybe. Whichever one lasts the longest represents the answer.

Natural Elements and the Sacred Space

To include plants in your sacred space, simply consider the symbolic value of the plant and its elemental correspondence. A variety of plants may serve as markers for the four elemental quarters of the sacred space. By choosing an item with the appropriate elemental association and putting it in the appropriate quarter, you honour the Watchtowers and support the energy of the sacred space. When using a living plant isn't possible, it is perfectly acceptable to use a decorative item or an aromatic made from the appropriate plant. The following list contains some common plants and their elemental associations:

EARTH (NORTH): Alfalfa sprouts, beets, corn, fern, honeysuckle, magnolia, peas, potatoes, turnips, vervain.
AIR (EAST): Anise, clover, dandelions, goldenrod, lavender, lily of the valley, marjoram, mint, parsley, pine.
FIRE (SOUTH): Basil, bay, cactus, carrots, chrysanthemum, dill, garlic, holly, juniper, marigold, onions, rosemary.
WATER (WEST): Aster, blackberries, catnip, cucumbers, daffodils, gardenias, geranium, iris, lettuce, roses, willow.

A plant's elemental association should also come into play with the time of the year. In the spring, air-oriented plants might decorate the altar, followed by fire plants in the summer, water plants in the autumn and earth plants in the winter. Of course, this correspondence may change according to their magickal tradition and is sometimes dictated by location and weather patterns, so this is only a generalized example.

Another application for plants in the sacred space is to honour the gods and goddesses (as discussed earlier in this chapter). Plants suited to whatever divinity the Witch plans to invoke into the space are placed on the altar or around the Circle. If, for instance, a Witch is working with Hera, a bowl of apples and a vase of irises would be suitable – not to mention visually appealing.

The remaining applications come in the enacting of the ritual itself. A Witch might use plants for asperging the sacred space (such as a branch of heather), wear them as headpieces (wreaths of flowers and vines) or incorporate plants into her spellcraft. The limits are set by the goals of magick and the green Witch's eye for creativity.

Sprouting Spells

At one time or another, nearly every plant on this planet has been used as part of a magickal spell. After all, the magick of plants and nature was always open to anyone who knew how to harvest its riches.

After the green Witch comes to understand nature's messages and symbols, it's natural to want to use that knowledge in spellcraft. All the traditional approaches to creating spells apply here (see Chapter 9), with the main difference being that the spell focus or key components are, of course, plants.

Exactly how the plant participates in the magick depends a lot on its symbolic value, the goal of the magick and the spell construct the Witch devises. Typically, plants may be bundled, burned, buried, carried, floated, grown or tossed to the winds as part of the spell.

☾ Bundling is typical of portable magick.
☾ Burning is a way of releasing a prayer or wish, and sometimes is also used for banishing.
☾ Burying occurs a lot with health-oriented spells.
☾ Carrying a plant is typically a type of charm or amulet.
☾ Floating can take energy away from or towards the Witch, depending on the water's direction.
☾ Growing supports progress and manifestation.
☾ Releasing plant matter to the winds carries the magick outward from the Witch.

Daisy, a very common flower, could serve as a working example. Herb Margaret, thousand charms, silver penny and cat posy are just some of the names that have been given to this flower; and the word 'daisy' derives from 'day's eye', because the top of the flower follows the sun through the sky. According to Christian mythology, the daisy is sacred to Mary Magdalene, having grown from her tears. The Victorian language of flowers says that the daisy represents fidelity and youthful innocence. Both the flowers and the leaves of this plant are edible, and they typically appear on the magickal altar during spring celebrations. The daisy often appears in spells for love or to encourage fair weather.

To incorporate daisies into your own magick, you could pick three flowers and carry them as a love charm. You could also burn dry daisy petals in incense for fair skies, or release them to wind or water to take your wishes for good companionship to the four quarters of creation.

Let's take pine as another illustration. Because of the heartiness of this tree, pine represents longevity, fertility, protection from evil and peace. Witches also say that its aroma brings joy and prosperity. Carry pine cones with you to improve your outlook, or bury them around the home to safeguard it. Pine needles are excellent additions to dream pillows, helping to bring a peaceful night's rest.

Although these examples are limited, they provide a good foundation on which any green Witch can build a spell repertoire using her favourite plants. Just one note: if you cannot grow your own plants, please make every effort to ensure that your components are organic – or at least very well washed: chemical additives impede or dramatically change the magickal energies in any natural item.

Magickal Herbcraft

Green Witches resort to herbcraft as an important part of their magick. While some Witches belief that herbcraft constitutes working with spices, other consider herbcraft to be the making of any useful item out of plant parts. This includes, but is not limited to, the following items:

AIR FRESHENERS	HEADPIECES
BOOKMARKS	INCENSE
BREAD	OILS
CANDLES	SACHETS
CREAMS	VINEGARS
DREAM PILLOWS	WREATHS

While you can certainly make any of these items without being a Witch, adding the magickal dimension makes the final product even more special. This doesn't take a lot of tweaking, just a little thoughtfulness.

For one, you could work during propitious moon signs or phases. Rely on the waxing moon for positive energy, the waning moon for banishing and a full moon for manifestation. And choosing the auspicious time of day will support your magickal creation as well: work at dawn to inspire hope, at noon to augment the conscious mind, at dusk for closure and at midnight when you need to rely on your subconscious.

Look at the instructions for whatever item you plan to make. See what ingredients already suit your goals and which ones should be changed. Obviously, if you're making something edible, you'll need to mix and match the ingredients for a good flavour and to keep the proportions right, or the item won't turn out correctly. Beyond those considerations, there are very few limits as to how you choose to devise your Craft item.

For instance, an incense recipe might call for mixing 125g (4oz) of cedar shavings (which are good for cleansing and contain healthful energies) with a teaspoon of cinnamon powder, a teaspoon of myrrh powder, and 30g (1oz) of dried gardenia petals. Looking over this recipe, a Witch might be inclined to use sandalwood shavings instead of cedar, because the rest of the ingredients are suited to the theme of spirituality, and somehow cedar doesn't fit. If this incense is for health, however, keep the cedar and cinnamon and substitute pine needles for the gardenia, and perhaps a bit of thyme for the myrrh.

There are a lot more herbs associated with healing and health. Get yourself a good magickal resource book and compare the applications listed to your instincts. Also consider reciting chants or prayers over the item while you work on making it. This vocalization directs positive energy into the object you are making and keeps your mind focused on the goal. Alternatively, visualize the item being filled with the white-blue light of Spirit, which will saturate the completed product.

Finally, if you give the item as a gift, enclose a card that explains its magickal significance. It's really nice for people to see the kind of thoughtfulness that went into a gift's creation; this will be doubly appreciated. Remember, kindness is true magick in itself.

CHAPTER 18
The Animal Kingdom

Although using animal parts as offerings and spell components is no longer practised, the power in each living creature (or its representation) has not been lost to modern Witchcraft. Magickal use of animals might include placing an image of an animal in the sacred space to represent the energy of a particular element, or enacting spells that protect beloved pets.

Animals: Messengers of Nature

Witches believe that the patterns and messages of the Divine exist in nature. The natural world is a wealth of knowledge that humans would do well to learn and integrate into their lives. Part of it is the knowledge of animals and their role in nature that Witches have relied on in their magick. There is a long-standing global tradition of animal magick that the modern Witch can tap into.

Familiar Friends and Spiritual Signposts

Many Witches choose to have a familiar – a spiritually attuned creature to whom the Witch turns for insights into nature's lessons and for help in magick. Today's familiars include cats, dogs, birds, rabbits and even the stereotypical frog, but really, any living creature with whom the Witch can have an ongoing relationship or rapport can fulfil the role of the familiar. Actually, the Witch doesn't necessarily choose this creature so much as the animal and the Witch seem to discover and bond with each other. No matter what kind of creature it might be, the familiar is no mere pet – the animal in question is the revealer of truths and a respected partner in every sense except being human!

According to global lore, nearly anything can become a familiar. In Lapp, Finnish and Norwegian stories, for example, flies are familiars. Amphibians – specifically, sea snakes – show up in New Hebrides stories. And among the Zulu, familiars can be made from reactivated animal corpses.

If a Witch wishes to put out a call for a familiar, he usually does so through a spell or ritual. Such a ritual typically takes place outdoors, near the home. The Witch begins by creating sacred space, and then meditates, prays and places the request in the hands of nature. During the meditation the Witch visualizes the living space so the right creature can easily find its way to the door.

Power Animals and Totems

Power animals and totems also serve as helpers to Witches (as well as shamans). Now, there is some disagreement on what constitutes a power animal and what constitutes a totem. For the purpose of this book, a power animal is a creature whose attributes you may take on for a short time, while that energy is 'in play': for example, when you need to protect a beloved project, a she-bear guide may come into your life. These animals have strong associations with protective maternal instincts. By comparison, a totem animal seems more strongly attached to a person's spirit and often becomes a lifelong spiritual companion.

Similar to finding a familiar, the process of discerning a power animal or totem often takes place in a ritualistic setting. Alternatively, the animal spirit may reveal itself in a stray encounter or a dream, through repeated sightings in a variety of media and so on. The key to success in this process is for the Witch to remain open to nature's voice and to avoid anticipating what her animal may be. While it would be wonderful to have a beautiful, graceful, powerful creature as a guide, that simply isn't always the case. Imagine the wonder of a Witch who discovered a bumblebee totem – it wasn't exactly an exciting discovery, but the symbolism made sense for her hardworking, buzzing personality.

What happens when you discover your totem or power animal? The value of these energies varies a lot from culture to culture. What's important to remember is that an animal's symbolism embodies the whole creature – both its positive and negative aspects. The otter, for example, is playful, but it can also be very nippy. A Witch with an otter totem, therefore, needs to be aware that her biting sense of humour might take frolicking a bit too far.

Wild Magick

Familiars, totems and power animals are part of wild magick, which covers a lot of territory. Wild Witches may include those from the fairy faith, shamans, earth healers, green Witches and proverbial tree-huggers. The main reason for such a broad diversity is the definition of wild magick. Essentially, the wild Witch seeks to defend nature, deepen her understanding of the wild, use this understanding as a spiritual tool and then educate others regarding the state of the earth and how to preserve it. That's a pretty big job, but one that many Witches, Wiccans and Neo-Pagans are glad to embrace.

Wild magick deals specifically with those moments when the 'wild' world touches our everyday reality in intimate ways. Animals represent a big part of that picture, especially the Witch's pets and familiars. Try the following strategy, a type of 'wild' divination that relies on reading signs. Observe your pet's behaviour with visitors in your home; this may give you some insights about your visitors that you wouldn't otherwise get on your own, perhaps because animal reactions are based on instinct.

Outside the home, wild magick transforms a bit, especially when you're in a natural environment. For example, if a Witch observes gulls circling above a group of fishermen with their daily catch, he might gather up a stray feather and add it to his power pouch, in order to inspire extended vision, especially when hunting (figuratively). This, too, is wild magick: taking a gift from nature and applying it positively to your spiritual life.

Certain precautions exist in accepting these gifts. All animal parts should be cleaned properly to avoid the potential for disease. Furthermore, there are laws governing what is legal to have in your home (in terms of animal parts). Please be prudent and cautious, and check with the relevant authorities if you're uncertain.

However, wild Witches would never 'harvest' animal parts for magickal purposes. A true gift isn't something you pick out for yourself or something you search for – it's something that comes to you freely and unexpectedly.

Greek Divination by Found Feathers

According to an old Greek tradition, you can get specific clues about your future from bird feathers that you find, depending on the type of bird the feather came from, the colour and where it was found. Here's a brief list of the interpretive values based on the feather's predominant hues:

BLUE: Love is on the horizon.

BLUE, WHITE AND BLACK: A new relationship blossoms.

BLACK: Bad news.

BLACK AND WHITE: You will avoid a problem.

BROWN: Improved or continued good health.

BROWN AND WHITE: Look forward to a joyful occurrence.

GREY: Battles or struggles ending; peace.

GREY AND WHITE: Wish fulfilment.

GREEN AND BLACK: Affluence and renown

GREEN OR PURPLE: Be prepared for adventure or travel.

ORANGE: Forthcoming happiness.

RED: Good luck.

YELLOW: Be careful: friends may be false.

Animal Omens and Signs

Diviners from all over the world, and from various religious persuasions, have observed animal movements and behaviour when trying to predict the future. Now, modern Witches realize that happenstance encounters with most wild animals are becoming increasingly unlikely, so they have come to consider other animal appearances instead. For example, a Witch who sees images of a lion on a business card, the side of a bus and in a newspaper advertisement might consider that a sign and look up possible interpretations in a book such as this one.

An animal appearance in your life, particularly if it is completely unexpected, is definitely something to ponder. Just please be careful. Wild animals are just that – *wild*. Report any potentially dangerous creature to the proper authorities and consider its message to you afterwards.

The following is a list of animals and their corresponding signs and omens.

ANT: Biting predicts a quarrel.

BEETLE: The larger the beetle, the better your luck.

CAMEL: Good luck.

CAT: Meeting a black cat brings improved fortune.

CRICKET: Domestic bliss.

DOG: Something new on the horizon (unless it's a black dog, which predicts misfortune).

DONKEY: Unexpected burdens (a lot on your proverbial plate).

FOX: Beginnings that get off on the wrong foot.

FROG: Matters of love or health (the condition of the frog will tell you more).

GAZELLE: A bad omen if it is moving from left to right.

GOAT: Fortunes will be improving.

HARE: Be cautious.

HORSE: Good news is forthcoming.

LAMB: Peace and harmony.

LIZARD: Disappointment or lack of closure.

MICE: Difficulties, often of a financial nature.

MOLE: Moving to a new home or apartment.

MULE: Business interests taking a downturn.

PIG: Worries.

SNAKE: Treachery and betrayal, or jealousy.

SPIDER: Financial losses (especially if encountered in the evening).

TOAD: The death of this creature portends increased tension.

WEASEL: Sickness or distress.

For more ideas about what a particular animal's appearance may mean, you can also use the list of dream harbingers in the next section of this chapter.

Dream Animals

Speaking of omens and signs, animals may wander into a Witch's dreams, and these nocturnal visits are often significant. A creature that appears to you in a dream could be your power animal or spirit guide trying to help with a specific situation. Alternatively, the symbolic value of the animal could have bearing on a personal or spiritual matter.

fact

> According to the Ainu, bats were made by the god of the world; they are courageous and wise, and battle disease. In China, five bats together represent joy, prosperity, longevity, happiness and contentment. Conversely, in Japanese Buddhist tradition, bats represent sadness and restlessness. For the Maori of New Zealand, seeing a bat is an omen of bad luck.

As with crystals and stones, any personal feelings you have towards the animal should be considered as part of the dream's interpretive value. For example, if you're afraid of dogs and you see a dog with someone you recently met, then there might be a reason to be cautious of that person (especially if you felt ill at ease when you met this person in real life). And if you really adore birds and see a dear friend with one in your dream, it might be time to call that friend or make some quality time for him or her (so that the 'adoration' between you does not fade).

Here is a brief list of animal harbingers and messages in dreams (for more information, see Chapter 8):

BAT: Making your way through an uncertain situation successfully; alternatively, improved luck and happiness.

BEAR: May speak of your mood (if you've been bearish); traditional symbolism is forbearance, protectiveness, fearlessness and possibly the need to rest for a draining situation.

BIRDS: Symbolic value changes according to the specific bird; in general, birds represent liberation, movement and the ability to distance oneself from a situation. A bird that's singing happily foretells success in its song.

BULL: Masculine energy, stubbornness, creativity, leadership skills, the ego/self (especially for men), moving forward too quickly and doing damage in the process.

CAMEL: Prepare for a time of stretched resources.

CAT: Quick, agile recuperation.

CHAMELEON: Transformation; knowing when to remain quiet and out of sight.

CRAB: Moodiness or misdirection; situations that seem to lead nowhere.

CROCODILE: Lies or misrepresentation.

DEER: Swift legal movement; gentleness.

DOG: Steadfast friends or companions.

DOLPHIN: Rapid movement and decision-making; messages that require attention.

DRAGONFLY: Improved health or fortune; balancing head and heart.

EAGLE: Solar energy; freedom, difficult goals and authority.

ELEPHANT: Memory retention; strength and devotion.

FISH: Abundance, fertility and the potential for miracles (note the specific type of fish and its condition for more insight).

FOX: Cunning, charm and craftiness when it's most needed.

FROG: Renewal (particularly in health-related matters).

GIRAFFE: Stretching yourself or being more open-minded.

GOOSE: Good news is forthcoming, possibly combined with improved communication skills and creative aptitude.

HORSE: Movement/travel; transitions, messages or ambitions.

HUMMINGBIRD: A blast from the past (possibly a former lover) is about to appear.

INSECTS: Small aggravations (the meaning can change dramatically depending on what type of insect appears and the dream's overall context).

LION: Authority, protection, ferocity (when necessary to defend something you love).

LIZARD: The ability to break away from the old and begin anew.

MONKEY: Playfulness or flattery (not always with good results).

MOUSE: Frugality through innovation.

OTTER: Frisky behaviour that causes you to overlook something important.

OWL: Messages and news; pay attention to your inner voice in reacting to these missives.

PEACOCK: Being egotistical (a show-off).

PIG: Overcoming and new beginnings.

PORCUPINE: Be on guard.

RABBIT: Abundance, creativity and overall luck.

RAVEN: A warning of some sort.

SHEEP: Passiveness that can lead to undoing.

SNAKE: Some type of new life or opportunity begins.

SPIDER: Fate's hand at work in something.

TIGER: Courage, competence, tenacity.

VULTURE: A predator nearby.

WHALE: A real or spiritual journey that aids enlightenment; regeneration.

WOODPECKER: A change in literal or figurative weather on the horizon.

Dreaming of animals in general implies an awakening of the tribal soul (humans are, after all, animals too). Aggressive animals warn either of danger in your life or that you feel threatened. Dreaming of an animal being tamed brings a warning to control your primal nature (for instance, curb your overexuberant physical passion). If an animal is killed in your dream, some type of literal or figurative death is going on around you.

More information can be gained by considering what the animal itself represents. For example, if a bull is killed by a matador who happens to look like you, a possible interpretation is that you are getting your bull-headed nature (and temper) under firm control. Or if an ant is being crushed by a huge foot, ask yourself if you feel as if your industrious nature is being squelched by someone in authority or someone who is purposefully trying to undermine your job.

Creature Craft: Spells

Anyone who has read Shakespeare is familiar with the idea of using animal parts in magick: 'Eye of newt and toe of frog,/Wool of bat and tongue of dog...' (*Macbeth*, IV, i). Where did this tradition come from? Quite simply, humans have always trusted animal spirits (and the spirits of plants and inanimate objects) for their powers. A magus who needed courage looked to nature's blueprint and found a lion, whose heart may be carried or otherwise used in a spell (thus the phrase 'heart of a lion'). When a Witch needed stealth, it made sense to use the chameleon's skin as a spell component. When he needed perspective, a variety of birds came to mind and he might harvest the eye.

Over time things changed, however. Only animal parts found in nature and properly cleaned are fit to be used magickally in Witchcraft. Modern Witches honour nature and her needs in their methods, and eco-consciousness is a top priority.

Here's a brief list of animal components and applications you would likely find on a random walk in nature.

EGGSHELLS: Traditionally, shells were buried or burned in healing spells (often after having been carried by the patient so the eggshells 'absorbed' the illness). Eggshells also make a good womb symbol in which energy can be nurtured to maturity. Make sure to consider the colour of the eggshell in the final application – for instance, you can use blue eggshells to nurture peace and joy.

fact

In Egypt, Finland, India, Phoenicia, Japan, China and Greece, the egg represented the primordial matter from which all things came. While the stories vary a bit, in essence this cosmic egg became the womb for the universe. Among Buddhists, breaking an eggshell represents getting past the world's ignorance and starting on the path of enlightenment.

FEATHERS: Use feathers for divination (as described earlier in this chapter), for moving incense around the sacred space or as a spell component in magick directed towards liberation and release. Feathers are also good for meditations in which you wish to connect with bird spirits or the air element.

FUR: Tufts of animal fur can often be found on burrs or other prickly bushes. If you can determine which animal lost the fur, you can apply the fur as a symbol of that creature and its attributes in spells and rituals. For example, a bit of rabbit fur would be a good component to put in your power pouch for abundance and fertility. (Any small pouch will do as a power pouch. Use it to keep special items, such as small stones given by friends and those that carry personal meaning.)

NAILS: Nails serve utilitarian purposes (for gathering food) as well as defensive ones when in the clutches of a foe. With this in mind, animal nails could be carried as amulets and talismans for providence and safety.

WHISKERS: According to an old bit of folklore, cat's whiskers that you find somewhere can be used in a wish-fulfilling spell. For this to work, burn the whisker and whisper a wish to the smoke. This spell might be accomplished with the whiskers of other animals too, like using a dog's whiskers to inspire devotion and constancy.

The Elemental Animal

Witches draw on animal symbolism to mark the sacred space. Specifically, they use animal images to denote the element of a quarter, to honour a god or goddess or to illustrate the theme of a working.

As with everything else on this planet, animals have particular elemental associations. These associations come out of the creature's environment and predominant behaviour. It's easy to see that fish are aligned with the water element, and therefore the western quarter. On the other hand, some animals have two common associations: a poisonous snake, such as an asp, relates to both the earth and the fire element, because it dwells close to the soil but is also native to a sandy, hot environment and has a lethal bite.

Within the sacred space, any of the animals aligned with the energies of a specific quarter can watch over that quarter as an appropriate representative. The following list provides the animals that embody characteristics of the four elements, as well as their combinations.

EARTH (NORTH): Bear, cow, deer, ferret, gopher, mole, mouse, rabbit, snake
AIR (EAST): Bat, most birds, butterfly, dragonfly, ladybug
FIRE (SOUTH): Desert creatures, lion, lizard, scorpion
WATER (WEST): Crab, duck, fish, seahorse, seal, whale
WATER/AIR: Dolphin, flying fish, seagull
WATER/FIRE: Electric eel

FIRE/AIR: Bee, wasp, other stinging insects

EARTH/WATER: Amphibians, beaver

Using Animals to Honour a Divine Being

Most gods and goddesses have sacred animals – animals they can turn into and whom they protect, and the following list is just a brief sample. (Animal statues meant to honour a divine being are typically placed on the Witch's altar.)

AKUPERA (HINDU): The tortoise that carries the earth on its back

AMATERASU (JAPANESE): She-crow

AMUN (EGYPTIAN): Animals that hatch; cows

ANUBIS (EGYPTIAN): Dolphin, jackal

APHRODITE (GREEK): Dolphin, goat, swan

APOLLO (GRECO-ROMAN): Horse

ATERGATIS (SYRIAN): Fish, snake

AVILAYOQ (INUIT): All sea creatures, especially seals and whales

BAST (EGYPTIAN): Cat

BENTEN (JAPANESE): Snake

BLODEUWEDD (WELSH): Owl

BULLAI-BULLAI (ABORIGINE): Parrot

CHINGCHINICH (NATIVE AMERICAN): Coyote

HERMES (GREEK): Swallow and all winged creatures

JANA (ROMAN): Woodland creatures

LOKI (SCANDINAVIAN): Fox (and other crafty creatures)

LUONNOTAR (FINNISH): Duck, eagle

MARI (CELTIC): Crow, ram, raven, sea creatures

ODIN (SCANDINAVIAN): Horse, raven

SADHBH (IRISH): Deer

SIGU (GUYANESE): All creatures of the forest

VESTA (ROMAN): Donkey, goat, fire-oriented creatures

ZEUS (GREEK): Bull, eagle, elephant, swan

Animal Imagery in Magick

Animal imagery may be used as a way of accenting a magickal working. Rituals for earth healing, for endangered species, for a sick pet, to connect with the wild magick within and so forth, would all benefit from this type of visual cue. The key is to choose the right animals for the goal of the ritual or spell – for example, when casting a spell for a sick pet, the images should mirror that pet (use photographs or at least images of a similar breed).

Bird's-Eye View: Animal Visualizations

What about the Witch's inner landscape? The beauty of visualization is that it requires no statues, no pictures, no real-life animals – just an awareness of what you want to see inwardly and why. Better still, the visualization allows you to see the animal in any situation that's helpful to the goal. Say, for example, a Witch needs to improve her courage to face a difficult situation. In this instance, she might visualize a lion sitting in the middle of her stomach (the area of the human body in which the centre of gravity resides); from there, the lion's image could slowly grow outwards in all directions, until it overlaps the Witch's aura, enveloping it in that energy.

Caution: do not give yourself over wholly to an animal's energy. To stick with the previous example, the result could be exaggerated bravery or wordiness (part of a lion's power is in its roar).

CHAPTER 19

Above and Below: Astrology and Numerology

This chapter explains the role of celestial objects (the above, the superconscious element) and numbers (the below, the conscious element) in magickal practices. Bear in mind that astrology and numerology are very complex systems, so what you're getting here is but a small portrait, meant for general reference.

As Above, So Below

'As above, so below' – what does that mean? Basically, this phrase, common among Witches, reminds them that everything in this world has a pattern that is reflected elsewhere in the universe and the astral plane. Conversely, everything in the universe and the astral plane has some shadowy symbology in the here-and-now. This point is very important to spiritual seekers; it allows for the possibility that there is something magickal but substantive 'out there' that may be seen and interpreted. It also provides some measure of hope that those mysteries that have been around for a very long time will slowly be revealed and understood.

Above: Where the Stars Guide Us

Astrology is a branch of natural omen interpretation that originated in approximately 2000 BCE in ancient Babylon. Written accounts dating to 1700 BCE explain how divine beings move the stars around the sky to warn people of forthcoming events. Subsequently, a complete collection of astrological omens and signs appeared, and not long after that, Mesopotamian priests came to see the connection between celestial objects and the order of the universe, including the pattern of the future. It was from this hub that ideas about astrology spread into Greece, Egypt, Syria and India.

Where and when did the first horoscope appear?
The earliest surviving horoscope dates to about 400 BCE. It appeared in the Cylinder of Gudea (Babylon), which recounts the author's dream of the Goddess reviewing a map of stars and then providing people with predictions based on what she saw there.

Aristotle developed the main ideology and methodology for astrology in about 300 BCE. His efforts were later supported by the Greek physician Galen, who was a strong advocate of celestial omen and sign reading. Nonetheless, early astrology bore little resemblance to what is presently popular: at this juncture astrology was really an early form of astronomy and was used as a rudimentary calendar and road map – by watching the stars, people knew when to plant, harvest and travel. In some respects, this practical foundation is more important to modern magick than are the birth signs. You'll see why shortly.

Birth Signs

In around 4 CE a Greek astronomer by the name of Eudoxus introduced the idea of natal astrology as a kind of celestial code for determining a person's characteristics and fate. That particular concept, however, only began to take off in the 19th century, when the first published horoscope appeared in a widely circulated newspaper. At around the same time, a number of almanacs became quite popular; these publications included sections of advice for sowing, planting and even cutting hair according to various astrological cycles.

The word 'horoscope' comes from the Greek *horoskopos*, meaning 'observer of hours or seasons'. Astrology was not limited to the Greeks: in the Islamic tradition, for example, specially trained astrologers taught children how to find their true star, the one that governs their destiny. Once found, the astrologer tracked the star's behaviour with other celestial objects and made predictions accordingly.

Both Wiccans and Witches will tell you that what appears in the horoscope section of newspapers today is a highly generic version of a very complicated art. Most people prefer to have a professional or a good computer program construct a detailed birth chart that considers various influences on their lives; these influences include the placement of the sun, the moon and various planets in the 12 houses of the chart. Some Witches then use this chart to plan important personal magickal events, such as an initiation or eldership rite. Some also use their chart to help determine the best spiritual group to join (based on other members' signs). And other people just enjoy comparing it to daily realities.

Birth Signs and Magic

Look for your birth sign below and read the generalized description. Does it ring true?

- ♈ ARIES (21/3–19/4): These people tend to become spiritual leaders, inventing new paths or magickal approaches. Alternatively, they may go off on wild adventures aimed towards enlightenment. This is a very fiery sign.

- ♉ TAURUS (20/4–20/5): People born under this sign love earth-oriented magick and make excellent druids. They also have a knack for expressing magickal ideas through art.

- ♊ GEMINI (21/5–21/6): The Gemini personality sometimes has trouble settling on one Path, especially a restrictive one. An eclectic approach to Witchcraft will likely be the best choice.

- ♋ CANCER (22/6–21/7): Cancers make good water-mages. They are very adept at memorizing rituals, spells and other procedures – the ideal combination for helping lead public events.

- ♌ LEO (22/7–21/8): Leos tend towards ritual or high magick, enjoying all the trappings and pomp that often accompany those arts.

- ♍ VIRGO (22/8–22/9): Virgos are the philosophers of Witchcraft, enjoying anything that's thought-provoking.

- ♎ LIBRA (23/9–22/10): Libras are great people to call on to handle the subtle logistics of any spiritual event, especially the décor. Their sense of balanced energy is unparalleled.

- ♏ SCORPIO (23/10–21/11): Scorpios have the charm and leadership skills necessary for coven work, but they have to watch their emotional natures and desire for introspection. The first aspect can cause imbalance, while the other may make them retreat from the group.

- ♐ SAGITTARIUS (22/11–21/12): Sagittarians are best at leading magickal groups, but should avoid being priests due to a tendency to pride.

- ♑ CAPRICORN (22/12–20/1): Let the Capricorns in your magickal group handle the money. Their even-minded temperament will keep everything in the black.

≈ **AQUARIUS** (21/1–19/2): The ideal chaos magicians, Aquarians like to be unconventional in life and in magick.

)(**PISCES** (20/2–20/3): Pisceans take on nurturing roles in the magickal community, often as teachers or healers. They also have highly attuned psychic abilities.

As an interesting aside, the Chinese have a system of astrology that names each year after one of 12 animals. The Rat, for example, is known for his or her strong financial cunning, honesty and creative energy, and comes into play during the years of 1984, 1996 and 2008 (12-year intervals). The other animals (following the Rat in chronological order) are Ox, Tiger, Cat, Dragon, Snake, Horse, Goat, Monkey, Rooster, Dog and Pig.

Astrology and Witchcraft

The birth signs play a very important role in the Witch's art, from the point of view of timing. A large number of spells, rituals and other magickal processes are timed according to propitious astrological placements. This practice is very, very ancient and can't always be used due to people's hectic schedules, but it is good food for thought when planning any magickal event.

Sun Signs and Correspondences

The characteristic energies of the sun signs (birth signs) are pretty well known. Those of you who may be unfamiliar with the metaphysical correspondences can begin here. The following list will tell you the effects of the sun as it moves through the 12 houses of the zodiac.

IN ARIES: Inspires strength and a sense of adventure.
IN TAURUS: Provides fortitude and devotion.
IN GEMINI: Manifests social skills or variety.
IN CANCER: Best suited to matters of hearth and home or the arts.
IN LEO: Supports magick directed towards bravery.
IN VIRGO: Promotes the rational mind.

IN LIBRA: Brings peace.

IN SCORPIO: Filled with ingenuity and tenacity.

IN SAGITTARIUS: Furnishes an abundance of energy.

IN CAPRICORN: Improves focus and discipline.

IN AQUARIUS: Offers a plethora of new ideas.

IN PISCES: Teaches flexibility and the power of kindness.

Moon Signs and Correspondences

Next, let's turn to the moon signs. These are seen more readily in magickal processes along with the moon phases. The overall idea is to perform a spell or ritual during the right moon sign so that the timing supports the goal of the magick.

IN ARIES: Purification, overcoming, personal development.

IN TAURUS: Abundance, devotion, fortitude.

IN GEMINI: Transformation, bringing symmetry to diverse energies/situations.

IN CANCER: Inventiveness, prosperity, any lunar-oriented working.

IN LEO: Acquiring new qualities, strength, any solar-oriented working.

IN VIRGO: Virility, monetary improvement, success.

IN LIBRA: Balance within and without, discernment, revealing secrets, air-oriented magick.

IN SCORPIO: Passion, sexuality, intense study.

IN SAGITTARIUS: Firm foundations, self-control, manifesting goals, fire-oriented magick.

IN CAPRICORN: Looking within (inner development), overall supportive energy, earth-oriented magick.

IN AQUARIUS: Fun, adventure, liberation.

IN PISCES: Movement, profuseness, water-oriented magick, developing psychic awareness.

To put all this information into an example, if you were trying to time a spell so it would help you manifest more money, you'd want to try to work when the moon was in Taurus, Cancer or Virgo; or you'd plan to do your accounts when the moon is in Libra (for balance).

Other Celestial Symbols

Astrological signs certainly weren't the only symbols the clever Witch applied to her bag of magick. You have already learned about the values ascribed to the moon's phases (new moon for banishing or rest, waxing moon for growth or positive energy, full moon for divine energy and manifestation, waning moon for waning energies). But what about falling stars, meteorites and eclipses?

Like many people, Witches still wish on falling stars or the first star appearing. Originally, this little bit of 'wishcraft' was an active prayer to Ishtar or Venus. As for meteorites, rock finders and geologists collect anything that doesn't burn up in the atmosphere, and Witches purchase what they can find at rock shows and specialist shops. The applications vary from stone to stone, but usually the energies are of a more spiritually adept order. For example, to improve empathic or telepathic abilities with people or animals, moldavite is recommended.

In times past, the appearance of a meteorite, falling star or comet portended some great event, often an unpleasant one. This concept seems to have some support if you look at the history of Halley's comet, which appeared before the demise of Herod, was said to influence the outcome of the Battle of Hastings, and showed when Elizabeth I took to her deathbed.

Eclipses are a little different. Our forebears were afraid of this heavenly occurrence because they didn't understand its cause. Sanskrit writings claim that a huge dragon flies between the moon and sun and blocks light. Even with misunderstanding and fear, however, mages recognized potential in a day that was not a day and in a moon going dark (an effective phase shift). Modern Witches likewise see an eclipse as a perfect in-between time, well suited to magickal gatherings.

Celestial Dream Images

The world above may appear in the Witch's dreamscape. If you dream of returning to the moon, and it is the predominant feature in the dream, a possible interpretation is that the Goddess is presenting herself to you. Alternatively, it implies the development of your intuitive sense.

An eclipse in dreams speaks of being in a kind of limbo, often between two different phases of life (such as the ending of one Path and the beginning of a new spiritual focus). A lunar eclipse is a warning that you might be trying to run from magickal arts or abilities. Conversely, a solar eclipse speaks of someone who doesn't put the foundations under his or her beliefs and who tries to hide from the light of reason.

Dreaming of Stars

A star appearing in your dreams may mean many things. It could mean realized or unrealized wishes or a tendency towards overly romantic outlooks (being starry-eyed); dreaming of a star could represent goals that may or may not be obtainable (reaching for the stars); perhaps it is an invitation from the fairy world to explore further – remember, the traditional fairy godmother has a star on her wand. Finally, if the star has five points, this could be an alternative pentacle, which denotes spiritual or magickal matters that you should watch.

Seeing a vast expanse of space rather than a single star or a small star grouping can be an alternative abyss dream. In the Tarot, the abyss is part of the fool's journey to enlightenment. There comes a point when you must simply leap, trusting in your magick.

It's All in the Numbers

Numerology is an ancient art that emerged in ancient Egypt, Greece, Rome and Arabia. In folkloric writings, the most common numbers that appear are 3, 4, 7 and 13. People considered 3 and 7 to be particularly fortunate numbers, and often used them to time the course of treatments throughout the Greco-Roman empire and during the Middle Ages. For example, in considering whether patients might live or die, healers checked their progress on the fourth, seventh and ninth days. Arabs took a slightly different approach, combining the numerical values of the healer with that of the messenger sent for assistance. If the sum of the two names was an odd number, the healer would go to the patient because the chances of recovery were strong.

The Hebrews based their number system on letters of the alphabet, devising a system of 22 letters in which each letter had both numerical and spiritual value. The symbolic value of these numbers has continued into modern times, and to Kabbalistic Witches and magicians, these letters and numbers, when properly utilized, are the key to understanding the universe.

The Great Pythagoras

Pythagoras, a Greek mathematician who lived in the 6th century BCE, is a great source for modern Witches, who look to him for insights into numerology. Pythagoras believed deeply in the mystical nature of numbers and taught that self-divisible numbers and those only divisible by one are the most powerful for magick. In addition, each number has its own energies, and each holds clues to the mysteries of the universe. In keeping with this reverence, he also devised a system of numerology to be used for telling the future. A myth credits this divinatory system with Cagliostro's success at predicting Louis XIV's death over 2,000 years later.

'Were it not for Number and its nature, nothing that exists would be clear to anyone, either in itself or in relation to other things.'

Pythagoras

Modern Numerology

Most modern methods of numerology are based on the numbers 1 to 9. You'll need to know how to use the basics of this system to apply it effectively to the next section.

Start with your name. For each letter of the name, work out its numeric value by counting its place in the alphabet (that is, *A* is 1, *B* is 2 and so on). If the number is higher than 9, add its two digits together. Then add together the numbers for each letter. Once again, if the resulting number is greater than 9, add its digits together; repeat this process until you get a number between 1 and 9. For example, the name Joe goes like this:

$$J = 10 \Rightarrow 1 + 0 = 1$$
$$O = 15 \Rightarrow 1 + 5 = 6$$
$$E = 5$$
$$1 + 6 + 5 = 12 \Rightarrow 1 + 2 = 3$$

If you have used your full given name, the resulting number is your destiny number, said to portend the future. Here is a list of personality traits and predictions associated with the numeric value of names:

1. A leader, not a follower; lots of fire and energy; creative ideas and hard work bring success.
2. A peacemaker; good at looking at both sides of a situation; will have true friends and a bumpy life.
3. Creativity, independence and versatility; anything set as a goal will eventually manifest.
4. Earthy, very logical, and organized; brings honour in life.
5. Adventurous and intense, but too trusting.
6. Enjoys the arts; idealistic and romantic; a Gypsy soul.
7. Philosophical and psychic; very disciplined; prominence is in the stars.
8. Individualistic; prone to both great success and great failure; a good life, but with lots of financial problems.
9. A fighter, often with a heated temper, but with many talents that people respect.

Working out the numerical value of any date works the same way. The year 2005, for example, bears the signature of 7 (2 + 0 + 0 + 5). In the same way, a birthday on 4 March bears a signature of seven (March is the third month, so 3 + 4 = 7).

Here is a list of energies associated with dates and years:

1. Transformations and new beginnings (for good or ill).
2. Improved communications; a great year to seek partnerships.
3. Opportunity knocks, if you have time to answer the door... lots happening.
4. A quiet, paced year (a relief from the last).
5. Unexpected surprises and unique circumstances abound.
6. Focus on hearth and home.
7. Adopt a meditative outlook to resolve things.
8. Financial improvements, but you'll have to work for them.
9. Closure or an ending.

You can also work out the energies associated with specific months. To do so, add your destiny number to the number of the month and the year. For example, if your destiny number is 3 and you would like to test February 1960 to see its energies, your calculation would look like this:

$$3 + 2 \text{ (for February)} + 1 + 9 + 6 + 0 \text{ (for 1960)} = 21 = 3$$

The following key is for your interpretations.

1. Consider starting a new project.
2. A month full of odd events.
3. Go on holiday (or clear up a financial matter that's hanging overhead).
4. Tie up loose ends; trust your judgment.
5. Move slowly and carefully; don't leap without looking.
6. Get out there and do it, but be prepared for a few delays.
7. A month to invest or manifest.
8. Lots of changes ahead, but hang on in there.
9. Openings and opportunities, make sure they're right for you.

Bear in mind that these vastly generalized meanings just provide a starting place. As you learn more about numerology, you'll see that the exact meanings of numbers vary from culture to culture, which makes it difficult to provide firm interpretive values. Once again, trusting your instincts will likely manifest far more positively than following a handbook to the letter.

Numerological Symbolism Applied in Magick

In a review of both Wicca and Witchcraft, numbers have some prescribed symbolic value and some pretty universal methods in which they play a role. Specifically, a Witch might enact a spell or ritual a prescribed number of times, use a set number of components in the process or repeat the method over a set number of days or weeks. She could also charge components for a specific number of hours in sunlight or moonlight and so forth.

How exactly does the Witch choose her numbers?
At least part of this equation is instinct, and the rest comes out of a long historical tradition of each number having metaphysical value.

A Quick List of Numbers and Their Magickal Values

1. Harmony, unity, the sun; the Monad (the ultimate atom or single indivisible substance). In the Arabic alphabet, the number 1 represents God (as it did in Egypt with Ra). The belief that 1 is a masculine number is nearly universal, so it can be an alternative 'god-oriented' number to 8.
2. Balance, truthfulness, duality, the waxing moon. This had an odd dichotomy of symbolic value. Since the unity of 1 no longer exists here, there can be conflict. Nonetheless, Christian ministers use two fingers to bless the congregation, and Egyptians used the number 1 to represent the nature of their land. As opposed to 1, 2 is feminine. (I wonder if that's why it's said that women can't make up their minds?)
3. Body-mind-spirit; luck, the Goddess. This is a charm (how often have you heard this phrase?). It was a sacred number to many triune gods and goddesses, including Ea and Bel in Egyptian traditions. Among the Babylonians, the entire model of the universe had three parts: heaven, earth and the underworld. Greeks had three Fates; Plato had three great principles (matter, idea and god); and dream authorities tell us that any dream that is repeated three times is

destined to come true. And, of course, there is also the Catholic Trinity.

4. Elements, directions, earth magick. This number ties into the earth because we have four winds and four directions. Even the annual cycle of Wiccans is depicted to this day as a circle with a unilateral cross extending to the circumference, making a hub around which the Wheel of Time moves. The Judaic name for God has four letters (YHWH), as does the generic name for God in many other civilizations (two examples being *Dieu* in French and *Diós* in Spanish).

5. Diversification, skill, the senses. This is a sacred number, especially among Islamic people who pray five times daily and have five sacred tasks (prayer, fasting, purification, alms and pilgrimage). In the Old Testament many altars were constructed by the measurement of five cubits, and Solomon's seal (the pentagram) has five points. The number might also represent the five senses. Overall, 5 is a number that supports protection on various levels.

6. Safety, fidelity, productivity. This is the number of the Star of David. The Egyptians felt this number deserved its own festival. It's quite possible that both the Star of David and the festival owe their origins to the figure of a star that a double triangle makes, meaning this number has the power of 3 x 2 (also see number 3).

7. Spiritual insights, versatility, synchronicity. This is an important number because it mirrors the moon in its phases. The week has been organized into seven days ever since ancient times. Seven knots featured heavily in Arabic spellcraft. There are seven heavens (Middle Eastern lore), seven seas, seven deadly sins, seven colours in a rainbow, seven notes in a musical scale and seven seals in the Bible. Everyone from the Assyrians to the Celts considered 7 a number with high spiritual vibrations.

8. Cycles, energy, leadership, the God. This is a powerful number. Being a double 4, it also represents the cycles (in this case the eight major holidays of Wicca that take place at pretty regular intervals throughout the year). In Egypt, 8 was the number of rebirth. Magickally speaking, it represents sound justice and anything else relating to solar energy.

9. Completion, closure, legal matters. This is a number that speaks of completeness. There were nine Greek muses, nine orders of biblical angels and nine degrees of mastery in certain mystical traditions. Some magicians even went so far as to draw ritual circles nine feet (3m) in diameter, in order to strengthen the protective powers.

10. Tenacity, following through.

11. Generally not used.

12. Durability, fruitfulness, purification.

13. Persistence, conviction, the full moon. This is the number of full moons in a year, the 13th of which is called a blue moon and is a time for miraculous workings. Nonetheless, 13 is considered very unlucky in many settings, which is why to this day many buildings do not have a 13th floor or rooms numbered 13, and why there won't be 13 people seated at a dinner table. This oddity in mundane settings may or may not deter a Witch from applying the better interpretive value to this figure – as always, it's all in that person's vision, and in the numbers (of course).

CHAPTER 20

Divinities Venerated by Witches

While discussions of gods and goddesses tend to fall heavily into the realm of Wicca (not all Witches are religious), exploring these archetypes is not without merit, regardless of your spiritual path. Divine beings can help you understand the mysteries of creation and the force that sparked that miracle; they fulfil the realm of faith.

One or Many? The Face of the Divine

Since the dawn of time, humankind has connected spirits with the wind, nature, the stars and the forces behind seemingly inexplicable phenomena. As times changed, people gradually came to see the world as much larger than previously thought and understood its workings better. In a similar manner, small personalized spirits also grew larger to embrace the vastness. Eventually many people around the world put their trust in one powerful being, although some polytheistic religions and beliefs are still functional today. These divine beings were said to watch over creation and guide destiny.

Before moving forward to considering specific types of gods and goddesses among Witches, think about how you view the Divine. Do you believe in many gods or one god with many faces? Answering this question will change how you integrate sacred energy in your life.

Try picturing the Sacred Parent as a great crystal with thousands of facets. What you see of that crystal depends a lot on where you stand. If you believe in a goddess (since women are the ones who give birth, a female creator has some logic to it), there are thousands of goddess figures in the world to choose from: for example, the Christian sees Mary, the young virginal goddess; a person who grew up in China envisions the caring face of Kwan Yin, a maternal goddess who brings children and teaches magic; an elder Wiccan might look to Hecate the Crone for inspiration. Are any one of these people wrong in their vision? Not necessarily.

Even as Christianity envisions God as having three distinct personalities (Father, Son and Holy Spirit), Wiccans similarly portray the Goddess as Maiden, Mother and Crone. This triune nature isn't unique to these two settings, either: Islam talks of the three daughters of Allah, the eldest of whom presides over fate; the Greeks had three separate temples to Hera – one for the child, one for the wife and one for the widow; the Zoryas (Slavonic warrior goddesses) represented dawn, dark and midnight in one power; and Carmenta (the Roman goddess of childbirth) had two sisters with whom she worked constantly: Antevorta (looking forwards) and Postorta (looking back).

It is ultimately up to each practitioner to decide whether the Divine is one great power or many (and if many, exactly how these personalities interact, if at all). It is also a highly personal decision as to what aspects Witches look to for guidance and support in daily spirituality.

Choosing Gods and Goddesses

It is natural for humans to want to make gods in their image, which is why there are literally thousands of names for the divine beings around the world. Each Witch would naturally want to discover the names and attributes of divinities that appeal to her and her spiritual vision. How does a Witch go about choosing a god or goddess? Well, it isn't exactly a time for drawing lots!

A Witch may turn to personal tradition for ideas. Some paths have defined cultural origins, drawing upon the gods and goddesses of their ancient cultures; Strega is one such example. Being from Italy, Strega priests and priestesses call on the Greco-Roman pantheon in their practices.

A Witch might feel drawn to a specific god or goddess due to a dream, meditation or divinatory message. People tell of hearing the name of a divine being whispered to them at such moments, seeing images associated with a specific being in their mind's eye or having a very particular being come out in a reading. It's possible that this power simply had a one-time message, but this may be a strong indicator that building a relationship with that god or goddess would be a good thing.

How Do Gods and Goddesses Reveal Themselves?

The answer depends significantly on the person in question. The Divine, a powerful being with a much broader understanding of the universe, knows how to deal with each person through a medium that he or she will understand. For example, if a Witch relates better to symbolism than to direct contact, the god or goddess might send her symbolic images while she sleeps. By way of illustration, Isis might send the image of winged arms (the traditional way in which she's depicted), and Apollo might send a dream that includes the powerful scent of bay leaf, one of his sacred plants. On the other hand, a rather matter-of-fact person would probably be happier with a vision or dream in which the being simply walked up and introduced himself or herself!

The third approach to choosing gods and goddesses is more eclectic. First, a Witch considers the attributes he most desires in a god or goddess and then seeks out one or more from the world's religious traditions. The research doesn't end once he finds suitable beings, however; just as you wouldn't ask for gifts from strangers, a god or goddess is a partner in magick, and you can't have a partnership without learning about each other and without understanding cultural contexts.

In addition, there are some instances in which the Witch may call on a god or goddess with whom she doesn't normally interact, because that being best represents the power needed for the success of a specific spell or ritual. In general, however, this approach is not recommended – according to most mythologies, most divine beings are jealous creatures; they like their followers' attention, and they don't share very well. And because the Witch had not worked on developing a rapport with that being, the outcome may be quite unexpected.

Feminine Divinities

It is impossible not to be aware of the re-emergence of goddess-centred art, books and songs, even in the popular public sector. Many Witches believe that this surge has a lot to do with overcoming 2,000 years of overwhelmingly patriarchal influences and a society where technological innovation is strongly emphasized. Considering that both stress yang energy, the human spirit now thirsts for the goddess figure to balance things out a bit.

The Maiden

As Witches rediscovered the feminine energies of the universe, they began to sort out commonalities among global goddess figures. The first commonality is the Maiden Goddess, who is young, innocent, hopeful, charming, happy, bold, flexible and full of enthusiasm.

Typically, the goddesses who fall under the Maiden category may have celestial connections, such as Luna the chaste moon goddess (Greco-Roman) and Knowee the aboriginal sun goddess, who circles the earth with her torch. Other symbolic associations for the Maiden include:

☾ Baby animals (before puberty)
☾ Children's toys
☾ The colours of silver and white (for purity)
☾ The early hours of the day (before noon)
☾ A clear quartz
☾ Plants such as the chaste tree, meadowsweet, thistle, narcissus
☾ The season of spring to early summer

This category also includes virginal goddesses and goddesses of the dawn and spring (the youthful part of earth's year): Persephone is the virginal goddess who landed in Hades for six-month periods (thus explaining winter). Other examples include the Greek goddess Eos (dawn) and the Egyptian goddess Renpet (spring).

The Mother

The general attributes ascribed to the Mother aspect of the Goddess are maturity, nurturing, fecundity and productivity. In this category you will find fire-keeper goddesses such as Pele (Hawaiian); earth goddesses such as Gaia (Greek), whose abundance was that of the whole planet; and fertility goddesses such as Isis (Egypt), whose fertility was that of the Nile. This category also includes goddesses of sexuality (Greek Aphrodite) and marriage (Roman Juno). The following symbols are associated with the Mother Goddess:

☾ Practical, functional clothing
☾ Rich colours: dark red, forest green, royal blue
☾ Geodes
☾ The hours of noon to sunset

- ☾ Plants such as cinquefoil, cowslip, parsley, pomegranate and tansy
- ☾ Pregnant imagery (trees budding, the pregnant goddess, nursing animals and so on)
- ☾ The season of summer to mid-autumn

The Crone

Traditional images of the ancient Crone seem to be anything but appealing, but that reaction is not surprising: humans are afraid of mortality, and the Crone is a harsh reminder of that irrevocable fact. This is why her images appear during the Halloween season, the Celtic New Year, which also happens to be a festival to honour the dead.

The Crone's symbolism is not limited to the turning Wheel of Life. She also embodies enrichment, shrewdness, steadiness and the attitude of wry wisdom towards life. That's why you will see goddesses of fate (such as the Navajo grandmother spider) and sagacity (such as the White Buffalo Woman of the Sioux, who taught humans how to pray) depicted as elderly. Other goddesses who carry the attributes of the Crone might preside over prophesy, transformation and the underworld (such as the Greek Hecate or the Butterfly woman of the Anasazi, who keeps the underworld in her breast and all the future children in her belly).

Symbols associated with the Crone aspect of the Goddess include:

- ☾ Heavier clothing (often robes)
- ☾ Dark colours: brown, black, midnight blue
- ☾ The hours of sunset to dawn
- ☾ Plants such as holly, mandrake and nightshade
- ☾ Smoky quartz, fossils
- ☾ The season of mid-autumn to early spring
- ☾ Withered or dry items

GODDESS ATTRIBUTES AND SACRED ITEMS

NAME	CULTURE	ATTRIBUTE	ITEM
Aino	Finnish	beauty	willow
Amaterasu	Japanese	sun, leadership	silk
Aphrodite	Greek	love and beauty	apple, myrrh, quince, rose
Artemis	Greek	moon	fir, ox-eye daisy, willow
Axo Mama	Peruvian	fertility	potato
Bast	Egyptian	life's goodness	catnip
Bona Dea	Roman	blessing	myrtle
Calypso	Greek	music	alder
Centcotl	Aztec	agriculture	corn
Concordia	Roman	peace	olive
Cybele	Asia Minoran	fertility	almond, pine
Danu	Indian	individuality	meadowsweet
Diana	Roman	hunting, purity	apple, vervain, willow
Freya	Norse	love, healing	apple, daisy, primrose
Hathor	Egyptian	love	myrtle, sycamore
Hecate	Greek	magic, death	almond, garlic, willow, yew
Hulda	Northern European	spinning, sewing	flax
Idun	Teutonic	youth	apple
Isis	Egyptian	moon	heather, lotus
Itchita	Siberian	great mother	beech
Lakshmi	Indian	wealth	lotus
Medea	Greek	magick	vervain
Siva	Slavic	fertility	wheat
Uttu	Sumerian	creation	cucumber
Wang-mu	Chinese	immortality	peaches
Yemaja	Nigerian	virginity	fish

On days when a Witch feels she needs more goddess attributes, she might warm up a set of clothing in a tumble dryer with goddess-centred herbs such as gardenia blossoms, heather, lemon balm, lemon rind, lily, myrrh, primrose, spearmint, vanilla bean and violet. This act will charge the clothing with the goddesses' feminine attributes.

Alternatively, she could pick out one herb sacred to a specific patroness and use it in perfume, incense or other aromatics in honour of that goddess; in this case, anointing candles is a good option. Finally, she may eat goddess-centred foods (such as coconut to internalize the lunar goddess) and wear clothing of a certain colour (for instance, white is the traditional colour for the 'yin' energy of the universe).

Overall, goddess energy makes you more aware of your intuitive, spiritual nature. She reminds you to nurture yourself and others, and to be creative in your magick so it doesn't become old and stale (destroying the energy). The Goddess gently motivates personal change, and sees the best in people (although she is always aware of the reality of every situation).

Masculine Divinities

The feminine divinity is not complete without its male half; together, they represent the greater whole. Before the goddess movement hit New Age and Wiccan circles, the male divinity's face was the only one present. As a result, many Wiccans and Witches concentrate on the feminine divinity. Others, however, believe that the divine figure is both male or female – or neither. Overstressing the goddess aspect is no healthier than overstressing the god aspect, because it leaves one gender feeling left out of the spiritual equation. Balance is very important to good magick.

Generally speaking, the energies of the God, the masculine, or the yang in the universe are personified as having strength, virility, leadership skills, logic and a heavily emphasized conscious element, as opposed to the more intuitive Goddess. For God and Goddess to create, to work together, they must be in balance with each other. Witches divide the god aspect into three types (equivalent to the three aspects of the Goddess): the youthful Son, the more mature Father and the elder Grandfather. Within each of these types you will find certain commonalities and characteristics, both in powers and in the way they interact with the Goddess.

Triune personifications of God include Mithras, the Persian sun god who worked hand in hand with Agni (the fire) and Vayu (the wind), and Siva, a friendly and gracious god of India, who has two other sides — Ugra (violence) and Mahakala (death). In this manner Siva embodies all energies of the universe, both creative and destructive.

The Son

The youthful aspect is playful like his female counterpart. He typically loves the world, good food, good drink, poetry and lovely women. He is a lover, in love with love. Among these gods, we find the young Horus in Egypt, who flies through the sky freely, with the sun in one eye and the moon in the other. An even better example is the Horned God of Witches, whose youthful wildness and passion make him brashly attractive. This deity strongly symbolizes the Witch's connection to nature, and all the primal magick therein.

A third image is the oak king. In magickal mythology, the oak king represents the waxing year. This rather cocky young man takes over from the elder aspect at year's end by battling him for the crown. The tale of Sir Gawain and the Green Knight is an excellent illustration of this concept, with the Green Knight being the elder god.

Also included in this category are the gods of sexuality and fertility. Cupid (the son of Venus) is the most easily discernible example; another instance would be Eros, who embodies raw sexual power.

Transition from Son to Father

As the youthful god grows older, his strength and prowess improve. Thus, just prior to becoming the Father God (or shortly thereafter), he often takes over matters of battle. Mars comes immediately to mind here, being an integral part of Roman life as a staunch protector of the land. Interestingly enough, another name for Mars was Marpiter (Father Mars), a name that implies an older, more experienced deity.

The Father

This god figure is a little different. Here we have a wiser man who has defined responsibilities. For one, Father God figures oversaw crafts, such as those of the smiths, who were regarded as magick workers in their own right. Hephaestus, originally a fire god in Lycia and Asia Minor, eventually became the god of craftspeople in Greece, earning this reputation by constructing palaces for the gods and fashioning Zeus's thunderbolts.

One of the most potent aspects of the Father figure is God the creator (the father of all things): Bahloo, the Australian aborigine All-Father, is one example, whose job was that of creating all animals and people with his consort. Another excellent example of the creator god is YHWH, God or Allah, as he is known in the world's monotheistic religions. After creating all living things, the Father provides for them by assisting in the hunt, providing the gift of fire and encouraging lush vegetation.

The Grandfather

The elder aspect, or Grandfather, is as wise and wily as his female consort. This aspect oversees things such as the underworld (the place where souls go between lives), destiny, death, resurrection and justice. The elder god who battles with the oak king is one type of the Grandfather, known as the holy king. Truthfully, the grandfather could win this battle with his wits if he so chooses. However, he allows himself to lose so that the Wheel of Life will continue to turn.

GOD ATTRIBUTES AND SACRED ITEMS

NAME	CULTURE	ATTRIBUTE	ITEM
Adibuddha	Hindu	ultimate male essence	lotus
Aengus	Celtic	youth, love	heart
Agassou	Benin	guardian	spring water
Ahura Mazda	Persian	knowledge	feathers
Aker	Egyptian	gatekeeper	lions
Anu	Babylonian	fate	star
Bes	Egyptian	playfulness	music
Bunjil	Australian	vital breath	rainbow
Byelbog	Slavonic	forest protector	greenery
Damballah	Haitian	wisdom, reassurance	plants
Ea	Chaldean	magick, wisdom	salt water
Ganesa	Indian	overcoming obstacles	elephants
Hanuman	Hindu	learning	sandalwood
Itzamna	Mayan	written communication	squirrel
Lug	Celtic	handicrafts	bread
Odin	Scandinavian	cunning, poetry	rain water
Pan	Greek	woodlands	orchids
Sin	Chaldean	time	lapis
Tyr	Teutonic	law, athletics	arrow

Although there are certainly more characteristics given to global gods than those listed here, this table should give you the general idea. Overall, it's the masculine principle of the universe that keeps people grounded in reality and helps them balance their spirituality with daily life. The masculine divinity provides courage and fortitude to handle life's all-too-common ups and downs.

Those wishing to connect with the god aspect can use all the hints provided in the goddess section of this chapter – just modify the ingredients to those that have masculine attributes, or those associated with a specific god.

Communing Meditation

Once a Witch decides her vision of the Divine, it's very important to develop a relationship with that being: guided meditation (see Chapter 6) is one way of communication. In the broad landscape of your mind, you can create an image of the sacred being and begin to better understand that power. The following is a sample meditation that you may use for this task. You may choose to tape-record it and then play it back while you are meditating.

Take a nice, deep cleansing breath now... In through your nose 1-2-3 and out through your mouth 3-2-1... Again. 1-2-3... 3-2-1. And one more time: 1-2-3... 3-2-1.

Release your cares, any thoughts of the world outside, to the Mother. Let her take your tensions... your burdens... and lift them for this moment. We are beyond space, beyond time. We are in the moment between breaths, and at the soul's horizon.

In your mind's eye, see yourself walking down a corridor of young trees, just beginning to bud. All around, the light of dawn is breaking across the earth, and spring is in the air. The birds are singing, the winds blow gently at your back and the world rejoices. The path is smooth... very few stones or holes, and – as if yours are the first feet to touch it – it seems to sing with each step you take. The joy of that music fills you. Stop for a moment and listen... listen to your heart beating and the whisper of life's blood within. Listen to the music of joy that exists as part of the Great Spirit – that spark of the Divine within you, around you, above and below you.

When you feel filled to overflowing with that energy, continue on your way down the path. The road is a little bumpier now... a little more travelled... and the trees beside you have grown into fullness. Flowers beyond them are open to a noonday sun, animals nurture their offspring, fruit is ripening on the vine. The breeze mingles the scent of rose and tansy, and excites your being. Stop here for a moment and reach your arms to the warm solar disk. Feel how it holds you, heals you and saturates every cell of your body with the strong, motivational energy of the god aspect. Let this power tend your heart, shine a light on the shadows and make you whole.

[Pause]

As you sense your body, mind and spirit working together in the Mother's harmony... you also know it is time to travel again. As you move down the path, the sky is turning towards night and the moon rises directly in front of you. All around you the trees have grown bare and silence falls across the land like a blanket of snow. Gather this silence into your soul, for it is in those moments of stillness that we can hear the wise voice of Spirit revealing tidbits of life's mysteries. The moon is so large before you, you can reach out and touch it – touch the ancient and eternal Goddess. She who is, was and will be. That silvery light engulfs you and whispers a message to your soul. Listen. Listen.

[Pause]

When you feel ready, continue walking past the moon. On the other side lies this room. Let your breathing return to normal, and slowly open your eyes.

Honouring and Invoking the Divine

Those of you who aren't used to considering a divine being as a partner in your spiritual pursuits may wonder about other ways in which Witches integrate this power into daily living. Here are a few:

☽ Calling on specific facets of the deity to energize spells.
☽ Calling on the deity before meditation to guide and direct the outcome (especially in pathworking).
☽ Choosing crystals or herbs for power pouches and portable magicks based on a specific deity's divine associations.
☽ Daily dedication/prayer at the deity's altar to bring the sacred into a more active role.

☾ Having rituals centred around specific deities with whom you are developing a relationship.

☾ Thematic ritual brews and libations that honour the god or goddess of your choice.

☾ Thematic postritual feasts such as Greek food for Athena-centred celebrations, or root vegetables for Hecate.

CHAPTER 21

Sacred and Magickal Places

Sacred sites celebrate the magick of Mother Earth and allow humans to reconnect with the divine Mother on a more intimate level, if they open their spiritual eyes and ears and really begin paying attention. This chapter will explain what makes sacred sites different from the rest of nature, and shows how to recognize them.

Sacred Sites Versus Sacred Space

Chapter 5 examined the significance and technicalities of creating sacred space, a temporary gathering of the energies for magickal purposes. However, Witches and Wiccans have also come to realize that sacred space could be around them all the time. Wiccans in particular advocate living a lifestyle that honours the earth as holy. Unfortunately, humans seem to have forgotten the unique language this planet speaks, and consequently can't always understand its signals – signals that communicate the extraordinary nature of some places and that sing the praises of this planet's wonders.

Planetary Aura

The first step to understanding sacred sites is to realize that the earth has an aura, just as people do. This aura contains hundreds of lines of energy, each connecting to another along a geometric grid. This grid represents the focal point to which sacred geometricians pay attention. These people, part scientists and part students of metaphysics, believe that if you unravel the intricate pattern of the earth's ley lines, you will find those that have been broken or disrupted by war, pollution and other sociological causes. Once you identify the wounds, you can learn to heal the earth's aural grid, begin renewing the human relationship with the earth's spirit and start interacting with the whole on a more positive level.

'Each Witch's way of honouring and invoking the Divine will have personal, cultural and traditional overtones. For instance, in the mornings you might light a candle to welcome Spirit (to say "good morning" if you will). It's a small but meaningful touch. As in all magickal things, simplicity isn't the issue – intention is.'

Louise Erdrich, writer

If you map the world's recognized sacred sites, you will notice that many of them lie along specific routes that create a defined pattern. For the most part, the patterns are circles, spirals, triangles, octahedrons and other polygonal forms that keep expanding until they embrace the whole planet. It seems that the ancients were aware of the earth's energy lines and built temples and other structures as one way of respecting, honouring and augmenting that energy. There is no reason modern Witches cannot do likewise.

Sacred Sites Around the World

Throughout the world there are literally thousands of sites that have been deemed holy to a group of people or have been honoured for their energies by visitors from around the world. Why would places not associated with the Craft be of interest to a Witch? Quite simply, because sacredness is sacredness. In the worldview of a Witch, Spirit is religiously neutral, so a Witch can visit any sacred place and honour the underlying power there without that area necessarily having to be connected to Wicca or Witchcraft in any way.

Here are just a few such sites:

AMARNATH, KASHMIR: Lord Shiva, the lord of the Dance, is worshipped in a cave here; it was at Amarnath that Shiva imparted the secrets of creation to Parvarti.

ANGKOR WAT, CAMBODIA: This archaeological site is covered with temples where pilgrims would come from miles around to make offerings and perform rituals. This site is sacred to Vishnu.

AVEBURY, ENGLAND: The village of Avebury, Wiltshire, has the largest stone circle in Europe.

BATH, ENGLAND: The springs here were sacred to the Celtic and Roman goddess Sulis and were reported to have the magickal ability to heal, which is why several of the pools were found to contain hundreds of gold coins as offerings.

BLUE GROTTO, CAPRI: This amazing grotto shines with blue light. Locals claim that it was once inhabited by Witches.

CALLANISH, SCOTLAND: Here is an ancient set of standing stones where lovers went to declare their vows.

COPÁN, HONDURAS: The Mayans used this site for an annual ritual to improve the priest's ability to walk between the worlds and receive guidance from spirits.

DENALI, ALASKA: In native tradition, this mountain houses a great god under whose dominion is all life.

EASTER ISLAND: This island is the home of great stone statues, each of which represents an ancestor or spirit whose power was channelled into the stone during the creation process.

ENCHANTED ROCK, TEXAS: This region is a fantastic place to witness ghost lights and other natural phenomena (such as the rock itself groaning).

EVEREST, TIBET: In native tongues, this mountain is called the 'mother of the universe'.

EXTERNSTEIN, GERMANY: An ancient site for worship and initiation to followers of the mystery traditions. According to tradition, this region was once the home of the World Tree (the Tree of Life). Sadly, the tree was torn down by Charlemagne. Sacred geometricians believe that many of Germany's ley lines connect here.

GIZA, EGYPT: Giza is the site of the Great Pyramids, one of the seven wonders of the world, and a much speculated site with regard to astronomy, psychic activities and other philosophies.

GLASTONBURY, ENGLAND: Legend claims that somewhere on these grounds the ancient Grail found a resting place. There is a strong possibility that the Abbey was built on an earlier pagan site of worship.

HENG SHAN, CHINA: Sacred to Buddhists and Taoists, the mountains around this region contain a powerful spirit that directs positive *chi* (energy) to this site.

KNOSSOS, CRETE: The infamous place where the legends of the Minotaur took place, the cliffs of Knossos were also a traditional site where Rhea (an earth goddess) was worshipped.

MAMMOTH CAVE, KENTUCKY: The calcite crystals in this cave have the amazing capacity to resonate due to the surrounding vaulted ceilings, making a womb of energy.

MONTE ALBÁN, MEXICO: For ten centuries, this region housed a ceremonial site that included pyramids and an observatory neatly aligned with the Southern Cross.

NIAGARA FALLS, NEW YORK: Native Americans called this place 'thundering falls'. Iroquois warriors worshipped at this great water-oriented site in order to strengthen their courage and vitality.

STONEHENGE, ENGLAND: Stonehenge, near Marlborough, Wiltshire, is the only stone circle in the world whose stones have lintels. It is set in a landscape of over 300 other prehistoric remains.

There are obviously many more places around the world that could be listed, but you get the idea. In some instances, local lore contributed to the manner in which the site was used; in other cases, the natural beauty simply inspired reverence. In either case, these and other sacred sites are definitely worth visiting if the opportunity affords itself.

Some places are very holy to a specific religious group and have specific protocols attached – ways in which visitors must dress, act and so on. It is very important to respect those protocols. The Witch's way is one of peaceful coexistence and respect for all Paths. So long as you honour the cultural and religious history of a place, you can then look beyond the details and find that source of energy that inspires such beauty.

Sacred Sites in Your Own Area

Although visiting famous sacred sites is an important experience, it is more important to the Witch or Wiccan to be able to discern places that house special energies where they live – not everyone can travel the world just to experience that natural magickal energy. In addition, by paying close attention to the world around you, you're bound to improve your overall rapport with nature, which is part of your goal. If you can multitask magickally – go for it, and more power to you!

Sacred places are perfect locations for meditation. Being at a sacred site is much like having an electric plug that goes directly to Spirit. When you connect yourself to that outlet, it's much easier to move into altered states of awareness.

Finding sacred sites is not as difficult as you might think. Look back on your childhood, for example. Where did you go when you needed private time or when you were upset? Perhaps a tree house, a cave or a nearby park? That's a great place to start looking.

Why do Witches look for sacred places?
Sacred locations have little bundles of energy in and around them. This energy can help refill the Witch's inner well for magick, and can also be used as a source of energy for spells or for charging magickal tools.

Indicators of a Vortex, Ley Line or Power Centre

As you look for places that house special energy, pay attention to these key indicators:

☾ Body heat increases (without the sun coming out or other environmental causes).

☾ Dowsing rods or pendulums react positively, as if finding a hit (see Chapter 4).

☾ The place appears repeatedly in your dreams, usually with something magickal or spiritual taking place there.

☾ An emotional sense of peace and tranquillity settles over you like a warm blanket.

☾ A feeling as if you're not alone (as if the animals, birds, trees or other living things are trying to communicate with you through motion or other symbols).

☾ Hairs on your arms rise, as if you've been exposed to electric current.

☾ Unusually lush displays of plants uncharacteristic for the region (for example, a streak of bright green grass was once called a fairy trail and usually follows a ley line).

☾ Regular greetings by totems and power animals (these creatures are naturally more attracted to earth's energy sources).

☾ A sense of timelessness – as if there is only now.

Buildings can also house sacred energy, so don't dismiss those intuitive nudges. Bear in mind that the ancients used the stone circles in Europe as people now use a church, and these sacred sites certainly weren't natural in their formation: human hands moved those stones into place, while remaining sensitive to the energies that surrounded them. We can do that too. Buildings that exhibit a sense of sacredness may have been built by someone very sensitive to mystical energy, or their location on a natural vortex, ley line or power centre may be a coincidence.

Taking the Next Step

Once you find a location that shelters this wonderful, warm energy, it stands to reason that you would want to visit as often as possible (as long as it's permitted). When you're away, you'll find that the area calls to you as if lonely for your presence. All human beings are part of the earth's energy matrix, and spiritually attuned people sense what it's like to mingle with that pattern, enjoying a sense of wholeness and connection.

What if you want to mingle your energy with that of a sacred place you've found? Begin by preparing yourself for a visit. Perhaps fast the day before, get plenty of rest, centre yourself and announce your intention to the universe at your personal altar. Consider anointing yourself with a special oil that accents spirituality (such as sandalwood), having a purifying bath or taking any other ritualistic approaches that put you in the right frame of mind for the experience ahead of you.

As you're going to this place, release your expectations about what may or may not happen there. Each area is unique, and each visit can likewise be unique. If you honour the partnership between yourself and the planet and simply allow it to speak to your heart, your experiences will be much more vital and complete. That doesn't mean you can't have special activities in mind, but allow the land and Spirit to guide and inspire you in how those activities proceed.

Remain attentive and mindful. The Witch should learn from the Buddhists, whose philosophy is seen in their language; in Sanskrit, the word for 'mindful' also means 'remember'. Being mindful means remembering your connection to the Mother, to Spirit, to your inner world and to magick. When spiritually inclined people move through this world mindfully, they maintain a sense of presence, place and being, a sense that is very difficult to describe with mere words.

In many ways, the state of being attentive and mindful is like a stretched-out meditation. At this moment you shine a light and shift your attention so it embraces the below, the centre and the above (the below being earth; the centre, self; and the above, Spirit). The knowingness and connectedness this creates is very powerful and transformational. In this moment, mindfulness can become your 'home', in the deepest sense of the term. Isn't that exactly what Witches want – to be truly at home with the self, others, the earth and Spirit?

When you get past the obstacles and struggles, you'll reach the point when whatever lesson you were meant to learn makes complete sense. In this moment your mind and soul are cleared, and you see the bigger picture.

Any road towards true personal change and manifested magick is going to have periodic obstacles and struggles. The possibilities are varied – you may not have a vehicle to reach your special place, or you may not be allowed to go there during specific times of the day. Obstacles may be spiritual in nature – you may feel as if you're not really making progress during your visits. When these kinds of issues arise, remember that no pilgrimage is struggle-free. These are the refining fires that test a person's resolve and devotion. This is not the time to be impatient: just keep on keeping on, and all will be fine.

When clarity descends, seize the moment to align yourself to that energy flow you're feeling. Take your time; there's no need to rush. Let your aura adjust to the energy and saturate your being. This is when meditation, integration and internalization become nothing less than essential. Without stopping to reflect on and honour what has happened, you'll also give up a valuable opportunity to be transformed by the experience. If you allow yourself to undergo the transformation, you will have this moment to carry within your spirit forever.

In general, take positive steps to be able to get to your special place regularly. The more you visit a region and work magick there, the more it becomes imprinted with your mystical fingerprint. As you spin spells, pray, weave rituals or meditate there, you will become more closely attuned to the energies and spirits around you. In other words, you will fulfil this place as much as it fulfils your spirit.

Reviewing the Steps: Visiting Your Sacred Site

While a Witch's journey to a sacred space is a physical one, the intention behind it affects the whole of being – body, mind and spirit. This is as much an inward quest as one that's upward and outward. The sacred site is a catalyst for that quest. Following are the steps you should follow.

1. Prepare yourself.
2. Release any expectations.
3. Remain alert in body, mind and spirit.
4. Overcome fears or barriers if they appear.
5. Tune in; wake up to the potential around you.
6. Align yourself to that energy and experience it fully.
7. Meditate on what you learn.
8. Internalize and integrate the experience.
9. Make notes in a spiritual journal.
10. Take positive steps to make these visits regular.

Discerning Elemental Energies in a Site

Just as every part of nature has a corresponding dominant element, so do sacred sites. If you think of each element (earth, air, fire, water) as a voice in a choir, each voice should work cooperatively with the whole for harmony. Humans, however, have faults and often are off-key in working with the natural world and each element therein. By learning to recognize the dominant element at sacred sites, you will be able to 'retune' yourself to better utilize the energies of that area.

Chapter 13 can help you with the basics of elemental energy. Bear in mind that the correlations made here are strictly Wiccan. In other parts of the world, the elements often have different meanings that reflect cultural myths and religious beliefs. If something doesn't feel quite right, trust your inner voice. This is only a guideline that provides a functional framework; add or take away whatever will make this framework meaningful to your Path.

f@ct

Elemental Locations:
Earth: Caves, farms, dense forest, grasslands, valleys.
Air: Cliffs, crags, hills, mountains, peaks, windy shores.
Fire: Desert, hot springs, the tropics, volcanoes.
Water: Geysers, lakes, rainforest, river banks, waterfalls.

Earth

Any region that makes you feel really centred, with your feet firmly on the ground, is a predominantly earthy site. If you extend your psychic senses in such a region, it often throbs like a drumbeat (caves, in particular, demonstrate this magickal response). Magickally speaking, working with an earth-oriented centre supports growth, steady progress, financial improvements and a sense of stability.

Air

The air element is a little elusive, but any region that manifests a playful, creative, liberated, communicative energy within you is probably ruled by the air element. Extending your psychic ears here often results in the sound of bells or chimes. Don't overlook the music of the winds; each wind has a unique voice and emotion. Magickally speaking, working in an air-oriented centre supports divinatory efforts, psychic abilities, motivation, happiness and inventiveness.

Water

The water element has a gentle, patient side. Typical sensations generated by a water site include peace, healing, nurturing, cleansing and fertility (literal or figurative). The astral sounds here are very similar to the rush of waves that you hear when you put a seashell to your ear. Magickally speaking, working in water-oriented sites supports your versatility, the ability to tune into your inner voice, improves overall wellness, honours lunar-oriented spells and rituals, and generally aids empathy.

Fire

Fire is strong and demanding and, according to shamans, the hardest element to master. It purifies, energizes, joins in kinship, destroys and creates. Typically, the fire sites have a distinctive 'crackle' to them like static or the sparking of a flame. Magickally, working in such a region offers a lot of power, but one that must be carefully controlled.

Spirit

Finally, there are some sacred sites that resonate with Spirit – the binding tie between all the elements and the source of magick. These places feel timeless: when you're there, they awaken in you a sense of oneness with all things, karmic awareness and a consciousness of your spiritual nature.

Listen for deafening silence. Spirit only speaks when you quieten your heart and mind, and truly listen. Magickally speaking, a spirit-oriented site is good for all forms of magick, particularly those moments when you need to reconnect with your soul-self and manifest a miracle.

Empowering and Honouring Sacred Sites

Witches have a propensity for wanting to decorate just about everything in some manner that reflects their faith and practices. These decorations are highly personal and frequently highly functional. This desire to deck things out certainly doesn't end at the Witch's doorstep – a variety of changes and additions applied sensitively to a sacred site will actually augment its powers.

How does a Witch go about honouring a sacred site and empowering it? Well, she looks to her ancestors for inspiration and ideas. In times past, people used sacred stones and stone altars as 'markers' of the sacred space. Usually situated in spirals or circles, these stones marked the entirety of the sacred space, often lined up with stars and also frequently marked ley lines. As the stones went into place, they created a web of power aimed at protecting and energizing that space.

Gardening in Your Sacred Site

People also practised the custom of planting groves and gardens on or near sacred sites. Trees were planted in circles, and specially designed gardens abounded. This custom was almost certainly a way to honour and support the energy of a sacred site and of all nature at the same time.

Here are some gardening tips for this magickal endeavour.

- ☾ Use only native plants so as to not upset the ecosystem.
- ☾ Plant medicinal herbs at water-oriented sites (to support the healthful energies).
- ☾ Sow elementally coloured flowers (or ones with the right correspondence) around the site.
- ☾ Consider planting four types of trees or bushes (one for each element) at the four directional points of a spirit site.
- ☾ Over vortexes, put your chosen array of flowers in the ground as an outward-moving spiral.
- ☾ Design a small mandala garden near the centre of the site so you have a special place to meditate.
- ☾ Plant culinary items in an earth-oriented site (honouring earth's providence).

Magickal Offerings

At many ancient sacred sites, people would leave a gift for the spirits of the land. Appropriate gifts typically included bread, milk, wine or something else the visitor felt would please the spirits. Witches often follow this lovely custom, especially when harvesting something from nature.

CHAPTER 22

A Witch's
Healing Touch

Spiritually minded people are no different from anyone else in wanting good health – if you have your health, you have everything! How do witchy or Wiccan ideals figure into the health equation? How do witches blend magick with the mundane when it comes to personal wholeness or helping a friend or loved one in need?

Historical Roots of Healing in Witchcraft

One of the primary and most sacred trusts for ancient shamans, cunning folk and priests or priestesses was that of healing – be it of a farm animal, a pet, a person or the whole community. To borrow the eloquent phrase of 18th-century author Dr Samuel Johnson, 'To preserve health is a moral and religious duty, for health is the basis of all social virtues.' Today, even physicians are rediscovering age-old methods of protecting, reclaiming and motivating health.

The Magickal Philosophy of Wholeness

Witches and Wiccans (along with a good number of Neo-Pagans) seem more open to trying 'newfangled' approaches to health. Why? For one, they know that a lot of these purported 'new' methods have ancient origins and a long history of successful application. Moreover, true wholeness depends on spiritual condition just as much as on the body and the mind. As Socrates aptly pointed out: 'There is no illness of the body apart from the mind.'

The vast majority of the Neo-Pagan community embrace the concept of holistics. In this healing philosophy, the healer becomes more than someone treating a symptom; he or she is also the conduit for universal energy, so the technique used to effect wellness is the conduit for that energy. Throughout this process, the healer remains mindful that if one part of the body-mind-spirit trinity is overlooked, the healing efforts will be only partially successful, if at all.

To understand this concept better, think for a moment of how your body feels after a long day at work. Even if you don't do a lot of physical labour, your mind is weary and that translates to bodily fatigue as well. Similarly, consider how you feel when you've been away from spiritual resources for a long time. That disconnection affects everything; you feel distracted, sad, weary and frustrated. Those negative emotions then seep into every part of your life – magickal and mundane. In consequence, when looking at various approaches to improve or safeguard your health, try to find those that serve all aspects of the body-mind-spirit trinity.

The Five Healing 'Gifts'

Many Witches believe that various people have talents or knacks that can be honed and employed towards improving the quality of life for others. These aptitudes manifest distinctly through a prescribed holistic or metaphysical method but originate somewhere in a person's spirit and natural abilities. For example, a good massage, a herbal tea or aural work will help alleviate stress, but the sensitivity of the person who provides the massage, tea or aural work has a direct impact on the quality and longevity of relief. For instance, depending on the healer, stress relief might be effected through energizing the patient, inducing sleep or relieving pain. Each of these results ties into a particular healer's aptitude.

If a Witch is interested in activating his spiritual potential as a healer, he can look to the following five types of healing gifts (as points on the pentagram) to determine where his best focus lies.

1. *Helping a person rest, de-stress, or sleep* (air energy). Some healers seem to have a natural ability to get a restless patient to rest. Bringing sleep is so important to healing that while it may seem like an insignificant skill, it's actually among the most important.
2. *Relieving pain* (fire energy). This gift is equally important, because the human body, mind and spirit can't accomplish what needs to be done when distracted and tormented by pain.
3. *Manifesting quantifiable physical results* (earth energy). Profound physical results from healing are more likely to occur with hands-on approaches such as acupressure or chiropractics.
4. *Caring for the emotional well-being of a patient* (water energy). Individuals who possess this ability are able to support and sustain their patients until their bodies are well enough so that emotions can return to a balanced state.
5. *Nurturing the spirit* (spirit or void energy). Whether it is someone who shares a new vision with you while doing crystal healing, or someone who combs your aural envelope back into balance during touch therapy, these people round out the holistic formula we seek.

The caregivers' calling is not an easy one. There are a lot of needy people in the world. Nevertheless, the capacity for love (which is amazing magick) shown by these people is truly admirable. Not all are born to heal, and even Witches who have the healing gift can't all approach it the same way. The uniqueness of each Witch's spirit and her Path will undoubtedly distinguish her healing methods and in turn allow her to better serve the whole, varied magickal community.

tips

Physical healers must take care to work with natural progressions and not push for too much too soon, or they will harm instead of heal. Holistic healing does not seek fast results; it seeks lasting results.

Holistic Approaches

The holistic approaches included in this section – just a few from the huge number available – are beginning to become established in the medical community. These particular methods require training and study to master and are some of the more common healing methods to which a Witch might turn for assistance under the guidance of his physician.

ACUPRESSURE AND ACUPUNCTURE: These methods focus on the body's own ability to resist sickness by redirecting the flow of energy (called *chi*) through physical points, each of which, treated alone or in tandem, affects another part of the body, mind or spirit. Acupressurists and acupuncturists both stress that ongoing maintenance is very important to the success of these methods – rather than waiting until the car breaks down, maintenance avoids dis-ease (hyphen intentional). Both methods have proved helpful to those trying to overcome addictions, struggling with chronic pain and suffering from joint disorders.

CLINICAL AROMATHERAPY: Using small amounts of diluted safe essential oil applied externally, this system works both on both the inner and outer person. External aromatherapy is considered noninvasive, and is very helpful with stress-related conditions.

HOMEOPATHY: Homeopathy is based on the law of similars. In treatment, homeopathists prescribe a small substance that would, in larger doses, have induced symptoms of the disease that is being cured. Basically, the theory behind homeopathy is that introducing something into the human body teaches it how to work with that 'energy', but the substance should be introduced in very small amounts. (Bach's use of flower essences relies on this idea as well.) To this foundation, trained homeopaths add advice on diet, exercise and lifestyle, to balance the rest of the body-mind-spirit equation.

MASSAGE: Massage therapy proves effective in many situations, including providing stress and pain relief, improving circulation and rebuilding strength in an area of the body. However, anyone who has received a bad massage knows how damaging it can be, so make sure you go to a professionally trained massage therapist who will concentrate on slow, steady results.

POLARITY THERAPY: Related to acupressure, polarity therapy attempts to excite or calm specific meridians (energy lines) in the body to restore balance, which in turn improves the body's capacity to heal itself. Dr Randolph Stone developed polarity therapy in the early 1900s. Dr Stone divided the body into negative and positive poles – the negative poles correspond to the lower parts of the body and the left-hand side, while the positive poles correspond to the upper body and the right side. The therapist uses light touch and manipulations to adjust these polarities back into balance.

Bear in mind that a world of options exists for anyone interested in wellness, not just Witches. Always ask questions, look around and explore the alternatives that appeal to you. It's well worth the time.

REFLEXOLOGY: This system of healing is all underfoot (or in the feet). Reflexology deals with points on each foot in which the body houses various illnesses and disorders. By breaking up the tension there, the reflexologist can relieve pain without ever needing to make physical contact with the afflicted part.

Metaphysical Approaches

Because Witches strive to bring magick into their daily lives, using metaphysical methods for health and healing makes perfect sense. Being already familiar with the basic processes of magick helps the Witch control the healing energy so that it flows more smoothly and naturally, in keeping with the practitioner's vision. In addition, there is a definite psychological edge gained by using magick: even when it seems that you can do nothing to help, magick gives you something you *can* do, engendering hope.

Aural Work

Portraits of saints and other holy people often show a halo; this depiction is part of what Witches call the aura. Basically, the aura is the body's atmosphere, a shell of energy that surrounds it. The shape or size of that shell varies according to the each person's physical, emotional and spiritual conditions.

The way each Witch perceives the aura varies: some feel textures, while others smell aromas, and still other psychically attuned Witches see the aura in colours. By examining those sensory bits of information, a Witch can learn what areas of a person are stressed, then add energy into the aura to bring everything back into balance.

The process for adding energy into the aura rarely involves direct touching. Most Witches simply project energy through the palms of their hands, which remain above the body at the outer edge of the aura. The idea here is to smooth out the energy levels externally so the body isn't working so hard and can focus on the main problem.

Colour Therapy

Chapter 15 examined the magickal significance of colour. As early as the 1400s, Paracelsus was using this idea by creating colour-coded curatives in the form of herbal mixes and elixirs. Witches use both the modern and ancient ideas behind colour therapy as part of the wellness equation.

The easiest way to apply colour therapy is to add specific colours to your wardrobe. The significance of 'putting on' energy shouldn't be overlooked here – when you're feeling blue, wear pink (to be 'in the pink'). In addition, try adding decorative touches to a room in hues that support your needs (like blue for peace), or eating foods of a specific colour to internalize the necessary energy.

Crystal Healing

Crystal healing is based on the idea that the human body is like a large fuse box with lines of criss-crossing energy. Each line of force is important to overall health – but what happens when energy is misdirected or cut off? There needs to be some way of reconnecting it and getting it back on track. That's where crystals come in.

A trained, sensitive crystal therapist knows which stones (by colour, shape and type) vibrate at certain frequencies, and how these vibrations affect the body, mind and spirit. She places the right crystal in the corresponding part of the body that needs the energy, effectively reminding the body of how it should be operating.

The ancient Chinese trusted jade to be a protective health amulet. Germans carried beryl to improve physical energy levels. Babylonians kept hematite close at hand to improve physical charisma. In the Middle Ages, blue topaz was used to cure vision problems.

Here are some modern recommendations provided by crystal workers:

AGATE: Improves the immune system and overall emotional harmony.
AMETHYST: Clarifies the conscious mind.
CARNELIAN: Relieves dietary problems, improves physical energy.
GARNET: Improves memory.
JADE: Relieves knee and joint pain; improves ability to give and receive love.
LAPIS: Increases sense of balance.
ONYX: Works well for ankle and foot disorders.

ROSE QUARTZ: Heart problems (physical and metaphorical).

SUGILITE: Helps to calm and alleviates fear.

TURQUOISE: Promotes honesty and creativity.

In terms of metals, copper was thought to clear circulatory problems, and gold was once used in water because it was so expensive people thought it *must* help magickally; other metals weren't as dominant.

Sacred Sounds

Religions around the world, including Wicca, use sacred sounds as a vehicle for energy (see Chapter 7). The tonal quality of words and music has the capacity to help maintain and encourage wellness – for instance, plants seem to grow better when exposed to happy or calm music (as opposed to harsh, too-loud sounds).

There are a variety of applications for sacred sounds. A healer may sing a special song to an ailing person, so the song's vibrations wrap around the patient's body like a bandage. Other methods include chanting to change internal and external vibrations, or singing a saga song (a song that talks of overcoming and wholeness).

Potions

What would any book about magick be without a section on potions? Although potions are not used exclusively for healing purposes, they certainly play that role often, and modern Witches rely on herbal preparations in their healing efforts. Some may make a tea over which they incant to focus energy, while others might create a crystal tincture (an interesting blend of crystal therapy, herbalism and magick) based on the vibrations of the stones. Not all such potions are meant for consumption. Some are poured out as libations, symbolizing the release of a sickness, or as an offering.

Rituals and Spells

Rituals and spells are two favourite methods in the Witch's kit, tried-and-tested ways of raising power for specific goals. If a Witch is doing a ritual or spell for someone else's health, he should request permission from the ailing person. For his own health, he can enact the spell or ritual any time he needs or desires it. However, if a Witch is very tired or ill, he may need to ask for another's help so the negative energy associated with his condition doesn't leach into the magick.

The beauty of using rituals or spells is that there is an abundance of examples to choose from, such as the *Abracadabra*, an ancient healing charm (see Chapter 7). A Witch can create meaningful health and healing methods by relying on the all of the magickal tools and approaches discussed throughout this book.

The most opportune time to work healing spells and rituals is during a waning moon so the sickness will shrink and disappear. In addition, working at noon banishes the darkness of disease.

Ethics and Legalities

Legally speaking, some metaphysical approaches have no public face; they require no licence or training. Ethically, however, most Witches believe that such methods should work hand-in-hand with modern medical knowledge and treatment. Additionally, they strongly believe that a person who wields metaphysical energy in an attempt to help another should always explain that his or her efforts are based on faith, not necessarily on provable facts.

Nearly every metaphysical healer I know has a defined code of ethics to which he or she tries to adhere closely. Healers should never forget that their calling is to help, not to harm. If there is ever an instance in which they're not sure of the effects of their magickal efforts, they should politely decline. In addition, healers should try to work in tandem with both nature and science, recognizing the power of both to bring about health and spiritual wholeness.

'I swear by Apollo Physician, by Asclepias, by Health, by Panacea, and by all the gods and goddesses, making them my witness, that I will carry out, according to my ability and judgment, this oath and this indenture.... I will keep pure and holy both my life and my art. In whatsoever houses I enter, I will enter to help the sick.'

Hippocrates, from the Hippocratic oath

Witches should never perform healing magick without express permission. Spiritual energy is such that a person must not only wish to get better but also be willing to accept the energy offered. To work without permission enters that territory of manipulation and disregard of free will.

Witches recognize that sometimes showing gentleness and concern improves things faster than any type of magick. People are people, with distinct emotional needs during times of physical duress, and the human dimension cannot be overlooked in matters of wellness any more than the spiritual dimension can.

Witches should decline to cast spells, engage in rituals or attempt other forms of energy manipulation if they cannot put aside ill will or uncertainties towards the person in need. They should also decline if they feel ill, tired or just out of sorts. Working with love, a positive outlook and good intention is a powerful combination – without these qualities, the effort could do more harm than good.

Witches realize that the outcome from their efforts may not be dramatic. Magick can be very subtle in its workings – perhaps a spell just helps a weary, sore person to sleep. Even in that small thing, the positive effect has value. Rather than waiting for a miracle, Witches simply seek to help when and where they can, so that the individual can make steady progress towards wellness.

Finding the Right Methods and Healers

Witches, being typically independent sorts, know that not all mystical or holistic healing methods are right for each person. When you need help, how exactly do you go about choosing which methods and healers are the right ones for you? At least part of this answer can come from people you know who have tried approaches that you might have not. Ask them how the method felt and whether it helped, and their recommendation for your particular problem.

Witches also rely heavily on instinct. Reading the information on a particular method, a Witch may get a 'feeling' for whether it's a good idea for her. On the other hand, the method may not really mesh with the Witch's overall practices – for example, if a Witch doesn't work with crystals very often and doesn't have a lot of faith in their energies, he probably won't turn to crystal therapy as a wellness aid.

As for which healer to choose, rely on good old common sense. For example, if you don't think a healer's office staff behaves professionally, on the phone and in person, you probably won't feel confident with that healer. Trust is very important to the overall wellness equation, and anything that sets off warning bells or stirs up doubts and worries will undermine any potential good any method might do.

Check the healer's credentials and references. Any reputable healer will have no objection to providing necessary phone numbers and/or addresses.

Write down all your questions and then interview each healer. When you're done, compare the results. Although this sounds like a lot of legwork, it's worth the sense of confidence you will have about the process you will be undergoing and the person who will be working with you.

Once you have chosen a healer, don't forget to:

(Follow through on the instructions provided by the healer.
(Tell the healer about any issues or problems you have with any part of the treatment.
(Ask questions about things that you don't understand or have concerns about.
(Communicate about your progress, or lack thereof.
(Continue with metaphysical support for your treatments at home.

☾ Get a second opinion if you feel one is necessary (or if it would give you greater confidence).

☾ Remain informed and involved in every part of the treatment (including changes).

These actions will acknowledge your role as an active participant in the curative process in particular, and in your destiny in general. To find out more about working with a healer, take a look at *The Healer's Handbook* by Patricia Telesco.

CHAPTER 23
Coven Craft

Some Witches choose to work alone, pursuing their Path and vision in a solitary way. Nonetheless, humans are pack animals by nature; we like companionship, especially with like-minded people. This chapter will help you decide whether you would like to seek out a group with whom to interact, and if so, how to go about finding the right group.

The Power and Problems of Group Dynamics

It is very important to remember that a coven is a group – and every group has dynamics. The typical coven has 13 members, although some may have many more. As you can well imagine, dealing with the issues and opinions that come up among 13 independently minded Witches can get pretty fraught – some covens explode and dissipate over trivial matters, while others seem to be able to work through problems by devoting time and effort to find solutions. The question is: are you willing to make the effort necessary to make the coven work? If being part of something greater than yourself is important, you'll have to be willing to recognize that the recipe for success in covens is anything but simple. As long as you go in with your eyes open on that point, you're less likely to be disappointed later.

On the positive side, groups offer a lot to practitioners of Wicca and Witchcraft – it's nice to have someone with whom to exchange and discuss ideas about magick and spirituality. Furthermore, there is no denying the vast amount of power a group can raise when the members work together for the good of all. The challenge is to get past egos, high expectations and self-esteem issues, and to allow the group connectedness to happen. Because, of course, it can happen – it just takes real work on the part of each individual in the Circle.

Historical Origins of the Coven

The word 'coven' originated from the Latin *coventus*, meaning 'assembly' or 'agreement'. The term first appeared in Scotland in around the 1500s to denote a Witch's meeting or a local group of practising Witches. Another Scottish document, dated 1664, mentions a woman who was tried for attending covens of 13, led by a little man in black clothing who made those in attendance sign a pact. However, other than rare side notes such as this one, the word was rarely used until the modern Witchcraft movement became more public and popularized.

Benefits of Working with a Coven

You can learn a lot if you work with a coven, especially when it comes to the foundation information that a well-established coven can provide. In particular, you will have the opportunity to:

☾ Learn what modern magick is in practice, as opposed to popular representations.

☾ Discover the history of a specific magickal tradition.

☾ Receive instructions on how to meditate and focus effectively in a group setting.

☾ Learn how to raise and direct energy through group spells and rituals.

☾ Explore divine images and their meanings to a specific group.

☾ Acquire the tools of Witchcraft and use them in a coven setting.

Of course, unless the group is eclectic, these points will be limited to the coven's particular traditions, but that doesn't reduce the value of learning at the feet of good teachers. Everything you glean can (and will) be easily applied to other methods and situations, both as a solitary Witch and within a group.

Finding the Right Coven

If a Witch carefully considers the pros and cons of joining a coven and decides to move forwards, how would she go about finding a coven to join? It's not as if covens are listed in the Yellow Pages!

The first place to look is on the Internet at *www.witchvox.com*, which is the largest repository of information about the Craft, including listings of groups around the world. You may find one or several in your own town or city, or at least in your area. Once you get in touch with a group's contact person, he or she should be able to give you more information about any nearby covens, study groups and gatherings.

In addition to using the Internet (there are dozens of online covens and groups on the Web), you can also check bulletin boards at book and music shops, health food cooperatives and New Age shops.

Leadership and Members

Once you find several groups to choose from, pay particular attention to two key points: the attitude of the leaders and the cohesiveness of the membership. These two factors can make or break a coven.

There are also several rules of thumb for reviewing a coven's leadership and members (in other words, if you see any of these warning signs, don't touch 'em with a bargepole!). First, any group that says you *must* do something in a particular way, even if it goes against a personal taboo or moral guideline, is not an ethical group. If one person is uncomfortable with a process, this will have a negative effect on the magick of the whole. There has to be some leeway for people to be people.

Second, seeing members grovel before the coven's leader should also raise a warning flag. A leader needs help and assistance, but not at a whim and not by demand without gratitude. Someone who orders coven members around like children or sheep is playing the ego game.

Third, be wary of any coven that charges for membership, unless there is a valid reason for such fees (and proper accounting is in place). Most Witches believe that learning should be free – it's OK to ask for help with travel expenses or snacks for a meeting, but there's a huge difference between this and making a killing from someone's spiritual thirst.

Fourth, a group whose members brag about their numbers, claim they are all-powerful or allege a 100 per cent success rate in their magick isn't worth your time. There is no such thing as fundamental Wicca, and no one group has the right to think that its way is the *only* right way.

The best leaders don't seem to need titles. They are great facilitators and communicators, and are very honourable diplomats. They remain sensitive to individuals and to the greater whole, and they work hard to teach, inspire and motivate the coven. When deciding between covens, ask yourself whether any of the leaders stand out as having these qualities, and whether they have earned the respect of the coven for tenacity and consistency.

The Coven and Its Culture

Similarly, the best covens are made up of individuals who take their responsibility to the group seriously. You want a group that respects both the person and the Circle in the way it interacts and sets up events – and you definitely want a group that isn't bickering all the time.

Consider the coven's tradition and the constructs that this particular tradition provides. Not every Witch wants to be Celtic or Egyptian, Dianic or Alexandrian, so if a coven holds to a particular tradition that doesn't interest you or is uncomfortable, you're in the wrong place.

Other points to consider: what kind of attendance and study requirements does the group have? Do these mesh with your mundane schedules and responsibilities? Does the group have a specific initiation ritual? What is this like? Is there anything in that ritual that doesn't fit your vision? Does the group require secrecy? If so, what's the thinking behind it, and how hush-hush is everything?

tips

If you are unsure about a certain coven's traditions, ask the coven leader for permission to attend an open Circle or other function. This will allow you to observe how the coven operates and get a feel for the words and actions involved in that tradition. Keep your senses open and imagine how it would be to work in that structure.

In the end, only you will be able to determine which coven is best for you, but take your time and don't rush. Bear in mind that every group you review will have its problems and idiosyncrasies; that is part of being human. The trick is to find the coven with whom you have the most in common and the fewest problems.

Joining a Coven

If you have found your ideal coven and would like to join, the next step is to have a chat with the group's leader. Tell him or her of your interest – specifically, what attracted you to this particular coven. Ask whether the coven is open to new members, and if so, when they hold initiations, and how to go about becoming more involved. The actual process from group to group will vary, but you probably have some studying ahead of you, and some things to learn before an actual initiation occurs.

During the learning process, start thinking ahead. What role do you see for yourself in this group? Do you want to have any specific function that mirrors your skills and talents? For example, musicians are a great asset to covens, especially if they can bring instruments for ritual work, as music can lend a special ambiance to a meeting. Alternatively, if you're a good writer, perhaps you could create some specialized spells or rituals for the group, using your knowledge of each person to guide the words. This attitude will show the prospective coven your sincerity – and that you're thinking in terms of the group and not just about yourself. In addition, this will help you define your place in the coven if and when you choose to take the next step of initiation.

There's nothing to prevent you from leaving a coven if you find you've made the wrong choice. While covens would like people to stay for continuity, Witches recognize that each individual's Path grows and changes every day. However, remember to try and part on good terms. As Witches say: 'Merry meet, merry part, and merry meet again!'

Forming Your Own Coven

Organizing a coven is rather like baking – you need the right ingredients and timing to make everything come together and work well. This isn't a club, and it isn't a way to show off to friends or freak out the parental units! A coven is a spiritually mindful group, and the process of making one should be taken with all due seriousness. Sometimes people form covens for the wrong reasons – for instance, as a power trip – so you really need to know yourself and be honest about your intentions.

If you still feel keen about giving it a go after a period of self-examination and meditation, there are some steps you can take to make your effort successful. First, decide how many people you want to be involved: 13 is the traditional number of Witches in a coven because there are 13 full moons in a year, but you don't have to follow that custom. Set a reasonable limit on membership, and remember that quantity is less important than quality.

Next, ask yourself what kind of coven you want. Do you want to focus on one specific magickal tradition? Do you want your group to be religious or secular? Do you want a rotating leadership or one defined leader? How will you choose the leader(s)? In other words, consider all the boundaries that will define and flesh out your group, as these boundaries will make it much easier for others to decide whether your coven is appropriate for them.

Other questions to consider include:

☾ What will the correct line of authority be?

☾ Will your coven work with magick for magick's sake, or will you be integrating religious aspects into your Craft?

☾ Where will your coven meet?

☾ Will you have requirements about how many meetings a year a person must attend to remain a member?

☾ Will you have study requirements?

☾ Will your members participate in activities together outside the coven setting?

☾ Do you plan to keep a Book of Shadows for your group – and if so, how and where will it be maintained?

☾ Will you need to have specific tools or regalia for your coven meetings?

☾ What seasonal festivals will you observe?

☾ What other types of gatherings do you want to have available to your members (for instance, to meet a member's personal needs)?

☾ What types of members' personal problems should the coven avoid getting involved in?

☾ How will someone attain the role of priest or priestess in your group?

☾ Who will make the decisions? Will you run your coven democratically, or will the leader's word be the final authority in every matter?

After these details have been determined, politely approach those people you think would be interested. Talk over the type of coven you envision, and listen carefully to the way each person responds. It's fine for them to ask questions – if they don't, you should be worried. Nevertheless, somewhere at the bottom line, their vision of the group has to mesh with yours, or there are going to be problems.

Once you've found a core group, the next stage is the trial period. Consider instituting a time period (for example, a year and a day) before anyone is considered a full, formal member of the coven (and before they are initiated into that group). The reason for this trial period is purely pragmatic: it gives everyone time to see whether the relationship between the members is going to work and to learn the skills necessary for working magick together – Rome wasn't built in a day, and neither is a good coven.

This is the time to try out a variety of rituals, spells and meditations, taking notes at each event. Find out what sensual cues work best for everyone; note what goes really wrong, and what goes really right. By reviewing these notes regularly, you will begin to see a spiritual pattern you can effectively use to build energy as a cohesive group.

At the end of the trial period, everyone should sit down and have a discussion: talk about your accomplishments and talk about what has and has not worked. Ask each person if he or she would like to continue in a more formalized manner. If the answer is yes, great! If not, part as friends and spiritual helpmates – just because you're not working magick together doesn't mean the end of the rest of your interaction.

Those who decide to move forwards now have an even greater task ahead, that of keeping things going. This is an excellent time to set up phone and e-mail lists for communication, create a line of authority,and really start organizing. And, of course, it's time to start meeting as a coven.

Planning Magickal Activities for Covens

Traditionally, the responsibility for planning coven events lies in the hands of a priest or priestess. However, since the leadership of some covens rotates, it's good to know how to design group activities. The following section makes some suggestions for an eclectic coven, because more traditional groups generally have standardized rituals and activities that you learn during the process of initiation.

When planning your event, consider the following points:

☾ The location date, and time of the activity should be accessible to the majority of the members (provide maps, if necessary).
☾ The focus of the activity should be meaningful to all members and be announced well in advance.
☾ The wording should be comfortable for those with speaking roles (I advise memorizing these; by doing so, you can focus on directing energy instead of reading).
☾ The people who want to participate actively should have some specific role or responsibility, and everybody should know what they need to bring (robes, food and so on).
☾ The tools and props needed for the activity should be brought to the site (having one person responsible for the care and keeping of 'community' tools is a good idea).

Initiation Rituals

Newly formed covens, in particular, need to consider what type of ritual they'll hold for new coven members. The initiation is a very important moment of bonding: you are about to extend your Circle, in all its quirky intimacy, to another person. Every person in the group should be present for this activity.

There is one really nice welcoming ritual that involves braiding or knotting. In this ritual, each new coven member brings a length of yarn, which is tied into the bundle created by the current members. In some cases, the coven's priest or priestess will keep the bundle or wear it as a belt as a sign of office. Symbolically, this ritual demonstrates how the new member's path is now tied in with the rest of the coven.

At the time of initiation, the new members can choose the magickal name they wish to use in sacred space. They then go to each person present, introduce themselves by that name and greet them as a brother or sister in the Craft (in whatever form the group wishes that greeting to take – a kiss on the cheek or a hug is pleasant).

Rites of Passage Celebrated in the Coven

Other types of rituals the group might wish to undertake include various personalized rites of passage for any member in need. These rites of passage include birth, death and adulthood rituals, as well as other dramatic changes in a person's life. Ritual can help internalize and cope with these changes. Divorce, a new career, a new home – all these situations are appropriate times for the coven to support its members in a viable, magickal way.

Group Divination and Dreaming

The idea behind conducting divination and dreaming in a group setting is to get the members of your coven more psychically attuned to each other. The following is a good example of a group divination activity.

You will need about 600g (1lb 4oz) of dry beans in as many colours as you can find, and a large sheet of clean white art or writing paper. Mix the beans well, put them in a bowl and decide what type of question the group wishes to pose. Get everyone to take three deep breaths together, then pass the dish clockwise, each member of the coven holding it and thinking about that question, focusing their intention into the blend. After the bowl completes the circuit, pour the beans onto the paper in the middle of everyone. Scry the patterns made and ask each person to give their impressions of the interpretive values. The results will be very revealing. (See Chapter 12 for other divination methods, and see whether you can use them to divine as a group.)

Group dreaming requires a little more preparation. First, you need to choose a date on which everyone can go to bed at the same time. Each member of the coven should eat the same foods, burn the same incense before bed and perhaps even have a specially prepared guided meditation tape to listen to at a set time so everyone is creating harmonious energy. Having a dream journal or a tape recorder next to the bed helps too – so that everyone records the experience. Basically, the idea is to try to 'meet' each other in the dream plane, which, like the astral plane, opens the door to infinite possibilities.

At your next get-together, compare notes to see how many people had similar dreams and experiences to report. A coven that has a high percentage of somewhat coinciding dreams is more psychically attuned to each other (see Chapter 8 for more on dreams).

Afterword: Living the Magick

Having read this book, you now know that Wicca and Witchcraft are nothing like the stereotypes portrayed in the media. Practising Witchcraft or accepting Wicca as your set of religious and philosophical beliefs won't solve all your problems; it won't give you perfect hair or physical attributes; and it won't do your housework or homework. So what is it all about?

Ultimately, being a Witch is really about fulfilment: you will reach down into a part of yourself that has been neatly tucked away, wake the magick there and then bring it back into your daily life. You will reclaim your birthright as a spiritual being and accept your potential in that new role. Mind you, it's not always easy – calling yourself a Witch brings out people's reactions: some will scorn you, while others just won't understand. Although this may create other interesting difficulties, it will also change your life in incredible ways.

The ultimate goal of becoming a Witch or Wiccan is to simply live and be the magick. This doesn't happen overnight. It takes time, patience, willpower and determination to reach that goal, but it is obtainable. Along the way the path may become bumpy, and on some days you may feel as if nothing whatsoever is happening. Don't become discouraged, as it is in the quiet moments that you really begin to internalize what you're learning and take it to heart. These moments also provide a necessary pause before the learning curve goes back up again!

Be persistent, stay alert and keep moving forward. As you do, you may discover that Witchcraft opens doors to other Paths that appeal to you. Don't ignore these opportunities. Each of us is cut from a different cloth, and perhaps your fabric is really that of a shaman or a Buddhist, for example. Allow yourself to become what you already are in your heart and soul – a powerful, magickal and spiritual person. The only difference in the long haul is how you express that reality. Express it joyfully – live the magick and be blessed.

Appendix A

Glossary

This glossary contains lists of magickal terms and their definitions, along with a number of historical and contemporary figures.

MAGICKAL TERMINOLOGY

ADEPT: Someone considered accomplished in at least one magickal art and able to teach it to others effectively.

ALL HALLOWS' EVE: An alternative name for Halloween.

ALTAR: A surface on which the witch's tools and other sacred items are placed; also an area around which many rituals and spells take place.

AMULET: An item worn or carried for protection or to deter negative influences.

ANIMISM: The belief that natural phenomena or items can have an indwelling spirit that can be appeased or called upon for aid.

ASATRU TRADITION: A northern European tradition of magick that also honours the old gods as described in the *Edda*, the ancient compendium of Icelandic lore, and legally recognized in Iceland in 1972.

ASPERGE: To sprinkle water in a ritual to clear a space of negativity and provide purification.

ASTRAL TRAVEL: The ability for the spirit to leave the body and visit other places and times.

ATHAME: The ritual knife of Wiccans, usually with two edges to represent the two-edged nature of magick (boon and bane). Some people prefer to use a sword, keeping their athame for working with magickal herbs instead.

AUGURY: The art, ability or practice of divination by signs and omens.

AURA: A term that means 'invisible breath'. Witches see an aura as a kind of energy atmosphere that surrounds each living thing. Some psychics can see auras. The patterns and colours within the aura are indicators of a person's physical, mental and spiritual state.

BALEFIRE: An outdoor fire Wiccans gather around for dancing and working of magick.

BANISHING: Turning negative energy or spirits away.

BARD: A formally trained storyteller often entrusted with the oral history of a group.

BLESSING WAY: The ritualistic dedication of young children (similar to a baptism).

BOOK OF SHADOWS: Also called a grimoire, this is a witch's or group's collection of practical magick. A Book of Shadows may contain recipes, spells, charms, invocations and rituals.

BOOK OF THE DEAD: An Egyptian treatise on the afterlife that includes hundreds of magickal instructions for everything from invocations to charms.

BURNING TIMES: A time in history when many people were punished and killed for purported acts of Witchcraft, which, at that time, was considered heresy.

CAULDRON: Any three-legged pot, which many Witches and Wiccans use to represent the threefold Goddess.

CHANT: A series of meaningful words that the Witch repeats to focus his or her will and raise energy towards a specific goal. A chant specifically designed for personal improvement is called an affirmation.

CINGULAM: A knotted cord worn with ritual robes; often denotes connection to a coven or degreed status (see also **MEASURE**).

CONJURATION: A means of invoking a helpful spirit for a specific task (note that this is most often seen, if at all, in **HIGH MAGICK**).

COVEN: A group of witches who practise together. A coven can be of any number but often includes 13 members (one for each full moon of the year).

CRONE: The third, and eldest, aspect of the Goddess. The masculine version would be **GRANDFATHER**.

CRYSTALLOMANCY: Divination using crystals.

CUNNING FOLK: An old name for people who practised folk magick and lived by cunning, insightful abilities.

CURSE: An appeal to supernatural powers for injury or harm to another.

DEGREES: Some witches have specific levels of skill within their Craft. Degrees designate progressive levels of skill and knowledge in Witchcraft.

DEOSIL: Moving clockwise (this generates positive energy).

DEVAS: A natural order of spirits with elemental essence (akin to fairies).

DIANIC WICCA: A sect of Witchcraft strongly tied into the feminist movement.

DIVINATION: The practice of trying to discover the future or other things unknown through a specific medium such as crystal gazing or Tarot cards.

DOWSING: Searching for water or precious items using a Y-shaped branch or other types of rods whose movements indicate a 'hit'. German miners brought this art to Europe in the 15th century.

DRUID: Priest or priestess of Celtic Europe who performed many social and religious functions.

EARTH MAGICK: A form of Witchcraft that focuses on natural symbols and components and attempts to remain very aware of our stewardship of Earth.

ELEMENTALS: The beings said to live within the energy force of a specific element. For example, **SYLPHS** are air elementals.

ELIXIR: A kind of potion used to energize, improve wellness and restore overall health to the person drinking it.

EQUINOX: A word meaning 'equal night'. Twice a year, the duration of daylight and night are equal. This is a traditional time for many Wiccan celebrations, marking two of the four major points on the **WHEEL OF THE YEAR** (the other two being the **SOLSTICES**).

ESBATS: Wiccan full-moon celebrations.

FAIRY TRADITION: A sect of Witchcraft started in the USA predominantly by Victor Anderson and Gwydion Penderwen, focused on the lore and magick of the fey.

FAMILIAR: An animal that acts in the capacity of a magickal partner, guide and teacher to a Witch.

FATHER: The second, more mature aspect of the God, similar to the Christian idea of God the Father. The feminine version would be the **MOTHER**.

FETCH: An old name for the ghostly image of a living person that appears outside the body just prior to death (it acts as an omen of death).

FETISH: Any object believed to have a specific magickal power for which that object is then carried, buried, burned or otherwise utilized magickally.

FOLK MAGICK: The practice of using natural symbols and the superstitions of common people combined with personal will to manifest change. Akin to a **HEDGE WITCH** in many ways.

RAIA: A name for the earth's spirit; also a Greek goddess who presided over the earth.

GRANDFATHER: The third, and eldest, aspect of the God. The feminine version would be **CRONE**.

GREAT RITE: A celebration of the God and Goddess in literal or figurative terms so the two can be united to create balance and increased power for magick.

GLAMOURY: The art of creating a sphere of energy within one's aura, akin to putting on an ambiance or atmosphere that presents a specific image to the outside world. Fairies are said to be highly adept in this art.

GREEN MAN: An image of the God aspect of Divinity that is strongly connected with nature. Many witches believe that the Green Man (who is often horned like a stag) is the image from which Christianity drew the portrait of Satan to try to frighten superstitious people.

GROUNDING: Shutting down psychic or magickal energy to return the self to a normal level of awareness and more mundane thought patterns.

GUARDIAN: Member of the security staff at various festivals.

HANDFASTING: A Neo-Pagan version of a wedding that does not necessarily correspond to a legal marriage. Many handfastings act as an agreement for the couple to be together for a year and a day (or other contract) and can also take place between more than two people.

HEDGE WITCH: A hedge Witch, traditionally, is a solitary practitioner who depends on self-study, insight, creativity and intuition as main guideposts. Such a Witch may be self-dedicated, but is rarely publicly initiated, with practices similar to those of the village shamans and cunning folk who provided spells and potions for daily needs.

HERMETIC TEXTS: A collection of books dated to about 3 CE, which contains information about astrology, rituals, education and much more. These books treat magick as a science of the mind, an outlook that continues to influence modern practices.

HIGHER SELF: A spiritual part of humankind that has access to the universal mind and all the knowledge and wisdom of our past lives.

HIGH MAGICK: The more elaborate and symbolic form of magick that deals with issues of the mind and spirit, as opposed to the more practical 'low magick'.

IMITATIVE MAGICK: Used a lot by ancient hunters and farmers, imitative magick involved enacting the desired outcome of the spell or ritual as a reality, such as drawing the image of a captured animal on a stone just before the hunt began.

INCUBATION: The practice of going to a sacred space alone for a time to receive divine inspiration.

INITIATION: A formal welcoming of a new Witch into a group (or a public dedication for a solitary Witch).

KABBALAH: An occult theosophy with rabbinical origins. It is an esoteric interpretation of Hebrew scriptures with strong ritualistic overtones.

KARMA: A concept borrowed from Eastern traditions, the law of karma is quite simply that of cause and effect. All our lives are said to balance out; all ills visit back on us, as do all good things, in this life or the next.

LEFT HAND PATH: Black magick, which is used to manipulate free will or cause harm.

LEY LINES: Invisible lines of force said to network throughout the earth in geometric patterns. When these lines are disrupted or injured, the associated land may suffer.

MAGI: Plural of magus

MAGICK: The unique spelling of this word came about to set this practice apart from stage magic.

MAGICK CIRCLE: The space within which many Witches and covens work their magick. This is a sacred space akin to a church, erected by words and actions (along with a variety of symbolic objects).

MAGUS: A sorcerer or magician. Also called a Mage. The plural is **MAGI**.

MAIDEN: The youngest aspect of the Goddess, characterized as energetic and beautiful. The masculine version would be the **SON**.

MEASURE: A practice that still takes place in some covens, this entails measuring various parts of a person's body with thread. This thread (or cord) is then kept by the group's leader in trust for the duration of a person's involvement, implying that person's promise to keep the secrets of that order.

MEDIUM: A person with the ability to become a middle ground between our world and the world of the dead, thus allowing the dead to speak through him or her.

MOTHER: The second, more mature aspect of the Goddess who is fertile and nurturing. The masculine version would be the **FATHER**.

OFFERING: Giving a small token to a god or goddess by way of thanks, or as a means of invoking assistance. This token should be meaningful and valuable to the person who gives it. Typical offerings include grains, wine, coins or handmade goods.

PENDULUM: An item suspended by string or thread that, when in motion, indicates the answer to specific questions. Romans used pendulums to try to determine the outcome of forthcoming battles. Witches use them for all types of divination, including trying to ascertain health problems. Up and down motion is generally regarded as 'yes'; left and right motion indicates 'no'.

POPPET: A figurine made to look like a person or animal to which specific magick is being directed. Historically, a poppet could have been a potato or lemon.

POTION: A liquid contrived with magickal components and through magickal processes to produce a specific result. Although most potions are meant to be consumed, some might be asperged, poured out to the earth or tossed on a fire, depending on their intended function.

RITUALS: Specific movements, words and actions designed to produce similarly specific results. Witches and Wiccans hold seasonal rituals, personal rituals, rituals for times of need in the community and so on; a ritual may be compared to a church service.

SABBATS: The eight main festivals of Wiccans, which take place throughout the year (also see **WHEEL OF THE YEAR**).

SACRED SPACE: Witches often create a sacred space in which to work their magick. This entails putting up a protective sphere of energy (sometimes called a **MAGICK CIRCLE**) that holds energy in place and keeps negative influences neatly outside. At the end of the working, the sacred space is dismissed.

SOLITARY: A witch who chooses to practise alone, outside a coven.

SOLSTICE: The two times of the year when the sun is either at its farthest northern or southern point of the celestial equator. Wiccans often celebrate the solstice as a fire festival to honour the sun.

SKYCLAD: A term used by Neo-Pagans to describe ritualistic worship without clothing (in other words, clothed in nothing more than the sky).

SON: The youngest aspect of the God, characterized as energetic and handsome. The feminine version would be the **MAIDEN**.

SUMMERLAND: The place between lives to which a soul goes after death to await reincarnation.

SYMPATHETIC MAGICK: This kind of magick relies heavily on the power of symbolism to create a specific magickal result. For example, a person who is ill might wash in a well known for its pure water to cleanse away her sickness. Here, the healthy/clear 'sympathy' of the water empowers the spell.

SYLPHS: Air **ELEMENTALS**.

UNDINES: Mermaids, or water **ELEMENTALS**.

WAND: A tool made of metal or wood used to direct or cast energy.

WANING MOON: The period following the full moon, when the lunar sphere gradually shrinks or wanes.

WARDS: Mystical energy patterns designed to safeguard an area (or person) from negative influences. Wards are often drawn in the air at the four quarters of a sacred space to enforce the protective energy.

WATCHTOWERS: A name for the elemental guardians of the four quarters of a sacred space (earth/north, air/east,

fire/south and water/west). These powers 'watch' over the sacred space when invoked and honoured.

WAXING MOON: The period following a new moon, when a small crescent appears and grows larger until it becomes a full moon.

WHEEL OF THE YEAR: The annual circle of eight major observances, fairly evenly distributed throughout the months, that are important to Wiccans and are also observed by many Witches.

WIDDERSHINS: Moving anticlockwise, widdershins is used in magick for banishing or decreasing.

HISTORICAL FIGURES

AGRIPPA, HENRY CORNELIUS: A 15th-century German physician, theologian and philosopher adept in the arts of astronomy, alchemy and magick, Agrippa wrote eloquently on the subject of occult apologetics and philosophy.

ALBERTUS MAGNUS: A German alchemist living in the 1200s. Magnus's writings on magick and alchemy are still considered valuable resources.

BLAVATSKY, HELENA PETROVNA: Russian mystic of the 1800s, Blavatsky was at the forefront of the Theosophical spiritualistic movement in the USA.

BÖHME, JAKOB: German mystic and philosopher of the late 1500s. Böhme'swritings on the eternal nature of the soul and the invisible world are still worthy of study by any Witch.

CAGLIOSTRO: A colourful figure in magickal history, this Italian adventurer's greatest contribution seems to have been introducing many nobles of the 1700s to Egyptian freemasonry.

CROWLEY, ALEISTER: A noted 19th-century magician, Crowley was considered a somewhat dark figure in the history of Witchcraft, but deserves credit for bringing a good deal of public attention to magickal arts.

CULPEPPER, NICHOLAS: A 15th-century English physician, herbalist and astrologer, Culpepper catalogued the use of hundreds of herbs along with their astrological associations.

DEE, JOHN: Court magician to Elizabeth I, mathematician and astrologer, Dee experimented greatly with alchemy and crystallomancy (divination using crystals).

FAUST, JOHANN: A 16th-century German magician of some acclaim, Faust's books reveal a great deal about medieval magick (even though Faust himself may have only been a legend).

FRAZIER, SIR JAMES: Frazier wrote *The Golden Bough* (1890), a thesis on magick as a religion. An expanded version of this book was published in 1922.

HERMES TRISMEGISTUS: This was the name given by the Greeks to the Egyptian figure of Thoth, to whom the hermetic texts were ascribed.

HUTINSON, FRANCIS: Writer during the 1700s whose work on historical Witchcraft helped to put an end to superstitious Witch beliefs among educated people in England.

INSTITORIS, HEINRICH: Author of the *Malleus Maleficarum*, or 'Hammer of Witches' in the 1400s, he was said to be one of the most influential motivators for the Witch hunts that followed.

JAMES IV OF SCOTLAND: The 16th-century ruler provided a fair amount of patronage to practitioners of occult sciences, and was himself a dabbler in the Craft.

LELAND, CHARLES: Author of *Araida the Gospel of Witches* (late 1800s). Although much of the veracity of this book is questioned in modern circles, its long-lasting effect on magickal practices (specifically ritualistic convention) remains.

LEVI, ELIPHAS: French occultist of the 1800s (sometime called the last of the magi). Levi wrote extensively about how magicians should (and should not) live in order to fulfil their power most successfully.

PLUTARCH: A 1st-century Greek philosopher, Plutarch believed that geometric figures had significance and could express divine patterns, an idea that is foundational in sacred geometry to this day.

PROCLUS: A 5th-century Neo-Platonic philosopher, Proclus was a staunch advocate of the old ways.

PTOLEMY: An Egyptian-born astronomer who lived in the 2nd century near Alexandria. He described the universe as a network of relationships that included the Divine.

VIRGIL: The greatest of Roman poets, Virgil lived from 79–19 BCE. He was thought to be a magician and diviner.

ZOROASTER: A Persian prophet who lived in the 6th century BCE. The magi were priests of his order.

CONTEMPORARY FIGURES

ADLER, MARGOT: Author of *Drawing Down the Moon*, Ms Adler brought the public a scholarly, broad-based look at modern witchery and Neo-Paganism.

ANDREWS, TED: Metaphysical author and lecturer on many topics, including hypnotherapy and herbalism.

BEYERL, REV. PAUL: Author of *The Master Book of Herbalism*, Reverend Beyerl founded the Rowan Tree Church, based on the Lothlorien tradition. In literature, the Lothlorien tree was a tree of knowledge and wisdom.; it comes from Tolkien's writings of the elvin kingdoms.

BONEWITS, ISAAC: Arch-Druid and founder of ADF, a neo-Druidic group.

BUCKLAND, RAYMOND: Occult student and writer for 30 years with a Gypsy background; Buckland has published over 20 books on metaphysics. He recently opened a Witchcraft museum in New Orleans, LA, USA.

CABOT, LAURIE: The famous official Witch of Salem, MA, USA, she has written several books.

CORRIGAN, IAN: One of the leaders of ADF, musician and author of much acclaim.

COWAN, TOM: Shamanic teacher and writer.

CUNNINGHAM, SCOTT: One of the most influential writers of the 1980s and 1990s, Scott communicated the ideas of Wicca and magick to the masses in down-to-earth ways.

CUROTT, PHYLLIS: Witch and lawyer of long standing, her *Book of Shadows* brought modern witchery further into the public eye.

FARRAR, JANET AND STEWART: Authors of many witchcraft and occult books, many of which Wiccans and Neo-Pagans consider essential.

FROST, GAVIN AND YVONNE: Founders of the Church and School of Wicca and authors of the *Good Witch's Bible*.

GARDNER, GERALD: Generally credited for kick-starting the modern Witchcraft movement in the 1940s, Gardner is the founder of the Gardnerian tradition.

GRAVES, ROBERT: Author of *The White Goddess*, which proposed the idea of an ancient goddess figure that had been worshipped widely throughout the ancient world. Graves argued that vestiges of this system still existed, particularly among Witches.

GRIMASSI, RAVEN: Editor of *Raven's Call* magazine and author of books on Strega (Italian witchcraft), Raven teaches about the Old Religion in the USA.

KNIGHT, SIRONA: Student of psychology, folklore and goddess beliefs, Knight is a published author and frequent lecturer on magickal arts and Witchcraft. She teams up with Patricia Telesco to write about 'Web witching' – celebrating the wonders of the Internet.

KRAIG, DONALD MICHAEL: Philosopher, teacher and writer, Kraig's areas of expertise include tantra, Kabbalah and psychic abilities.

LAVEY, ANTON: Leader of the Church of Satan. Wiccans and Witches both oppose the idea that there is any connection between Satanism and the Craft, because they do not worship or recognize any such being.

LEEK, SYBIL: A hereditary Witch, Sybil Leek is among the best-known Witches in England.

MORRISON, DOROTHY: High priestess of the Georgian tradition, lecturer, Wiccan teacher for 20 years and well-respected author.

MURRAY, MARGARET: Well-known feminist and mystical writer. Many of Murray's 'historical' accounts have come under fire in recent years. However, her public image helped support the modern Witchcraft revival.

PATHFINDER, PETE: Founder of the Aquarian Tabernacle Church, based on English Wicca, Pathfinder is also the president of the Interfaith Council of Washington State in the USA.

RAVENWOLF, SILVER: She recently rocked the USA with a *Teen Witch* book and kit.

SANDERS, ALEX: A prominent English Witch, Sanders started the Alexandrian tradition of Wicca.

STARHAWK: Author of the *Spiral Dance*, a widely read book on magick and goddess spirituality, Starhawk continues to be a strong, politically active figure who writes and speaks regularly on socially significant subjects.

TELESCO, PATRICIA: Author of over 50 books on witchery, Telesco is an active speaker and strong supporter of various magickal community projects.

WATERHAWK, DON 'TWO EAGLES': A Native American magickal toolmaker, drummer and teacher on both the Neo-Pagan and powwow circuit in the USA, and co-author of *Sacred Drumming* (with Samuel Weiser).

WEED, SUSAN: A green Witch who founded the Wisewoman School of Herbal Healing.

WOOD, ROBIN: Visionary artist and teacher of ethics.

ZOLAR: Writer and philosopher on the subject of magick and the occult (1970s).

Appendix B

Resources

Further Reading

Abadie, M. J. *The Everything® Candlemaking Book*. Adams Media Corporation, 2002.

Adler, Margot. *Drawing Down the Moon*. Viking Penguin, 1997.

Andrews, Ted. *Animal-Speak*. Llewellyn Publications, 1993.

Ash, Steven. *Sacred Dreaming*. Sterling Publications, 2001.

Beyerl, Rev. Paul.
  A Compendium of Herbal Magick. Phoenix Publishing, 1997.
  The Master Book of Herbalism. Phoenix Publishing, 1985.

Bonewits, Isaac, and Philip Emmons Bonewits. *Real Magic*. Red Wheel, 1991.

Budapest, Zsuzsanna. *Grandmother of Time*. Harper San Francisco, 1989.

Budge, E.A. Wallis. *Amulets and Superstitions*. Dover Publications, 1978.

Campanelli, Pauline, and Don Campanelli. *Ancient Ways: Reclaiming Pagan Traditions*. Llewellyn Publications, 1991.

Cavendish, Richard. *History of Magick*. Penguin USA, 1991.

Cooper, J. C. *Symbolic and Mythological Animals*. Thorsons, 1992.

Cunningham, Scott.
  Cunningham's Encyclopedia of Crystal, Gem and Metal Magic Llewellyn Publications, 1988.
  The Magic of Food: Legends, Lore, and Spellwork. Llewellyn Publications, 1996.

Currot, Phyllis. *Book of Shadows*. Broadway Books, 1999.

Drew, A. J. *Wicca for Men*. Carol Publishing Group, 1998.

Frost, Gavin, and Yvonne Frost. *Good Witch's Bible*. Godolphin, 1999.

Gordon, Lesley. *Green Magic: Flowers, Plants, and Herbs in Lore and Legend*. Viking Press, 1977.

Graves, Robert. *The White Goddess*. The Noonday Press, 1997.

Green, Marian. *Natural Witchcraft: The Timeless Arts and Crafts of the Country Witch*. Thorsons Pub., 2002.

Hall, Manly Palmer *Secret Teachings of All Ages*. Philosophical Research Society, 1994.

Hutton, Ronald. *The Triumph of the Moon*. Oxford University Press, 2001.

Knight, Sirona. *Dream Magic*. Harper San Francisco, 2000.

Kunz, George Frederick. *The Curious Lore of Precious Stones*. Dover Publications, 1972.

Leach, Maria, and Jerome Fried, eds. *Funk and Wagnall's Standard Dictionary of Folklore, Mythology, and Legend*. Harper San Francisco, 1984.

McArthur, Margie. *Wisdom of the Elements*. Crossing Press, Inc., 1998.

Matthews, John. *The World Atlas of Divination*. Bulfinch, 1992.

Roche, Lorin. *Meditation Made Easy*. Harper San Francisco, 1998.

Starhawk: *The Spiral Dance*. HarperCollins, 1999.

Telesco, Patricia.
  Dancing with Devas. Crossing Press, 1996.
  Exploring Candle Magick: Candle Spells, Charms, Rituals, and Divination. New Page Books, 2001.
  The Healer's Handbook. Samuel Weiser, Inc., 1997.
  A Kitchen Witch's Cookbook. Llewellyn Publications, 1994.
  The Language of Dreams. Crossing Press. 1997.

Waterhawk, Don 'Two Eagles', with Samuel Weiser.

Wilson, Colin. The *Atlas of Holy Places and Sacred Sites*. DK Publishing, 1996.

WEBSITES

www.avalonia.co.uk/
Source of articles and links for Wicca, Witchcraft and Goddess Spirituality including free lessons on Wiccan practices.

www.witchcraft.org
Site for The Children of Artemis, publishers of *Witchcraft and Wicca* magazine.

www.twpt.com/about
Site of the *Wiccan/Pagan Times*, online Wiccan/Pagan book reviews.

www.witchcraftinfo.info/
The witchcraft information centre and archive.

www.witchfest.net
Listing of events and festivals in the UK.

www.spellements.com/bos.cfm
www.newmoonoccultshop.com
www.pagansunite.com
Online shops for magickal supplies.

www.witches.org.uk
News and links on female Paganism.

www.outofthedark.com
Information and events relating to Wicca, Witchcraft and Goddess Spirituality.

www.ukpaganlinks.co.uk
Pagan resources and information for the UK.

www.tylwythteg.com/dynionmwyn/dynionmwyn23.html
Site dedicated to the traditional witchcraft of Wales.

www.ukpagan.com
An Internet community for Pagans in the UK.

www.witchvox.com/vn/hm/ukgb2
The English homepage of witchvox.com gives information about magickal festivals and groups.

www.geocities.com/sarcencircle
Sarcen Circle Protogrove, a druid fellowship in Nottingham dedicated to holding inclusive, open-to-the-public rites.

www.paganfed.org/news
The Pagan Federation website includes news and events listings for all areas of the UK.

www.geocities.com/kentpagans/ASP1
Association of Kent and Sussex Pagans.

www.norwichmoot.paganearth.com/body
Norwich Pagan group.

www.sagecatmoot.paganearth.com
Pagan events based in Mildenhall, Suffolk.

www.gippeswic.demon.co.uk/mootprog
Pagan events based in Chelmsford, Essex.

easyweb.easynet.co.uk/ ˜rebis/index.
Talking Stick group meeting in Central London.

home.clara.net/syrbal/home
News on groups and events in Birmingham and the West Midlands.

myweb.tiscali.co.uk/rainbird/paganfed/pagan
Groups and events in the East Midlands .

uk.groups.yahoo.com/group/Bristol_Open_Circle_Moot
Bristol-based group for anyone following a 'Pagan, Heathen, nature-based, magickal or alternative spiritual path.'
www.twistedtree.org.uk/moots

Groups and events in Gloucestershire, Wiltshire, Dorset, Somerset, Devon and Cornwall.

hometown.aol.co.uk/bonawitch/myhomepage/celtic
Site for the Pagan Federation in the North East of England.

www.paganfed.vscotland.org.uk
Site for the Pagan Federation in Scotland.

www.fellowshipofisis.com
Website for the Fellowship of Isis.

www.geocities.com/annafranklin1/hearth
Website for the Hearth of Arianrhod, a coven of the Coranieid Clan of Traditional Witches, based in the Midlands.

www.paganfestivals.fsnet.co.uk
Listing of Pagan festivals.

www.merciangathering.co.uk
Annual Pagan summer camp.

Index